4/29/11

John -

Thanks for reading
my book of memories.
You're a big part of them.
Please stay in touch.

Joe

P.S. Thanks for the
spirited plug.

ECHOES IN THE GANGWAY

A Catholic Boy's Trek Through The Fifties
Memories Of My Family And St. Leo Parish

JOE MURPHY

iUniverse, Inc.
New York Bloomington

iUniverse books may be ordered through booksellers or by contacting:

iUniverse
1663 Liberty Drive
Bloomington, IN 47403
www.iuniverse.com
1-800-Authors (1-800-288-4677)

ISBN: 978-1-4401-3748-8 (sc)
ISBN: 978-1-4401-3749-5 (ebook)

Printed in the United States of America

iUniverse rev. date: 10/18/2010

To my loving and selfless parents, John and Margaret Murphy

Mom and Dad in 1951

Contents

Acknowledgements

I am grateful to the many thoughtful people who helped me compile this bundle of recollections. First among them is my brother Jim, who proofread several drafts and made valuable editing contributions. Also deserving thanks are my other siblings: Joan, Dan, Margaret Mary, Tom and Pat. They checked to make sure that my memories did not lapse into fantasy. Equally valuable was the careful proofreading furnished by my wife, Mary and daughters, Bridget and Eileen.

More thoughtful help came from my grammar school classmates, Agnes Doherty Groskopf and Rose Trahey Breckenridge. Agnes provided photos, countless newspaper articles about St. Leo parish and a decade of encouragement. Rose sent me class photos with names, as well as the names of several nuns who taught us. Thanks are also due to my cousin, Mike Doyle, for his memories of our high school days.

In addition, I'm indebted to Eileen Stenzel and Father Bill Stenzel for providing the names of several neighborhood places. And finally, I want to thank Dave O'Donnell, Jim Brankin, Ado Rugai and Sister Ann Flanagan for their recollections about neighborhood businesses, St. Leo Church and St. George's Hospital. Help from everyone mentioned here enhanced the accuracy, color and character of this book.

Introduction

By some wonderful stroke of luck I was born into a big Catholic family. There were nine of us Murphys sharing three bedrooms and one bathroom. We were a bit cramped but life had a zest and urgency that I miss today. Things happened fast; personalities clashed. It helped to forgive and forget. My brothers were my best friends; my sisters were pretty and pleasant but on their own girl track.

Mom and Dad struggled to keep us kids fed, scrubbed and schooled. They taught us the same values their parents had drilled into them. Regular chores helped instill a helpful attitude and a rudimentary sense of responsibility. Our dusting, mopping and sweeping took some of the burden off Mom and kept our two-flat on Peoria Street looking good.

Playtime found my brother Jim constructing things. Two years my senior, he advised me on the fine points of building forts and push cars. Dan, a year younger than me, was always seeking opponents to face him in checkers or chess. I made model airplanes on the kitchen table while younger siblings throughout the house played with their toys or broke things that didn't belong to them.

Toddlers, teens and in-betweens confronted Mom and Dad with an ever-changing scenario. Fun and laughter were intermingled with strife and tears — a blanket of bliss was not in the cards. My pleasant morning could be upset by Jim's nasty teasing. If he provoked a fight Mom or Dad would step in to restore order. But, for the most part, we kids were a peace-loving lot. Our good-natured parents raised us to get along, help each other and stick together.

They sent us to St. Leo Grammar School to make sure we got a good Catholic education. Here the Sisters of Providence instructed us in the three R's. But above all, they focused on the redeeming R of Religion. The nuns taught from the Baltimore Catechism with missionary zeal. They led each class in prayer several times a day. And putting their teachings into practice, we kids confessed our sins on Saturday and received Holy Communion at mass on Sunday.

Luckily, the innocent Fifties were good times for raising kids. America was tops in everything. Fast food franchises were new on the scene; our local business district still had a mom-and-pop character. Popular music was upbeat with lyrics we could understand. My mother took pride in her (often) well-behaved children and neat home. Dad picked up groceries on the way home from his pipefitting job. On weekends he enjoyed making household repairs. We kids were happy. Life was optimistic.

Then one day I looked back and all of it was gone — the houseful of brothers and sisters, the happy holidays together, the birthdays and graduations...double features and doo-wop, ponytails and high school football games. So much that I loved was history. The old neighborhood had changed completely. We'd moved west. Years passed, then decades. Whither had flown those happy days in St. Leo parish?

Seeking the answer I took a ride back to Auburn-Gresham in 1988. That trip churned up a wealth memories about my family and childhood that had been hibernating in my head. I've pieced together some of these scraps from the past, hoping that they will help you recall how much fun it was to be alive during the Fifties. And if you missed that magic era, don't feel bad. These memories of Peoria Street still might leave you with a good warm feeling.

Chapter 1

Seems like yesterday

"There's no time like the present."
— John J. Murphy, my dad

It felt good to be heading back to Leo High School, retaking the one class that kept me from graduating years earlier. *It shouldn't be too difficult this time*, I thought. I was more mature and my family still lived on Peoria Street, less than a block from the school. Sitting in the kitchen finishing lunch, I tried to remember the room number for my class. *It'll come to me*, I assured myself, grabbing my textbook and exiting the house. As I walked toward Leo a soft breeze whispered through the elms lining both sides of the street. What a gorgeous September day! I cut left into the alley behind the school and entered through the rear doors as I'd done back when I was a regular student.

Climbing the stairs, it hit me that I still didn't know the number of my classroom. As I reached the second floor a scrawny snotty-looking kid stopped me. "Are you Murphy?" he asked in a clipped voice. "That's me," I answered, trying to act friendly toward this twerp. "The principal wants to see you — I'll take you to the office!" *What the heck is this about?* I wondered. *Am I in trouble already?* Well, maybe my class had been changed to a different time or something like that. I followed this kid, probably a freshman, through the hall, then down some stairs that ended in front of a huge oak door. "Here's the office," he snapped. Turning, he scampered back up the stairs.

I knocked nervously and waited. Nobody answered. I tried again. Still no response. Finally I gripped the brass handle and pulled the door open. Entering, I saw the stocky principal silhouetted against the window. Looking out onto 79th Street he seemed oblivious to my presence. Did I have the nerve to interrupt Brother Regan, the

Irish Christian Brother in chief? I waited a moment then risked it: "Excuse me brother, I'm Joe Murph..." "You're late!" he shouted hoarsely, still looking out the window. "I'm sorry, brother," I started to say. Regan cut me off. "I have your record here Murphy — you had a bad habit of being late for class." His voice sounded weird — different than I remembered. "I don't know who let you back into Leo, but let me just give you fair warning…" The blackened figure turned toward me and — oh my God — Brother Regan was a nun! A massive hulking nun!

"Things have changed around here!" a puffy, red-face screamed at me. "You're late once this semester and you fail the course. Do I make myself clear?" "Yes sis...sir...yes!" I stammered. "Good. Now, what classroom should you be in this period?" My mind melted. "The algebra room," I blurted. "Algebra room?" thundered the fearsome figure, "We haven't taught algebra here for years!" I panicked. *It must be the Latin room I'm looking for,* I thought. Glancing down at the textbook in my hand, I read the title on its cover: **Basic Auto Mechanics**. *What???* My knees turned to rubber as the brother/nun gripped my shoulder and started shaking it. "No," I shouted. "No, stop, no, no, no!"

"Joe, Joe, Joe, wake up! Joe, you're having a nightmare." Opening my eyes, I saw the face of my wife, Mary. She was still jostling my shoulder. "Were you having that 'can't graduate' dream again?" she asked. "Yeah" I told her. It was a new iteration of the same old thing. Nearly three decades after graduating I was still having bizarre confused dreams about Leo High School, St. Leo Grammar School and the whole experience of growing up in St. Leo parish on Chicago's South Side.

That summer morning warmed into a hot sticky afternoon. I'd just finished a freelance writing job and wanted to escape our un-air-conditioned house. *Could all these dreams about people and places from the past be trying to tell me something*? I wondered. Over a tall cold glass of iced tea I decided to visit the house on Peoria Street where I grew up. The drive from Oak Park wouldn't take long. Besides, I hadn't been back since Dad sold the house in August of '65. It had been twenty-three years since my family moved from the Auburn-Gresham area to Mount Greenwood, farther south and barely within the Chicago city limits.

Heading east along 79th Street I didn't recognize much until I approached Ashland Avenue, about a mile west of our old house. But the huge tan brick building that had housed the Highland Theater was easy to spot. It had been converted into a church. Nothing else along 79th looked familiar. As I crossed Racine I looked for signs of places I'd known as a kid — Glider's Hobby Shop, Lang Lee Chinese Takeout, Mrs. Hughes' Flower Shop. They were gone; their spaces filled by different businesses or empty storefronts. Nearing Peoria Street, I spotted Leo High School, looking very presentable after standing there for sixty-three years. The big iron gate bordering 79th Street was in good repair and the statue of the Blessed Virgin Mary still stood in the grass out front.

I turned down Peoria Street and drove to 7947, the handsome brick two-flat where my family lived for so long. Pulling to a stop, I sat for a few moments, pondering that span of thirteen and a half years. Out of Mom's seven kids, five of us lived there for the duration. Pat, the youngest, came along in '54 and Joan, the oldest, left when she married in '63.

Memories flooded my mind — some very happy, some less so, but all of them were tinged with melancholy: riding in a push car my brother Jim and I made from boards and buggy wheels, coasting down the street on my bike with the wind hitting my face, buying a new pocket knife at the cigar store, snagging a long pass in a game of touch football. I recalled fall mornings when breakfast was accompanied by the rat-tat-tat of drums as the Leo High School Band marched down the street, practicing for Sunday's football game. I saw myself with my brothers sitting on the roof of the A&P on a cold Sunday afternoon, watching the St. Patrick's Day parade strut along 79th Street.

Exiting the car I surveyed my surroundings. The mighty elm that shaded our balcony was gone; so was our tall maple. Replacing them were two small tidy trees that looked about fifteen years old. It would take many more summers for them to grow tall enough to form a canopy over the second-storey porch. The house was still in great shape. Its dark face brick appeared as sharp and clean as it did when my family departed for a less impressive home farther south. I looked up at the balcony, recalling warm summer nights when I lay there on a blanket, gazing at the stars and talking to my brothers about Davy Crockett and Godzilla, heaven and hell, the Big Dipper and sputnik.

I crossed 80th Street and walked halfway down the block to the house where a girl named Eileen once lived. What a heart-pounding, all-consuming crush I had on her! I thought about our few innocent dates and the emotional overload that accompanied them. Returning to reality, I noticed that the front of that house had been completely changed.

Time to get going I thought, walking back to my old house. Looking up the block, I remembered the great neighbors we had — the Schmids next door, the Carolis across the street and the O'Donnells up toward the high school. The kids in those families were friendly, like their moms and dads. I recalled the Burkes, our first-floor renters, and Patricia and Carol McCarthy next door, who both became nuns. Dave O'Donnell, my high school pal, came to mind; so did Jim Brankin, who helped me with my algebra. I recalled the milkman and the mailman who came each morning; the Fuller Brush Man at the front door.

My drifting mind caught glimpses of colorful characters from Peoria Street past: Spanky and Mickey Gamowski, who scared the hell out of me; the lady with purple hair who couldn't stop sweeping her sidewalk; the tall intellectual gent who watched us toss a football around, studying the trajectory of our passes.

I had to get back to Oak Park, but I couldn't leave the old neighborhood without a quick look at St. Leo Church and the grammar school. Heading north on Halsted I was shocked to see a blank space where the stately Mutual National Bank had stood. It looked as if some colossal dentist had extracted that big stone structure from the block. As a I kid I had a savings account there. And I loved to watch the yo-yo contests held in the alley behind the building. The young contestants did "Around the World," "Rock the Cradle" and other stunts over and over — sometimes until their strings broke.

A minute later I was on 77th & Emerald in front of the church. It looked smaller than I remembered, but seemed to be in good repair. The school appeared a bit worse for wear. I wondered if it was still in use. As I crawled by in my car the bright sun that was bleaching Emerald Street made me squint. I envisioned the same sun-drenched street filled with hundreds of noisy happy kids and the clanging of a hand-shaken school bell.

Circling the block for a second pass, scenes from grammar school flashed through my head: talking in class with Mike Dolan and Chris Skourlis, who sat near me; carrying a crate of small clinking bottles upstairs for morning milk break; opening a giant Valentine from the girl who sat ahead of me in fourth grade; drawing a Tsetse Fly during Friday afternoon "Art" period. I thought about all the times I'd walked with Jim Dunbar on the way home from school. Recalling how he had everything and everybody all figured out made me smile.

I passed the church, then pulled over across the street from the school. The image of a big cottonwood tree came to mind. It was just barely visible from my seat in fifth grade — I had to turn my head hard to see it through the rear window. But what a sight! Its glossy leaves shimmering in the spring breeze a block away made my soul ache for freedom.

School letting out was something to see — hundreds of kids filed into the street, some breaking left to go north, others turning right to head south. I thought about patrol boy duty with the pretty young crossing guard at 78th & Halsted and remembered folding my white patrol belt into a tight bundle that hung from my waist.

Shrugging my daydreams, I felt a strong urge to see more of the neighborhood, so I headed south on Halsted. Walgreen's was still in business at 79th but nothing else looked familiar. Then another shocker — the Capitol Theater was gone! That majestic movie palace was now a concrete slab. What the hell had happened? I'd read that the building had served as headquarters for Operation Breadbasket in the late Sixties but I couldn't fathom its demolition.

I saw myself and my brothers coming in midway through a black-and-white movie. Fumbling our way toward some empty seats, we climbed over folks young and old, spilling popcorn on their laps. Then I was on the Capitol roof, looking up a steel ladder as my brother Jim climbed higher. I was sitting next to my very first date, wondering if I had enough money to take her to the Capitol Annex restaurant after the show.

My focus shifted as I spotted the store where I'd worked in high school. Back then it was Auburn Food & Liquor, but now I couldn't see a name on the front. Entering, I walked past the register to the end of the aisle, where the big cooler was humming just like it did decades earlier. Most everything else had been moved around, but just standing there in the aisle rekindled memories of the feisty owner and the people I'd worked with. I recalled the countless cases of beer I'd loaded into the cooler and the hundreds of grocery orders I'd transported on the store's beat-up delivery bike. Pumping that one-speed contraption made my thighs burn.

Way overdue to head home, I drove back to 79th and turned west, recalling what a booming, thriving street it was in the Fifties. I envisioned the frantic newsstand at 79th & Halsted and bustling shoppers everywhere. Saturday mornings brought droves of people to the A&P and National supermarkets, Widen's Bakery, the Spic'n Span Swedish Deli, Frank's Department Store and Woolworth's.

Reality nudged me again as I reached Cicero Avenue, prompting me to turn north toward Oak Park. For the rest of the way home old scenes of family life flickered through my mind: Joan on the phone talking to a girlfriend...Marg on the phone talking to a boyfriend...Tom punting on fourth down in a grammar school football game...Dan hunched in a booth at George's Record Shop, listening to a new Connie Francis single...Mom reading aloud my letter of acceptance to Leo High School...John Keating and myself at Mallatt's store gulping down cold Cokes...

The rush of happy recollections came with a sad note. Those special moments that returned with such intensity were history. Had they all come and gone so very long ago? How could they still churn up such powerful feelings?

My memories of family life on Peoria Street span the period between Christmas, 1951, when we moved to St. Leo parish, and September 1961, when I entered college. The decade in between was packed with church, school, chores, games, relatives, TV, after-school jobs, bike adventures and family vacations. The hopes, joys, hurts and disappointments from those days were intense.

Life for us Murphy kids continued on an even keel. Occasionally, one of us whined about the nice things other kids owned or the places they went. But, in truth, we had it very good. It was our parents who had their work cut out for them. Mom and Dad worked and prayed hard trying to raise us right. They gave it everything they had, but were all their efforts worth it? One can hope.

Chapter 2

Family snapshots

"Charity begins at home."
— Dad

My mother raised her brood of seven kids on the second floor of a brick two-flat. Anchored at home, she kept us warm, nourished and out of harm's way. Of course, Dad played a major role in our upbringing as well. Working as a pipefitter he put in long days to stay ahead of the bills. Growing up, we kids were blissfully ignorant of the real-world stresses on our parents. I'm afraid we didn't often share their worries or appreciate the sacrifices they made for us.

Mom worried

When we moved to St. Leo parish in December of 1951 my mother had six redheaded kids, aged three to thirteen. She got four of us out to school each day, then made beds, cleaned and did the wash while keeping an eye on her two youngest. The surrounding Auburn-Gresham area was unfamiliar to her. Speeding busses, autos and streetcars on Halsted Street were dangers facing her offspring.

There were busy intersections with slippery ice. Even worse, the holiday rush made everything more hectic and hazardous. No wonder Mom worried about us. For divine protection she made each of us carry a rosary.

Loving but overprotective, Mom was happy when we kids were home. If we were in the next room doing homework, playing checkers or vacuuming the carpet she didn't worry. And at home we could help her with chores, which were plentiful. Shirking or laxity in this department was reported to Dad.

Dad provided

Dad got up early, went off to work and came home tired but with enough zip left to enjoy his family. He worked out in the elements, installing steam and hot water lines on big construction jobs. It was hard physical work and often dangerous. Most nights he arrived at the back door about six, hungry and ready for a little R&R.

At supper Dad got Mom's daily report: who brought home a paper with a gold star on it and what came in the mail, plus over-the-phone news from Aunt Martha. He also learned who got out of line or neglected their chores. Work and respect were important to Dad, so mouthing off to Mom or neglecting chores could merit a few licks of his belt after supper.

Jack soared

From my earliest memories Jack was my fun big brother. Actually, he was my half brother, but I'll explain that later. For a long time we younger kids just knew Jack as our much older, much bigger brother. He combed his hair in a tall wave, joked around a lot and was constantly in motion. If he were out somewhere I missed him and couldn't wait for him to get home.

Driving way too fast, Jack took us younger brothers on fun adventures — to the playground, the museum and the Jackson Park Lagoon. Even if we just went with him to the grocery store it was an adventure. If we were walking he sometimes carried one of us on his shoulders. If we were driving he let us sit up front and honk the horn. He bought us hot dogs, popcorn and popsicles. What a guy! Jack was a snappy dresser, especially on Saturday nights. When he took me with him to the drug store on Saturday morning he made the lady at the counter laugh.

Joan prevailed

The oldest of Mom's kids, Joan had a four-year jump on me. The age gap made her seem like an adult. She was always on the go — rushing to a lesson or a rehearsal; to the drug store or the dentist. When our family moved west to the Auburn-Gresham area Joan was already light-years ahead of us younger kids socially. Attractive and popular, she was eager to escape the house and explore new horizons. Meanwhile, the rest of us were happy with TV, toys and touch football in the alley.

Through high school and college Joan's after-school jobs kept her occupied so much of the time that seeing her around the house was rare. When Joan was home she was usually sleeping. Throughout her college years she seemed like a boarder. Soaking in the outside world like a sponge, my big sister acquired good street smarts and a firm grip on reality.

Jim befuddled

"What if cars could fly?" "What if clouds were pink?" "What if it rained Kool-Aid?" As a young kid Jim drove Mom and Dad nuts with a steady barrage of "What if" questions. He definitely had his own view of things. I thought Jim's questions were odd but fun.

Back then Jim and I built things together — everything from Lincoln Log cabins to scooters to push cars. Jim's introspective nature sometimes gave him a "far off " look that invited teasing from kids at school. The hurt he felt from this helped to shape his escapist outlook. He loved to scale tall brick structures and go on long bike treks by himself.

Jim explored several musical instruments, as well as foreign languages and exotic cultures. Through his teen years he fixated on far-away places — first Oklahoma, then France and then Hungary. It looked as though his wanderlust might take him away from us at any moment.

Dan focused

Who was this kid with the gold curly hair? Dan? Er, OK. Until I was five I was barely aware of his existence. Then he seemed to appear out of nowhere. Dan, who was sixteen months younger than me, liked to talk and ask questions.

Dan had a talent for creating skits — little talking dialogue pieces that he played with our younger sister Marg. And he loved board games like *Sorry!* and *Monopoly.* Dan read all the rules, so if there was an argument over some minor point, he won.

Reading was a pleasure for Dan. He explored South America and Africa long before his geography class at St. Leo got there. Three things that really grabbed his interest were big jungle cats,

American Indians and Notre Dame football. His deep-rooted love for Notre Dame was almost religious. And that hasn't changed.

Marg glowed

"Murph, you sure have a cute sister!" "Hey, your sister is a doll!" "Think you could introduce me to your sister?" I heard many comments and questions like these from guys in my senior class at Leo. Margaret Mary was sure getting noticed. But flattering words about her were not new to my ear. Aunts, uncles, friends and neighbors had always raved about Marg. She was a cute kid, but as a young teen she was a knockout.

From my lackluster perspective Marg's life was a fairy tale. She was attractive, that was obvious. But what made her so good at everything — so light on her feet, so graceful and coordinated? Roller-skating, ice-skating and dancing all came naturally to her. If she tried out for something she always made the cut.

Beyond this, Marg was Miss Popularity. She had a few regular girlfriends, but as a young teen her universe expanded exponentially. After her thirteenth birthday she needed desperately to be out having fun.

Tom persisted

As a toddler Tom had a voice so deep that we older brothers called him "Froggie." He was tough-minded at a tender age. In fact, as soon as he started forming sentences, it was clear that he had a staunch stubborn side.

Young Tom was eager to get involved, making sure that he was included in what we older brothers were doing. If Dan and I were setting up the tracks for our electric train, four-year-old Tom was right there helping. A few years later, when we played touch football in the alley, Tom made sure he was part of our team.

Tom loved wild things — forests, streams, frogs, snakes and raccoons. If he spotted a blue jay or a nighthawk, he nearly jumped out of his skin, shouting and pointing excitedly. At school, however, this fervor was lacking. Tom brought home unspectacular report cards year after year. Then, in seventh grade, he suddenly became the best of students. What's more, his fascination with nature began to include a concern for the environment. If his interest in the natural world kept growing, who knew where it might lead?

Pat romped

Pat was a miracle, born when Mom was forty-seven. We kids were surprised to have a new baby brother, but where to put him was a challenge. With the kid count now at seven and only three bedrooms in our flat, we were short on sleeping quarters. My parents had to find a place for Pat's crib, but where?

A happy little guy with blonde hair, Pat got loads of attention from us older kids. We played with him constantly and bought him every crib toy we could find. We picked him up so often that his little armpits were red. At six months Pat was standing in his crib, clinging to the rail with one hand and reaching out with the other. He couldn't wait to escape that wooden cage.

Right from the start Pat's hands-on approach to life was remarkable. The way he took his very first steps caught the whole family off balance. And after sleeping in a baby crib for the first six years of his life, Pat's escape to a bigger bed was ingenious and hilarious. This kid knew how to get things done — his take-charge attitude was prescient.

Martha, Lee and Mike

Three people were so close to us Murphys that they were almost immediate family. Aunt Martha, her husband Lee and her brother Mike visited our house all the time, bringing news, birthday presents, surprises and advice as we kids grew up. Mom conferred with Martha about everything. If we'd been extra good a couple of us kids might get to spend a weekend with Martha and Lee. When a family emergency came up Martha took charge, contacting people, arranging things and making sure that everything came out right.

Her spouse, Lee, was a friendly funny man who read to us kids from *Tom Sawyer* and told us spooky stories. Lee sometimes razzed us good naturedly in order to make a point. We loved it. He ran a small print shop that churned out invitations, posters and fliers for neighborhood businesses. It was always a fun place to visit, even when we had to help Lee finish a rush job.

Mom and Martha's brother Mike was an ex-marine and pipefitter who boarded with Martha and Lee. He had a tough-guy manner that melted when Mom placed her newest toddler on his knee. Mike dropped by on Saturday mornings to chat with her and check on us kids. A confirmed bachelor, he enjoyed the footloose freedom to work in exotic places, like California and Hawaii. Mike was gone for months at a stretch, staying in touch via postcards. When he returned to Chicago he always brought presents for everyone.

Chapter 3

Mom

"It's a great life if you don't weaken."
— Margaret Doyle Murphy, my mom

My mother was blessed with a sweet disposition and the ability to keep several balls in the air at once. Surrounded by kids of different ages, sizes and temperaments, she kept her composure and maintained harmony. Mom's good-natured prodding helped us to finish our homework, do our chores, stay organized and get out to school on time.

Mom felt comfortable within the confines of our second-floor flat, especially when all of us kids were safe at home. The physical perils of our metro area went beyond busy streets and speeding cars. There were dangerous people out there as well — bullies and bad companions; perverts, atheists and Republicans. All good reasons to come straight home from school.

Mom roused us in the morning with a gentle "Time to get up," and had breakfast ready. If I beat the rush to the kitchen I might catch her seated at the table with the morning sun highlighting her red hair. A brief uninterrupted chat with Mom was a treat. It ended with encouraging words from her that gave my day a pleasant start.

Seeing Dad off to work then getting a flock kids out to school was a half-day's work packed into an hour. As the time to leave for school drew near minor emergencies erupted. Margaret Mary was taking too long in the bathroom, I couldn't locate my fountain pen or one of us found jelly smeared on a homework paper. At times there was yelling and name-calling — even pushing and shoving — that Mom had to break up. It must have been a major relief for her to see the last of us kids head across the porch and down the back stairs.

So much to do

Of course, the fun was just starting for Mom. She carried full baskets of laundry across the porch and down the back stairs four flights to the basement. The laundry room, right inside the door, was home to a commercial-size Norge washing machine and a big Hamilton clothes dryer.

Mom scooped cups full of powdered detergent from a big cardboard container (Dad bought it in 100-pound drums) and poured them into the trusty Norge. To keep white things white she used Linco bleach from a gallon glass jug and Rinso Blue from a saltshaker-sized bottle. She was on her feet for hours, often handling double loads. (As a grownup I learned that the varicose veins in her legs from childbearing were very painful.) After everything made it through the wash/dry cycle, Mom carried the clean warm laundry back outside and upstairs for ironing.

To help her, Dad bought a huge ironing machine called a Mangle, that pressed clothes between a long padded roller and a curved metal shoe. Using knee controls Mom closed the ironing shoe and set the roller in motion. It was fun to watch the machine swallow a whole trouser leg in a few seconds. The Mangle was a big help to my mother and, of course, we kids were eager to play with it, but this was not going to happen.

Mom warned us that the Mangle was dangerous and not a toy. We had to content ourselves with watching her operate this humming, heat-producing wonder. She had a ready willing labor force at her disposal and couldn't use it — what a waste! After a few weeks Joan, who was in high school and fussy about her apparel, got to "Mangle" a few of her things. Envious, I imagined myself churning out pants and shirts with razor-sharp creases.

Chef Margaret

Mom had meals down to a system. Right before supper she ran through a list of items that had to be on the table. Under her breath she uttered a rapid-fire litany, "Sugar, butter, milk, salt, pepper, bread..." I never caught the whole thing because Mom was always in motion when going through this drill. It prompted her to tell us kids what to bring from the pantry. When Dad got home it was time to eat. He sat at the south end of our stretched, Formica-topped kitchen table. Mom seated herself at the north end.

We ate hearty, meat-and-potato meals. Mom always fried round steak with onions and canned mushrooms. I loved that chewy steak. In fact, other cuts of steak I've eaten as an adult seem like sissy meat compared to Mom's chewy round steak. I was twenty years old and shocked when a waitress served me a salad with raw mushrooms. I feared that they might be poisonous, like toadstools. Mom boiled the bejeezus out of vegetables, so they were always good and soft. The "al dente" veggies served in restaurants still seem half cooked to me.

My mother's forté as a cook was her baking. She made great puffy loaves of yellowish bread that was still warm when we buttered it. What a wonderful taste! And I loved biting through the thick crunchy crust. Mom's raisin bread, with swirls of coffee running through it, was even better. She baked spectacular lemon meringue pies, sweet spicy apple pies, tart rhubarb pies and Devil's Food cake with dark, tangy chocolate frosting laid on good and thick. None of these oven delights ever lasted a full twenty-four hours. By suppertime the next day not a crumb was left.

Mom loved horseradish on her pot roast. I liked a tiny bit of it but she had a real craving for this volatile stuff. She was usually pretty careful, however she occasionally dropped too big a glob onto her meat and paid the price for it. Her face turned beet red; her eyes glazed. She buckled over the table as if someone had slugged her in the solar plexus. We kids scrambled to get her a glass of water. After a few gulps Mom straightened up and resumed normal breathing, but supper would be over before she regained her normal color and composure.

Mom in a zany mood

The comforts of the couch

After dinner Mom liked to recline on the living room couch and watch TV. She enjoyed *I Love Lucy* and *What's My Line?*, with its celebrity panel that tried to guess the occupation of a "Mystery Challenger." *Name That Tune* was another show she viewed occasionally. Mom not only named most of the tunes, she had sheet music for many of them.

Too bad her television viewing was so often interrupted by us kids asking for help with our homework. Our mother showed infinite patience, never complaining as we bugged her again and again. She loved English, so helping me with an essay was fun for her. When she was in the right mood Mom recited chunks of speeches she'd delivered in high school elocution contests. She went to business college, then worked as a bookkeeper for thirteen years. Mom was deft with digits as well as words.

Relaxing on the couch, Mom often read the *Extension,* a monthly Catholic missionary magazine. And she subscribed to *The New World,* a Catholic newspaper published by the Archdiocese of Chicago. She checked the Legion of Decency movie ratings inside to make sure the movies her kids saw were approved.

Any film receiving a "C" rating was CONDEMNED by the church — Catholics were forbidden to see it. Classics, like *La Dolce Vita, Never on Sunday* and *A Streetcar Named Desire* made the "C" list, so I didn't see them until I was out of college. Of course, our neighborhood theaters wouldn't let kids in to see movies like that, anyway. However, Joan, who was dating, might have occasion to view an off-color film playing at the Capitol or Cosmo on Halsted.

After everyone else had gone to bed, Mom watched the *Tonight Show,* then hosted by Jack Paar. She got a kick out of regular guests, like Genevieve, the dizzy French lady, Hermione Gingold and Jonathan Winters. But late-night TV viewing didn't prevent her from rising early each morning. She was in the kitchen at six a.m., making coffee before Dad got up.

I wish my mother could have found more ways to let off steam — maybe bowling or walking. But she was a very private person, happy in her home. She didn't see a need to get involved socially with other parents in St. Leo parish. Mom's one sure safety valve was her sister Martha. Each day one phoned the other and they enjoyed a nice long chat. Mom told Martha what was new with her kids; Martha updated Mom on the Doyle side of the family. Some minor domestic crisis, like a fight breaking out or the sink overflowing, might interrupt, but these calls were a sanity break for Mom.

Help from above

Our mother's strong religious faith gave her the stamina to keep up with seven growing kids. When a tough situation developed she sighed and said, "It's a great life if you don't weaken." And if things got worse she might spout a religious blurb like, "Jesus, Mary and Joseph" or "Mary, mother of God." But when she was truly at her wit's end, Mom folded her hands, looked toward heaven, and pleaded, "God give me patience and resignation!"

There's no doubt that Mom's religion influenced the overprotective care she gave us kids. When one of us was about to travel beyond the few streets familiar to her, she made sure we were packing some extra protection besides the rosaries we all carried. She might pin a Miraculous Medal, adorned with the Virgin Mary, to our clothing or maybe a four-in-one combo medal shaped like a cross.

On really dangerous missions, like ice-skating at the lagoon or a bus trip to Riverview (Chicago's giant amusement park), we might not escape the house without wearing additional protective armor. A Miraculous Medal might be teamed up with the combo cross plus a Sacred Heart badge or square woolen scapular that hung around the neck like army dog tags. With a world of perils, bullies, and weirdos out there, Mom armed us with every defense in her heavenly arsenal. What's more, she urged us to remain in a constant state of "grace" and reminded us to go to confession and communion every week.

When her sister Theresa had surgery to remove a brain tumor, Mom prayed hard. She went to mass and communion at the Leo High School chapel every morning for several months — maybe a year. And, together with Martha, she made "Novenas" for Theresa, traveling to a distant church nine days in a row for special prayer services.

Gene and Theresa at Martha's wedding, 1949

Music for the masses

After religion and family my mom's great love was the piano. To make her life complete Dad bought her a Baldwin spinet soon after they were married. She enjoyed making music when she could escape housework for a few minutes or when visiting relatives made requests. They might ask to hear anything from *Yankee Doodle Dandy* to *The Notre Dame Victory March* to *Begin the Beguine.*

Mom was good at musical arranging, so the sheet music for a pop tune was just a basic blueprint. She added accent notes, riffs and glissandos that dressed up a song. The tune that really got to me was *I'll See You Again* by Noel Coward. When my mother played it and sang the words I always got a lump in my throat.

Folks loved to hear her play *The Irish Washer Woman.* This lively ditty made young kids (my siblings, their friends or visiting cousins) jump and dance with delight. And when the holidays rolled around Mom played Christmas carols for us kids, along with requests from relatives and friends. Year after year folks asked her to play *Jingle Bells, White Christmas* and *Walking in a Winter Wonderland.* She enjoyed the extra music making, even though it left her with less time to handle the normal crush of holiday duties.

Keeping up appearances

My mother had a terrible fear that neighbors or passers by might hear any discordant noises emanating from her house. She was overly concerned about what the people on the block thought. So when Jim, out of pure devilment, shrieked or howled in one of his bizarre voices she was mortified.

Even crying too loud was unacceptable. If Mom hit me and I started bawling, she clamped her hand over my mouth right after I'd expelled every atom of oxygen from my lungs and they were burning for air. Her hand not only covered my mouth, it sealed my nostrils as well. I tried frantically to pull her hand away so I could breathe. Finally, when it seemed that my lungs had imploded, she loosened her grip. Ahhh... Air! AIR! I gasped great lungs full of it. Mom never seemed to realize what a suffocating effect her mouth-covering maneuver had.

Mom had taste

Able to tell the real thing from the shoddy, my mother had strong preferences regarding décor. Wall-to-wall carpeting was a must.

The patterned maroon carpet she chose for our home ran from the hall off the kitchen through the dining room into the den and living room — wall-to-wall all the way. It was one of the nicest features of our house.

But with five boys running from room to room, the furniture took some hard knocks. When one of us broke a corner off something Mom got out the Old English Polish and did her best to disguise the damage. She kept the big picture in mind. Everything looked good as long as you didn't scrutinize the scratches.

We were allowed to sit on the couch and the big overstuffed chair in the living room but the Chippendale chair was off limits. My mother liked that chair so much that she had it reupholstered with gold fabric. She told us emphatically not to sit on the gold chair. So when an encyclopedia salesman or insurance agent got to dock his duff there, I felt that he was getting away with murder.

When Margaret Murphy bought something new for her house it was good stuff. Occasionally she went downtown by herself to shop for new furnishings at Marshall Field's or Carson Pirie Scott. To my great surprise, she took me with her to Field's one Saturday when I was eight or nine. She picked out a huge watercolor painting in a gold frame. The image showed big leafy trees shading a house on a small town street. After delivery arrangements were made Mom and I took an elevator to the toy department. Here she bought me a white plastic ambulance with rear doors that opened. And inside was a removable plastic stretcher. I was thrilled.

Before our ride home on the "El" Mom held my hand and we crossed Wabash Avenue to the famous Blackhawk Restaurant. It was dark and exotic with geometric Indian blankets on the walls. I got to order Chicken ala King on Toast. Wow! It was all very exciting, giving me a grown-up feeling I'd never had before. A few days later a green truck from Field's delivered the painting, all wrapped up in brown paper. That night Dad hung it on the living room wall with Mom directing to make sure it was straight and level.

Don't mention it!

My mother's ideas about sex were identical to those held by the nuns at St. Leo Grammar School. Sex was almost never mentioned at home or in the classroom. Still, I picked up smatterings of the Jansenistic notions Mom got from her Irish mother. According to Grandma Doyle, sex was "rotten." In line with this belief, Mom told Joan and Marg, "Don't let any guy start pawing you." And when I was dating she cautioned me against feeling "passion" for a girl — as if passion were something disgusting.

Like her own mother, our mom was proud. She wanted all of us kids to excel in school and pursue successful careers. All five of my mother's brothers became pipefitters like Dad, so Mom didn't discourage us boys from learning a trade. But she said that if we wanted college educations we should get them. She cautioned us against becoming photographers or commercial artists. "They're a dime a dozen," she insisted. "They're walking the streets." This caveat struck me as a warning she'd heard from her parents. To them real work was done with hammers, wrenches and saws. They'd probably known some "artsy" folks who couldn't earn a dime during the Great Depression of the Thirties.

Dedicated helper

Nobody went above and beyond to help us like our mother did. When we Murphy brothers were in high school she typed term papers for all of us. Unfortunately, none of us took typing — something we regret to this day. Mom came to my rescue time after time. Seated at the dining room table in front of the old Underwood manual typewriter, she waited patiently while I dictated what I'd scribbled out on notebook paper.

There were mornings when we both got up at three-thirty or four a.m. and worked straight through till eight-thirty. Somehow we finished with just enough time left for me to dash up the street and beat the bell at Leo. When I dictated to Mom I had the habit of starting each sentence with the word, "Put." I'd tell her: "Put Emily Dickinson was a Transcendentalist," expecting her to type everything but the word "put." However, when proofreading I'd find a few sentences starting with "Put."

What's more, "Transcendentalist" might be typed out as "transit dentalist," suggesting that Emily Dickinson was a dentist who made house calls. But despite these minor pitfalls, I would have been sunk without Mom's typing help. And I had a hunch that I'd be needing more of it if I went to college.

Chapter 4

Off to school

"Those nuns are backward!"
— Mom

"Hey! That's a sacrilege! You're going to the office!" The fat officious kid screamed at Jim and me as we stood in front of St. Leo Church. We were passing the church on our way back to school after lunch. Noticing that the doors were wide open, Jim stopped and took a small mirror from his pocket. I watched as he reflected a bright round spot of light into the dark church. It darted about, then came to rest on the golden tabernacle atop the altar.

At that moment the heavyset older kid appeared out of nowhere. In a loud righteous voice, he told Jim and me what a terrible sin we'd committed. I wondered what sin I'd committed by just watching. Our accuser seemed so well versed in sin, I figured he must be an eighth grader. When he asked our names Jim and I were mute. But an eager snitch standing nearby blabbed the needed info.

Sure enough, Jim and I were summoned to Sister Superior's office that afternoon. The hefty bully testified against us with righteous fervor as the head nun listened patiently. Jim looked scared and my hands were sweating. I thought we'd be flogged soundly with a heavy belt or paddle. Then we might be expelled and forced to go to the public school. I heard that word "sacrilege" blast from the fat kid's lips. A lump came to my throat. Sacrilege! Jim and I could be excommunicated and thrown out of the church. We might lose our souls and never get into heaven!

These thoughts were throbbing in my brain while Sister Superior spoke with our captor. She turned and said something to Jim. He was walking away. I stared with amazement. Then I heard, "What are you waiting for, Joseph? Get back to your classroom." I couldn't believe it — I was free to go. Jim was already out of sight as I stepped into the hall. I had to wait until I got home to ask him what punishment Sister Superior had given him. "None." he said. "She just took my mirror away."

Better days ahead

For the most part, attending St. Leo was a pleasant experience for us Murphy kids. With school a few blocks from our house we got there in no time, joining a throng of about a thousand other kids. Our teachers, the Sisters of Providence, were aided by a few female lay teachers. There were usually three classrooms of about fifty kids for each grade. The good nuns placed heavy emphasis on spelling and grammar. Periodic classroom spelling bees pitted the boys against the girls, with the girls almost always winning. The words were selected from the soft-cover red spelling books that we called "Spellers."

We often had to stand and parse verbs — first person, active voice, past perfect tense, etc. This was pure torture. But phonics was fun — the whole class stood and read lists of words together loud and clear. We learned religion from The Baltimore Catechism and did arithmetic word problems that never got harder after fifth grade. History was boring but our geography books had nice maps and color pictures of places like China and Australia. Simple facts still stick in my mind about our neighbors in this hemisphere — beef from Argentina, tin from Bolivia, the Panama Canal.

Morning rush hour

Mom made sure we were dressed, scrubbed, fed and out the door in time for school. She herded the younger kids into the bathroom and soaped their faces with a washcloth, finishing with a strong pinch on the nose that really smarted. Ouch! I was glad to escape that morning stinger at age eight.

Breakfast was hectic. A few kids at a time ate in the kitchen. Joan had likely left already for a music lesson at school. More siblings arrived at the table in no predictable order. Mom made sure we ate hot oatmeal or Cream of Wheat in winter; corn flakes, Cheerios and such on warmer mornings. I kept asking Dad to buy Kellogg's Pep (extinct for decades but much like Wheaties) so I could get the free Tom Corbett prize inside the box. Pep sponsored the *Tom Corbett, Space Cadet* episodes on TV, which I watched faithfully. Even better, the back of the box was printed with nifty rocket ships and spacemen that kids could cut out.

Getting back to breakfast, Mom varied the menu, serving poached eggs on toast, scrambled eggs, pancakes, waffles — most any breakfast fare under the morning sun. A couple of us might be munching on toast and jelly as we finished homework papers, adding sticky droppings that enhanced their flavor and texture. We drank our milk and orange juice while little Tom sipped a cup of coffee. Margaret Mary sometimes mashed a banana into a pulp and ate it for breakfast. On other mornings she ate Pabulum — the same pap that Mom was feeding the baby.

Mom cautioned us boys to be careful and not get food on our ties. Along with tan shirts, royal blue ties were part of our school uniforms. Purchased at Frank's Department Store, these ties sported a permanent double Windsor knot. Under-the-collar straps hooked together in back to hold them on. When Mom reminded us, we rotated our ties so they hung down our backs as we ate. Even so, they absorbed a polyglot assortment of stains over the school year. Our mother worked on them with a wet washrag or cleaning fluid before ironing them. And every ironing made the shinier, so that by spring our glaring ties made us Murphy boys easy to spot from a block away.

The way home

With school so close to our house it didn't take us long to get home. If I were alone I'd often cut through the two neighborhood dime stores. Kresge's and Woolworth's. Kresge's was on 78th & Halsted; Woolworth's was just a block south. I could enter Woolworth's on Halsted and exit on 79th Street. This was a great route home on biting-cold winter days.

Both five-and-dimes had long counters with stools where folks could relax and sip a Coke or order food. Once in a while I stopped by after school for an orange soda or a Green River. The elderly counter lady pushed a plunger, squirting flavored syrup into a glass (or paper cone in a metal holder). Then, pulling a handle, she added a stream of fizz water. A quick stir and it was ready to be sipped.

Woolworth's roasted peanuts and cashews, displaying them in a large glass case. The tilted display window facing the aisle was always loose, so it was a cinch to slide it up and filch a few cashews. As a third grader I walked by long counters where everything was displayed at eye level — plastic spacemen with clear removable helmets, pocket knives, pen lights (pint-sized flashlights), board games like *Clue* and *Parcheesi*, cap guns and squirt guns, Duncan and Cheerio yo-yos...

Pet departments in the dime stores sold parakeets, tiny turtles with painted shells and goldfish that traveled home in little paper cartons like the ones from the Chinese take-out joint. At Kresge's a Hohner Marine Band harmonica, made of wood and metal with real brass reeds, cost fifty-nine cents. It came in a hinged paper box and was wrapped in waxed paper printed with instructions for playing *Old Folks at Home.*

Each store had an aisle devoted to school supplies: three-ring binders, loose-leaf paper, art gum erasers the color of brown sugar and wooden rulers with cheap metal edges. I recognized some of the more sophisticated items, like compasses and protractors, because Joan, who was four grades ahead of me, was using them to do her homework.

The most coveted of all school supplies was the Parker fountain pen with a filling lever on the side and a two-tone metallic cap (the clip looked like gold). I longed to own one of these beauties for years. But only by mastering the Palmer method of penmanship could I transform this fantasy into reality. What a thrill it was when my lucky day arrived. Striding boldly into Kresge's I picked my Parker from a colorful array fanned across a cardboard display. I chose a manly metallic purple, paying ninety-eight cents plus tax.

Snowy lunches

On snowy winter days Mom told us to use the sidewalks going to and from school. Most folks in the neighborhood shoveled faithfully, so the sidewalk was the best route. But on the way home it was fun to cut into the alley between Green and Peoria Streets and trudge through the crusty unplowed snow. Garbage cans topped with round snowcaps looked like giant cones of frozen custard from the

Tastee Freeze stand. And it was quiet. All we could hear was the crunch of our boots against the snow.

Entering the back door, we took off our wet drippy galoshes and stood them in a corner near the pantry. Coats and gloves were tossed onto the nearest bed while Mom turned up the burner under a pot of cocoa. Crunchy toasted cheese sandwiches would soon roll out of the broiler. That lunch combo brought sunshine to a cold gray day.

We always had enough time to eat without rushing. In fact, if we ran out of milk or Silvercup bread, one of us would dash up the block to the A&P and be back in a few minutes. Somebody usually brought home a paper from school for to Mom to look at — a spelling test that got 100% or a drawing adorned with a gold star. And there was always some sheet or form needing a parent's signature. Mom would sign these and send them straight back to school in the afternoon.

Go ye forth and sell this stuff

For kids with natural sales ability St. Leo provided a terrific training program. Our Pastor, Patrick J. Molloy, kept the student body busy hawking religious and seasonal merchandise. We sold Christmas cards and holiday wrapping paper; turkey raffle tickets and religious statues. The annual turkey raffle brought in the most cash. Every kid in every class was supposed to sell at least one book of one-hundred tickets at a nickel apiece. Selling a whole book earned you a trip to the circus in the spring. I didn't like the circus so this was not a killer incentive for me.

Mom usually bought a quarter's worth of chances from each of us kids, but that still left our raffle books with ninety-five left to sell. What a drag. I'd make a halfhearted sales effort, hitting the 79th Street business district on a Saturday morning. But after an hour or so I'd be out of patience and itching to see a show at the Capitol. My siblings had more hustle, selling all their raffle tickets in short order. Mom got lucky once, purchasing a ticket that won her a nine-pound turkey. So we enjoyed our Thanksgiving turkey and the bonus bird a week later.

Coupon king

One year the school ran a drive for American Family soap coupons. Mom gave me a few coupons that she'd saved from bars of that foul-smelling brown soap. Then I checked with Mrs. Burke downstairs. She asked me to wait while she looked. A minute later she came to the door with a grocery bag filled with coupons. She told me that she'd been using American Family detergent for years. Wow! What incredible luck! I thanked Mrs. Burke and thanked her again. Seeing me so happy brought tears to her eyes. What a sweet kind lady she was.

The next morning I proudly plopped the bag on my nun's desk. She peeked into it, then stared at me in disbelief. As it turned out, I brought in more coupons than all the other kids in my class combined. At the end of the week Sister announced that Joseph Murphy had collected the highest number of coupons. I forget the number, but it was in the hundreds. I heard astonished murmurs all around me — "Holy cats," "No way," and "Wow!" I felt like I'd run ninety-nine yards for a touchdown.

Mr. Brain

In seventh grade I started walking home from school with Patrick Brogan, who was in my class. He was a tall bright kid who made good conversation. One day I invited him over after school, which he really enjoyed. In fact, he took my invitation as a permanent one. Brogan came over after school every day for weeks. He walked in with me and took a seat in the kitchen or strolled into the den to peruse our encyclopedia.

At first I was glad that he felt so much at home. But Brogan began taking liberties, like going to the refrigerator and pouring himself a glass of milk without asking. And he liked to joke about how much smarter than me he was. His arrogant comments didn't help our friendship.

On one occasion Mom was working a newspaper crossword puzzle and didn't know which word would fit. The clue was something like, "Ancient poet," and the answer was B_ _ D. As Mom set the puzzle aside, Brogan drifted out of the kitchen. Returning a few minutes later, he suggested that the mystery word was "BARD." He seemed to recall that in ancient Ireland a bard was a composer and singer of verse. After Patrick left I agreed with my mother that he had stolen into the den and found the answer in our encyclopedia.

A few weeks later I had a falling out with Brogan. He was wearing brand new glasses as we walked home from school. My little brother Tom, who was tagging along, kept bugging Brogan by jumping up and pulling off his new specs. Patrick caught his glasses again and again as his face turned redder and redder. Over and over he told Tom to cut it out. I should have stopped my pesky brother, but it was fun to watch Mr. Know-It-All not knowing what to do. Finally, picking his glasses out of some bushes, Brogan screamed at Tom in a trembling voice that was almost crying: "Lay off the glasses! They cost twenty dollars!" Holy cripes — he was more than just pissed. He'd really flipped. I didn't say anything as he went on ahead of us. About a year went by before Brogan and I walked home from school together again.

The Dunbar perspective

Jim Dunbar had everything and everybody figured out. I'd known him since I was in fifth grade, when he and my brother Jim worked together building scooters out of orange crates and roller skates. Dunbar and I wound up in the same classroom in the seventh and eighth grades. By this time scooters and bikes were ancient history to him. A handsome kid with the James Dean look, Dunbar was in a hurry to grow up. His folks were divorced and his dad seemed to be out of the picture. This probably contributed to Jim's unsettled persona. He talked a lot about girls, making references to things I wouldn't learn about for quite a while.

Dunbar had my number. He observed how I faked headaches to skip school and how I feigned stomach problems to get sympathy from my mother. Amazing! For years I'd imagined that my headaches and stomach problems were real. At school Jim liked to make things interesting. Our nun was constantly calling him into the hall for something he'd done.

One day at lunchtime someone stole into our classroom and placed an atom pearl (a small explosive pellet) under one leg of Sister's chair. When class resumed, she rested her hand on the back of the chair. BANG! The loud noise scared the hell out of everyone. The usual suspects were interrogated in the hall. I don't remember if Jim got nailed for this stunt, but I thought it was something only he would attempt.

Dunbar and I lived near each other, so we took the same route home from school. When our seventh-grade nun learned that we were walking and talking together she sent me home with a sealed note addressed to my parents. Curious, I opened the envelope and found a message warning them that I was keeping company with one of the school troublemakers. The note cautioned Mom and Dad that James Dunbar would be a bad influence on me. I threw it away before reaching home, but then I started to worry. Sister would be expecting a reply from my parents. What would happen when she didn't hear from them?

Weeks passed. I kept walking with Dunbar. Then one night after supper, my teacher phoned our home regarding the note. "What note?" I heard my mother ask. After a pause she explained that she wasn't worried about who her son walked home with. "I trust Joe to pick the right kind of friends," Mom said, adding that Jim Dunbar was a "good kid." That ended the conversation. Both of my parents gave me hell for keeping the note from them, but they didn't tell me to avoid Jim Dunbar.

I didn't see much of Dunbar after grammar school. He went to a public high school and joined the "greaser" crowd that hung out at a pool hall on Halsted. Jim D. had good street smarts and knew how take care of himself. I thought he'd do just fine for himself in the world outside of school.

Classroom highlights

Valentine's Day was a big deal in the lower grades at St. Leo. It seemed like every kid gave a card to every other kid in the class. In fourth grade I bought a big plastic bag of valentines at Kresge's to make sure I had enough for all the kids in my room. The tiny cards were loaded with red hearts and smiles. Their simple messages said things like, "I LUV ONLY U," "IT'S U 4 ME" and "I'LL B FINE IF YOU'LL B MINE." These cards had little tabs that folded back so kids could stand them up for display. The envelopes holding some of them were smaller than a wallet-size photo. That year I sat behind a pleasant olive-skinned girl with black hair named Ann. When it came time to exchange cards on Valentine's Day, kids scrambled all over the room, delivering and collecting. As I returned to my desk Ann turned around and handed me an envelope as big as a magazine. Wow! I opened it and thanked her heartily. What a super card! What a surprise! I still think about it every Valentine's Day.

"Do I hear ten cents?"

In seventh or eighth grade our class donated items for an auction to benefit the missions. This event was held right in the classroom, with Rose Marie Trahey serving as auctioneer. An attractive girl with red hair, Rose Marie was the smartest kid in the class. She had a serene unpretentious persona that was pretty classy. So I was flabbergasted at the way she took command of the auction. What force! What energy! She kept things moving at a brisk pace, selling each item with good-humored hype. "This isn't some piece of flimsy aluminum — it's tempered steel — the real McCoy!" It was a great a performance. And she really moved the merch. The next day Rose Marie was back to her calm controlled self.

Frosty fun

As the holidays approached the nuns always put up classroom decorations focusing on the nativity and the true meaning of Christmas. But there were Santa faces, jingle bells and candy canes as well. Even the windows were decked out for the season. I was jealous one year when some kids got to stay after school and apply Christmas designs to the windowpanes with Glass Wax.

Using stencils, they dabbed on the liquid Glass Wax window cleaner with sponges. The pink liquid dried to a white film, leaving frosty-looking snowflakes, snowmen and reindeer. The Gold Seal Company that made Glass Wax sold stencils with instructions for using their product to make windows cheery. If Jack Frost finked out Glass Wax would save the day.

Melodic twins

Occasionally, the class was entertained by vocal stylings from the Walsh twins, Kathleen and Eileen. They were cute, with clear sweet voices. It was a treat to close my history book and listen to their rendition of a song the McGuire sisters had just recorded. And though the twins loved to sing, they always seemed a bit shy, which made me like them all the more. Kathleen and Eileen were the most identical of identical twins. I couldn't tell them apart, but they were equally pleasant.

The lost Luger

After half a century I still feel bad about what happened to my cousin Jim's gun. Visiting us one Sunday afternoon, he brought along a full-size replica of a German Luger pistol. It was black cast metal, solid as a rock. What a great-looking gun! I was surprised when he let me borrow it on condition that I return it soon. At home we kids took turns picking it up but being solid metal, it was way too heavy to play with. After a few days I gave in to the temptation to show off the Luger at school. Toting it in a cigar box I joined my classmates in the morning as they lined up beside the school, waiting to enter.

With a minute or two left before the bell would ring I opened the box, giving some kids near me a peek inside. Big mistake. As soon as the class was seated our nun asked which boy had brought a gun to school. I raised my hand, assuring her that it wasn't a real gun. "Bring it up here, Joseph," she said. Handing it over, I tried to explain that it wasn't mine. She took the Luger and deposited it into a deep desk drawer. "I'll hold onto this for a while," she murmured. "Now go back to your seat." After a few weeks I forgot about the gun. In fact, when the school year ended I didn't think to ask for it back.

Years passed. Then one day in high school John Keating and I were reminiscing. "Remember that German Luger our nun took away from you?" he asked. "Yeah — she never gave it back," I answered. "She gave it to me on the last day of class and told me to give it to you," he admitted sheepishly, "But I sold it to a kid." *What? Are you kidding?* I wondered. Keating sounded so pathetic I couldn't even get angry. But wanting to distance myself from him, I found an excuse to take off. What a pal!

Our candy room

For several years the nuns set up a table in a small room on the first floor for selling candy during lunch hour. Later they moved the table into the auditorium, but I still think of this little operation as the "candy room." Most of the candy was the penny variety. A few items were two or three cents. Red gummy coins were a penny apiece — so were little nonpareils (dark chocolate wafers covered with sugary white beads). SNAPS came in a red box. They were hollow licorice cylinders with a sugary coating. Some were pink, some were white. They were good — and set you back only two or three cents.

Rows of candy dots stuck to shiny paper came in several colors and flavors. The kid at the candy table just tore off a strip holding the number of dots you wanted. The yellow dots tasted lemony but identifying the other flavors was a challenge.

In fourth grade I started buying airplane cards from the candy room. They came with a flat piece of bubble gum and were the same size as the baseball cards that kids still collect. On one side was a nice color photo of an aircraft — maybe an American fighter or a Russian bomber. The flip side was loaded with data about size, speed, performance, etc. I collected quite a pile of these cards, and even traded some with kids at school. The brittle bubble gum was so-so. I often gave it away or tossed it.

Every so often I bought a box of salted pumpkin seeds. They were just a few cents and fulfilled my salt needs for a month. Their colorful box was illustrated with an Indian chief wearing a big war bonnet. After chewing a few seeds I'd be dying for a drink of water and telling myself never to buy those nasty seeds again. But I always came back for more. Maybe it was that nifty box they came in.

Milk crate high-rise

In sixth grade Michael Dolan and I were responsible for bringing a wire crate filled with little bottles of milk up to our classroom for morning break. After the kids were finished and all the empty bottles were back in the crate, we carried it downstairs and out to the side of the school. The milkman picked up the crates when he made his deliveries the next day. On a bright spring morning one of us, I can't remember which, got the idea to see how high we could stack the milk crates sitting beside the school.

We used two or three crates to make a base. Then we added a pile of several more, so our finished structure stood higher than the roof next to it. As we admired our work kindergarten kids started running to the window and pointing. We beat it back upstairs to class. The milkman must have complained, because a few days later our nun called Dolan and me up to her desk and fired us from the milk detail. She said he was giving the job to two responsible boys.

My boxing career

I was a peace-loving kid. I didn't look for fights. Even so, I had to defend myself several times in grammar school. Mom influenced my attitude about fighting. She said a boy should not be a chicken. Mom's kind of boy stuck up for his brothers and sisters, and if the situation came to blows, he put up his dukes and fought. My mother spoke fondly of her brother Joe, who had been quite a neighborhood scrapper as a kid. In fact, she told us that none of her five brothers took crap from anyone.

I took Mom's message to mean that if some bully was picking on my brother or sister, I was honor bound to defend my sibling and make the troublemaker beg off. As a result, I lived with a certain amount of fear, being constantly on call to stand up for other kids in my family. If certain punks at school had stopped picking on Jim my life would have been easier.

Graduation

As eighth grade drew to a close I still had faint hopes of winning a scholarship to Leo High School. There were a few contenders in my class, but Patrick Brogan was the odds-on favorite to win. He certainly thought so. In the spring we eighth graders received long blue-and-gold ribbons known as "class colors." We pinned them to our clothes to advertise the fact that we'd soon be graduating. Our nun chose me to give a memorized spiel explaining the meaning of St. Leo's school colors to the kids in my room. I saw this honor as a sign that I might still be in the running for a free ride to high school.

I got a great final report card and graduated a day or two later at the church. The ceremony was after supper on a weeknight. Dad couldn't make it — he had to work overtime. After obsessively shining my shoes to a mirror gloss I was running late. Mom handed me my freshly pressed gown. I threw it on quickly and bolted to the bathroom, where I scrubbed my face. Then, leaning over the sink, I put my mouth to the faucet for a drink of water. After a few gulps I felt something cold on my right elbow. Yikes! Water had run down the sleeve of my gown. It was soaked.

No time to dry it. I darted out the back door and dashed to the church. Rounding the corner near the entrance, I snagged my left sleeve on a cyclone fence, ripping a big hole in it. Now both sleeves were a mess. Oh boy — I reached down and gathered in my sleeves, shrinking their size to conceal the double damage. Then, trying to look composed, I walked into the church and up the center aisle. Reaching my assigned pew, I made my way past a few classmates, sat down and dropped my sleeves. There were speakers but I don't recall their inspiring messages. The warm June night made for a sticky ceremony. At one point we graduates sang *Faith of our Fathers*, which gave me goose bumps.

The diploma moment

Before I knew it kids were walking up to get their diplomas — boys on one side of the aisle, girls on the other. Up near the altar a boy knelt next to a girl as they received their diplomas. Suddenly the kids in my pew were standing. I hiked my sleeves and headed up the aisle, shoulder to shoulder with the lovely Patricia Bartkus. We knelt next to each other and I let go of my wet sleeve to take my diploma. Grappling to readjust it, I forgot to let her go first — and almost ran into her. She looked surprised. Wow, she was even prettier up close. I let her precede me and we returned to our pews.

Finally, the priest announced the scholarships for each of the three eighth-grade classes. Patrick Brogan was the winner from my room. It shouldn't have surprised me but I felt bummed. With the exercises concluded, we fresh diploma owners proceeded down the middle aisle and out of the church. On the stairs and sidewalk folks clustered together, hugging, kissing and taking pictures. Then we grads walked over to the school to turn in our caps and gowns.

In the auditorium I said good-bye to a few kids I liked. I didn't want to loiter, fearing that someone would nail me for the rip in my gown. Mom and I exited the hall and walked south. On the way home she treated me to some ice cream at a little restaurant on Halsted. "You're not feeing bad about the scholarship are you?" she asked. "No," I lied. "I thought Brogan would get it." Later that night, when Dad got home from work, he gave me my official graduation present — a Timex watch. "Congratulations!" he said, as I opened the box. I wound my new timepiece and set it before turning in for the night.

Left behind

A day or two after graduation a bunch of kids from my room got together for a fun-packed day at Riverview. Chris Skourlis, who sat near me in class, told me about the outing. I thought it was a terrific idea and said he could count me in. I felt confident that the nine bucks I'd saved from my paper route money would get me through a day at the big amusement park. But fearing that Mom's answer would be "No," I put off asking her if I could go until the morning of the trip.

"Nothing doing," she answered briskly. I begged and begged, telling her about all the other kids who were going, but she wouldn't yield. With tears in my eyes I headed out the back door, telling myself I should disobey and go on the trip. But I was afraid to defy Mom, whose authority would be backed up by Dad when he got home. I felt I was missing an important event in my life and it really hurt.

Jumping on my bike, I rode over to Foster Park and circled the cinder track a dozen times or so, then flopped onto the grass. Looking up at the sky, I tracked the floaters moving through my eyes while pictures of my classmates at Riverview flickered through my brain. After an hour of this I biked over to Wimpy's Grill on Halsted, where I ate three pieces of boysenberry pie. I ordered a fourth, but the counter man refused to serve me, saying he didn't want to make me sick.

Behind the CTA bus pocket I did figure eights on my bike for a while, then rode to the hobby shop. With the money I would have spent on rides and hotdogs at Riverview I bought a boxed kit for an enormous glider. Arriving home, I was still too angry to talk to my mother. I went down to the basement and started working on my airplane, determined to avoid Mom for as long as possible. But about four p.m. the worst heartburn of my life drove me upstairs. All that boysenberry pie had turned to red-hot lava.

I was reaching for the baking soda when Mom entered the kitchen. She asked what was ailing me. "I'm fine," I grumbled, dumping some of the white bicarb powder into a glass of water. "You don't look too good," she said. "Why don't you go lie down awhile?" I took her advice. In fact, I went to bed for the evening.

The next morning I got up, finished my paper route and took a cup of coffee with me out to the front balcony. *This is my last summer before high school!* I told myself, thinking I'd better make the most of it. Looking up the block I could see the imposing silhouette of Leo High School.

Chapter 5

Dad

"Be a man or a monkey!"
– Dad

Dad had a full head of silver-white hair and a nose that resembled a natural rock formation. He'd broken it more than once, giving it a unique multi-sided shape. Looking at that nose you might get the impression that it had been applied to the grindstone regularly. Truth is, Dad worked very hard, often putting in overtime hours to provide for his growing family.

Most of the pipefitting he did was outside work on construction jobs. There were nights when he came home red and raw after a full day of freezing or subzero weather. On most weeknights he "brought home the bacon," arriving at the kitchen door with a bag of groceries. Somewhere in that bag was the coveted dessert that would top off our supper. Dad had a sweet tooth that he passed on to us kids. Cookies, cakes and such were precious cargo that disappeared quickly and needed constant replacement.

Enter the breadwinner

Dinner was ready when my father got home. He washed up, took his seat at the south end of the table and said grace. Then, as we ate, he got a rundown from Mom on her day at home. Dad contributed a bit of news from the outside world. My parents always spoke respectfully to each other, setting a pleasant tone for supper. Dad squelched any petty arguments that flared up between siblings. And if Tom or Marg wouldn't eat their spinach Dad made sure they didn't leave the table until they'd chewed and swallowed every bit of it.

If Mom told Dad that one of us deserved a "licking," he administered the punishment right after supper, doing his best to look angry or disappointed. As a parent I can see why he got this unpleasantness out of the way fast. What father likes to get home from work to learn straightaway that this or that kid needs a good thrashing? Joan and Marg, being girls, were exempt from physical punishment, usually getting by with a scolding from Dad, Mom or both.

After-dinner hours were usually calm. Dad sat in his big cushiony chair in the living room looking through the paper, his lips moving with each word he read. Meanwhile, in the kitchen, we kids cleared the table and did the dishes. An older sibling washed while two younger kids dried and returned items to the pantry.

It was wise to do the job right because we never knew when Dad might pop in to check on things. If he saw one of us carrying a teetering stack of dishes we'd hear, "That's a lazy man's load. Never take a lazy man's load!" In John Murphy's book doing a job right was important — and good training for the real world. When our kitchen chores were finished it was homework time. Some of us kids worked at the dining room table, while others took their books out to the kitchen.

On certain nights after dinner our provider in chief worked on paying the bills. The rest of the family was in bed as he sat at the dining room table with his little green "strong box" open. He made his calculations on notebook paper with a lead pencil before writing out checks to settle the Murphy accounts. Before Dad turned in at

night he knelt beside the bed and prayed. With a growing family to provide for he sought guidance from above.

Keeping up the castle

Come Saturday, Dad worked on the house. I'd see him up on a ladder or sitting on a windowsill washing our second-storey windows — his legs inside, the rest of him outside. The house was my father's big investment so he tried to keep it in good repair.

If the transom over the back door was sticking, he oiled it, while one of us boys "helped" him and learned. If someone complained of a draft in the winter, Dad quickly located the source — most likely the corner of a window. Deftly removing the trim, he stuffed some insulation (usually rags from old clothes) into the leaky space. Replacing the trim, he hammered the narrow finishing nails most of the way in, then carefully countersunk them, tapping his hammer on a little steel pencil called nail set.

While working around the house Dad whistled or sang old tunes, like *I Love You Truly, My Wild Irish Rose* or *I'm Looking Over A Four Leaf Clover,* with the family as his captive audience. He enjoyed weekend projects, like repairing the back porch floor or putting a tar patch on the roof. If he was in a playful mood he might sing: *"Mares eat oats and doeseatoats — andlittlelambseativy..."* or a peculiar tune about *"my cockeyed consumptive Mary Jane."* Dad worked variety into his routine, sometimes sliding from a whistle to a vocal or vice-versa. Occasionally, he'd even slip from a vocal to a whistle, then back to a vocal.

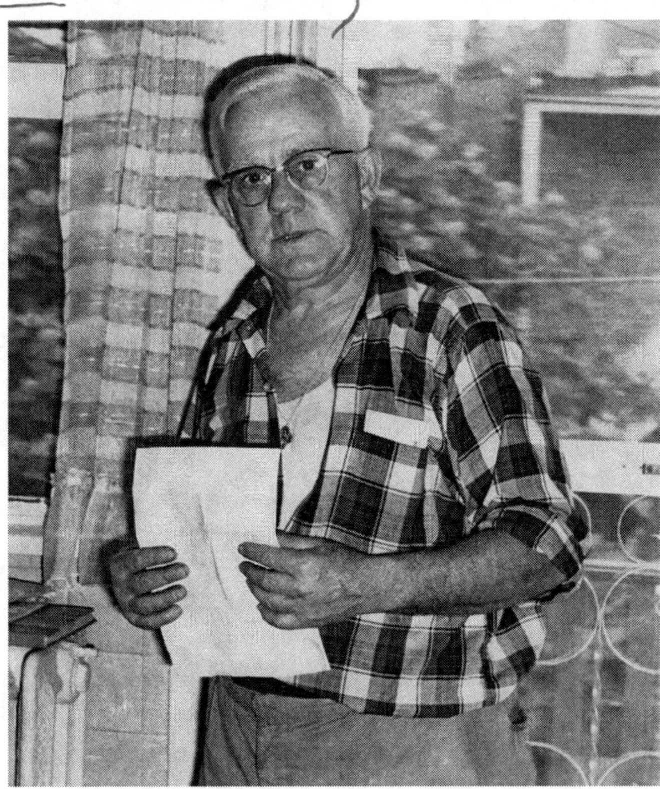

Dad reflecting on bank statement

The long cold winter

When winter arrived Dad wanted a warm house for our family and the Burkes, our downstairs renters. We enjoyed hot water heat and wonderful, old-fashioned radiators. My pipefitter father kept a close watch on the boiler and furnace in the basement. He was right at home with pipes, valves and gauges. All these mysterious marvels were concentrated inside the coal bin. Dad got the old furnace roaring and for the first few years in our two-flat he handled the coal-stoking duties.

John Murphy didn't like the thought of slipping on ice — maybe because the leg he'd broken on a construction site made him a bit unsteady. So he made sure our sidewalks were well shoveled. If snow was in the forecast we Murphy boys were on alert — Code White. And after a couple of inches were on the ground, Jim, Dan and I grabbed shovels from the basement (a big snow shovel and two coal shovels) and got to work.

We hit the front sidewalk first (somebody who slipped and fell could sue us) then did the front porch steps, gangway and back porches with their stairways. If we were still working when Dad got home he'd grab a shovel and help us finish. Whew! After an hour or more in the cold lifting and heaving snow I felt extra warm seated at the kitchen table. Supper tasted so good that I asked for more. If I felt sleepy from all the shoveling I might slip off to bed early, skipping my homework.

The nunfrontation

Neglected homework was noted by the nuns and reported to parents. Student problems came to a head on a certain Sunday, always in the dead of winter. In the afternoon we kids were required to come to the convent (accompanied by one or both parents) for a talk with the nun. Dad, stuck with permanent meet-the-teacher duty, had a memorable chat with my fifth-grade teacher. She told him that I didn't complete my homework assignments and didn't pay attention in class. "Joseph seems to daydream quite a bit," she said.

Dad listened patiently as I piled the fingers of my right hand on top of each other, forming a shape that resembled a conch shell.

My observant nun pointed this out to Dad. She told him that I did the same thing in class. A little annoyed, Dad asked me why I was playing with my fingers. I had no answer. Of course, in the Fifties Obsessive Compulsive Disorder had not yet been diagnosed. But behavior like my finger piling would be recognized today as a sign of OCD (God knows what drugs, counseling and therapy sessions would follow). Before we departed the convent Dad told my nun that he'd make sure I finished my homework. And he made me promise to pay attention in class. Oh boy.

I was worried. Now Dad the taskmaster, who watched to see how well I did my chores, would be applying the same vigilance to my schoolwork. *This will make regular chores seem like fun,* I feared. When we got home he told me to get started on my assignments while he talked to Mom. Then, after supper, I got a good dressing down from both parents. They said there would be no TV for me until my homework was finished. Even worse, I had to check with them while I worked on my lessons to prove that they were getting done. This marked the start of better study habits and higher grades for me.

A word to the wise

Dad kept an eye on more than my schoolwork. He could tell when I was preoccupied or worried. When my teenage compulsions were causing me angst he gave me this advice: "Never worry worry until worry worries you." He backed it up with a short story about a guy who kept hitting himself in the head with a hammer. Someone asked him, "Why do you keep hitting yourself in the head like that?" "Because it will feel so good when I stop," the hammerer answered. Blue-collar philosophy like this made me think.

At supper one night I told Dad about a kid at school who was badmouthing a friend of mine. I asked him if I should let my friend know about this. "Never pass up an opportunity to keep your mouth shut," he advised me.

One Saturday afternoon Dad and I were in the front vestibule struggling to jockey a heavy steel cabinet into place. When we stopped to catch our breath I suggested a different approach. Dad agreed to try it. We tipped and turned the cabinet and, hey, it landed right where we wanted it. Dad smiled and said, "Two heads are better than one."

Strictly on the level

Dad's home repair projects went smoothly except for the time he tried to "level" the house. When the limestone steps on our two-flat started sagging to one side, he decided to shore them up. Near the front of the basement he placed a big screw jack under a steel ceiling beam. Dad worked patiently, giving the jack a quarter turn every day for a week. Son of a gun — it was working! The stairs and house were slowly coming into alignment. Then on Saturday, as I entered the front stairwell, I nearly scraped my face. What the heck? A chunk of plaster was protruding a foot from the wall.

I ran down to the basement and told Dad. He looked at me blankly for a moment, then shook his head. "Let's take a look at it," he groaned. Surveying the damage in the hall, he said soberly, "I might as well keep cranking till everything's level — I'll have to get the wall fixed anyway." And so he did. Our front stairs lined up with the house again but paying for a new wall must have left Dad's finances a bit out of kilter.

A modern miracle

A few years later Dad bought Mom a dishwashing machine that liked to gobble up our silverware. Knives and forks kept shaking loose from their holding baskets and sliding down into the works. We heard thundering convulsions before the motor died. Dad made repeated repairs, but free-falling silverware caused the same problem over and over.

As I left the house one warm summer night Dad was sitting on the kitchen floor with his shirt off. He had removed the front of the machine and was ready to do battle. *Not again,* I thought as I started up the block toward to the O'Donnell's house. I was sitting on their front steps talking to Dave and Bill when a blood-curdling scream stopped me in mid-sentence. Coming from the direction of our house, it could only be my old man. I scrambled to the sidewalk and sprinted home.

Dad was still sitting on the kitchen floor when I arrived. Mom was fanning him with a dishtowel. He looked dazed and sweat was rolling down his bare chest. Mom advised him that he'd done enough repair work for one night. She urged him to take a bath and get to bed. When I asked Dad what the heck had happened, he said he got a shock and couldn't shake loose from it. "I could hear you at the other end of the block," I reported. Mortified that the neighbors should hear any noise coming from our house, Mom clasped her hands and looked toward heaven. Dad smiled and rose from the floor, waving off my offer to help him up. Then, taking Mom's suggestion, he hit the sack early.

The Maxwell Street excursion

When the clothes dryer kept breaking down Dad identified the cause. Heavy loads from the washing machine were proving too much for it. Items like cotton sweaters were still too water soaked after the spin cycle. He advised Mom that using an old-fashioned hand wringer would squeeze some of the wetness out of the heavy items before they went into the dryer. But where to find one? "Maxwell Street!" Dad declared assuredly. "You can find just about anything there." He asked if anybody wanted to come along with him on that cold mid-winter Saturday. I volunteered just to get out of the house.

As we drove north on Halsted Dad told me that the Maxwell Street area was really something to see. On weekends several blocks stretching east and west of Halsted became a colossal open-air market nearly a mile wide. After a straight twenty-minute drive we parked on a side street and continued north on foot. A few blocks later we encountered an endless sprawl of vendors.

Folks were hawking shoes, tools, typewriters, televisions, toys, auto parts, fans, toasters — almost anything imaginable. Some of the merchandise was on folding tables; some on blankets or tarps spread on the street. Still other goods were sold out of car trunks. Most of the stuff was used and beat up, but some of it looked brand new. Where any of it came from (especially the new items) who knew? A lot of the wares sold on Maxwell Street were reputedly "hot."

Dad and I trekked up and down a two-block swath that stretched west as far as I could see. We didn't find a single wringer but I was enjoying the sights, sounds and smells. Tired, cold and hungry, we stopped at an outdoor vendor for hot dogs and coffee. Then, with our batteries charged, we pressed on. It was getting dark when we came upon a middle-aged black fellow who was selling junk from the back of a truck.

Dad asked if he had an old hand wringer for clothes. The peddler said he'd take a look, vanishing into the blackness of his truck. A minute later he was back. And hallelujah! He was carrying just what we needed. The guy wanted six bucks for it. Dad offered four. The junkman came back with "five." "Done!" Dad carried the heavy wringer back to the car and set it in the trunk. As it turned out, I was lucky to have visited this thriving market in its heyday. A few years later construction of the Dan Ryan Expressway cut Maxwell Street in two.

Arriving home, we took the wringer down to the basement. It was in good shape and what luck — it locked in place neatly between our twin washtubs. Now Mom would be able to press the water out of those heavy items and, hopefully, Dad would get a break from dryer repair duty.

Hard work never hurt anyone

My father lived an arrow-straight life, heading off to work each morning and returning to base at night. He had foresight and kept the big picture in mind. Dad knew what had to be done now to make the right things happen down the road. He fostered a strong work ethic in us kids, insisting that we always do our best on any task, no matter how small. Beyond this, he encouraged side jobs, like paper routes and mowing lawns in the neighborhood.

Dad told us a little about his own father, who emigrated from Ireland and found employment with the Chicago Police Department. Working as a truant officer he earned the nickname, "Juvenile Pat." Dad's father was a strict humorless character who kept his five sons in line. If one of them questioned his authority the answer was a box in the ear. From Dad's description of him I saw Grandpa Murphy as an arrogant jerk.

Like his old man, our father tried to keep his sons on the right path, but Dad's tactics were a mite friendlier. One spring he hung a basketball hoop off the rear of the house to keep us boys within

Mom's hearing range. Reassured that we were in the yard, she didn't worry about where in the neighborhood we might be.

The basketball hoop was fun, but dribbling the ball on grass was impossible. After a few weeks, however, our little games killed the grass, creating a good-sized bald spot in the yard. Bouncing the ball on dirt was difficult. but at least it was possible. The hoop Dad installed kept us around the house that summer. Over the winter months, however, our interest in basketball faded. Come spring, we were no longer shooting baskets. I think Mom was happy to see fresh green grass closing up the black smudge we'd made in her yard.

Putting a ping-pong table in the basement was a better idea. We used it frequently year after year. One side of it ran parallel to the wooden wall of our coal bin. Jim and I hammered nails into the wall so we could hang up our paddles. We tacked up a coffee can to hold the balls.

We older brothers played some good games. I got most of my points with a fast serve. Once the ball was flying back and forth I had trouble tracking it with only one good eye. If the weather was lousy, Jim Bradley might drop in for a game or two. Even John Sullivan and John O'Leary, our touch football rivals, slapped the white ball back and forth on occasion. Tom, who wasn't much taller than the ping-pong table when we first got it, could beat anyone a few years later.

Of course, it was always more fun to be outside, so when warmer days arrived we boys were out biking or knocking around the 79th & Halsted area. As teens we'd be in the alley or street chucking a football around. None of us could get into baseball. With our myopic vision that game just wasn't in the cards.

Breezy Sunday drives

When most of us kids were still pretty young Dad took the family out for drives on warm Sunday afternoons. Sitting up front, my mother held the baby in her lap as we cruised Lake Shore Drive. These outings were fun, especially when I could get a window seat. Who got to sit next to the door and look out the window was a constant source of back-seat scuffles.

On one occasion Dad ended a fight by taking a backhanded swipe at us. The car swerved into the oncoming lane and tires screeched. A fading voice shouted "You jackass!" Then, with his eyes back on he road, Dad blurted something like: "Damn kids! Take 'em out for a ride and all they do is fight!"

But for the most part, these Sunday excursions were terrific. With the windows open we caught cool breezes off Lake Michigan and counted the white sails dotting the blue water. I ogled the expensive yachts anchored at Monroe Harbor with their polished mahogany and shiny brass hardware. Spotting the Goodyear Blimp overhead was another big thrill.

We looked forward to shakes and burgers on these outings. Dad usually found a drive-in stand and placed our family order, requesting some small cups for the younger kids. He divvied things up so that they got half a shake and half a burger. I was thunderstruck the day he handed me a whole chocolate shake. I wondered if I could finish it, but I did, thanks to several gulps surrendered to my thirsty brothers.

One sunny Sunday when we stopped at a gas station, a well dressed family was getting into their car. Mom remarked to Dad, "That's Paul Harvey!" "Which one?" I asked, lurching forward for better view. "The man, dummy," shouted a voice from behind me. I had no idea who Paul Harvey was but I liked the way his family was dressed. Wearing a suit and tie, his young son looked like a little adult. I thought he must be suffering in all those clothes on such a hot afternoon.

It didn't occur to me that Paul Harvey would be driving an air-conditioned automobile. Quite a few years passed before I realized what a famous radio personality I'd seen that day. And decades after that I had a brief chat with Mr. Harvey as we rode an elevator together in Chicago's Stone Container Building.

Pungent picnics

When I was a teenager Dad sometimes took our family on Sunday picnics to a big city park near Gary, Indiana. We loaded the trunk of our black Buick with blankets, balls, Frisbees and a big red cooler filled with pop and ice. On the way we got a whiff of the Whiting oil refineries — the first of many heady odors we'd inhale on the way to Gary.

I can't imagine what attracted Dad to this dismal park. It always smelled terrible. Not only was it near the refineries, but there was a big smelly soap factory just a few blocks away. When we arrived Dad set up a small portable grill and got the charcoal glowing. Then, while we kids horsed around on the park's large old-fashioned swings, he cooked hot dogs and hamburgers.

After we ate Mom and Dad sat on portable lawn chairs from home. It was good to see them enjoying a little R&R. Tossing a football around, I'd glance over at them now and then, wondering if they were talking about past memories or current worries.

The sky at this park sometimes had a strange orangey cast. And the air always smelled like burnt rubber. If I were running and breathing hard, the odor would get to me. I'd feel nauseous and develop a headache. What ever tempted Dad to take us here? And how did he get Mom to go along? I don't remember Joan or Marg ever coming along on these trips, but I can't blame them for begging off. Anyway, their dance cards were pretty full on weekends.

Onward to victory!

To an Irish Catholic boy growing up on Chicago's South Side, Notre Dame football was like religion. Victory brought euphoria! Ecstasy! A loss produced abject disappointment. Traveling to South Bend, Indiana to watch the "Fighting Irish" play was beyond my wildest dreams. So it was a major thrill when Dad took us older boys to a game.

On a bitter-cold Saturday in late November we rode the South Shore Railroad all the way to South Bend. The Irish were up against their archrivals, the Trojans of Southern Cal. And Notre Dame was coming out of a slump, having beaten top-rated Oklahoma a few weeks earlier. With the Irish leading at halftime it was a good day on the Notre Dame campus.

At halftime Dad unpacked the turkey sandwiches Mom had made for us. Then, with his breath steaming in the frosty air, he poured a cup of coffee from his thermos and passed it around. It was hot and heavy with cream and sugar. That wonderful taste out there in the frigid concrete stands made me a coffee lover for life.

The second half started with Pat Doyle running the Trojan kickoff all the way back for a touchdown. Six more points for Notre Dame! The home crowd went berserk, cheering, shouting and chanting, "Cheer, cheer for old Notre Dame..." The Irish squeaked by the mighty Trojans 40 to 12 that day. Gloating with pride, we filed out of the packed stadium and trekked to the South Shore station for the train ride back to Chicago.

Independent spirit

Dad valued independence. He liked to see his kids show a bit of enterprise. So if Jim and I were late for supper because we'd been out shoveling neighborhood sidewalks to earn money, he didn't take us to task for it.

Like Mom, Dad wanted all us boys to accomplish something in life. He told us that even if we earned college degrees, we should get union pipefitter cards as well. Dad stressed that a key advantage of owning a union card was independence. If you didn't like the job you were on you could walk across the street to another one, show your card and go right to work.

Dad dreamed that one of his sons, armed with a degree and a union card, would rise through the pipefitter ranks to become the Union Business Agent. And to make this possible, he put our names on a list for pipefitter apprenticeship when we were youngsters. Sure enough, our names came up when we reached our late teens. Too bad not one of us was inclined toward that honest good-paying trade. As the years wore on I could sense Dad's disappointment that none of his sons became fitters. He would have loved talking to us about the best way to run the pipes or ductwork for a big heating-and-cooling installation.

Getting your money's worth

Though none of us boys took up a trade like Dad, all of us kids, including the girls, learned lessons from him about shopping smart. Dad, the shrewd provider, knew where he could get a break from local merchants. He set up a charge account at Frank's Department Store and negotiated a family discount. With seven Murphy kids to clothe, there was plenty of potential for business. Sure enough, our family gave that charge card a good workout over the next decade.

On occasion, Dad took one of us grocery shopping with him to the busy Hi-Lo supermarket on 77th & Halsted. The store had an old-fashioned butcher shop with sawdust on the floor. Customers took tickets and waited until their numbers were called. Standing there it really upset me when I saw that the butchers were missing parts of their fingers. On the way home I asked Dad why a guy would keep a job that made him lose the ends of his fingers. "Because that's his trade," he informed me in a serious tone that made the word "trade" seem worthy of reverence.

One night Dad brought me with him to Star Electronics, his source of replacement tubes for our black-and-white TV. Calling a repairman every time our set went on the blink was too costly. Instead, Dad unplugged a bunch of tubes and tested them himself at Star. There was a testing unit near the front door where thrifty customers could find out for themselves which tube was dead.

Before we left the house Dad carefully placed four or five tubes from our set (the usual suspects) in a brown paper bag. The bag sat on the front seat of the car between Dad and me as we drove over to Halsted, then north about two blocks to Star. Once inside, Dad methodically tested the tubes, plugging each one into the proper set of holes — until an indicator needle showed which one had fizzled.

He bought a replacement tube and we drove back home. Then, before we missed Sid Caesar, he plugged in the new tube, along with he others he'd removed from the TV, hoping that none had been damaged in transit. Usually things worked fine, but on one occasion two tubes blew at the same time, causing great confusion and multiple trips to Star.

Harrowing haircuts

TV repair was only one area of Dad's expertise; he also gave haircuts on Saturday afternoons. The haircut victim was summoned to the kitchen and seated on the tray portion of the baby's high chair to be at a convenient level for Dad. He wrapped a sheet around his customer and reached for the clippers.

Dad alternated between electric and hand-operated clippers. When the electric ones got too hot, he gave them a rest, switching to the hand-powered shears for a while. I cringed when he gripped those old manual clippers. They were missing two or three teeth, so every in-and-out squeeze of the handles delivered a jolt of sharp pain. If I complained, Dad blurted some incoherent phrase which, translated, meant "Shut up if you know what's good for you."

Luckily, these haircuts didn't take long and we boys were too young to know if they were any good. Mom was Dad's biggest critic, offering occasional comments like, "You really scalped the kid" or "He has no sideburns at all." When our haircuts were over we helped our resident barber clean up. He swept the hair and the kid who'd been clipped held the dustpan and dumped the sweepings into a paper sack. We boys were Dad's unwilling patrons for years — until we got too big for the high chair.

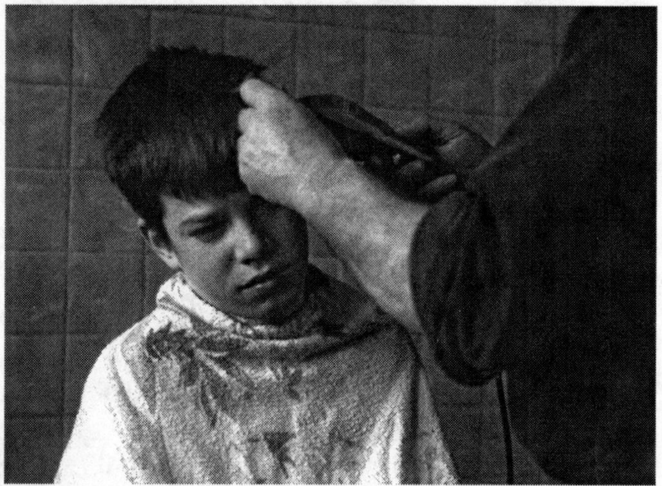

Young Tom delights to the caress of Dad's clippers

Summer haircuts weren't too bad. Dad just buzzed everything off, giving each of us boys a "Baldy Sour." Also, these haircuts were quick because he didn't have to be too precise. But things gradually got better for us boys. Starting at about age ten we were sent to Frank's Department Store to get our heads shorn. And when we reached our teens we were earning enough from neighborhood jobs to afford the barber of our choice.

I was jealous of Joan and Marg, who escaped the indignity of Dad's clippers. I don't know where they got their hair cut, but it was always on the long side and neat looking. Long hair for girls was the norm. They wore ribbons in it, tied it back, braided it in different ways and sometimes put it up in a ponytail. A ponytail was cute and tidy, not frazzled or frizzy. And watching it sway from side to side was fun.

Chapter 6

Work is good

"Many hands make light work."
— Dad

In 1953 Dad's work hours became completely predictable when he took a job with the City of Chicago, working at the 49th & Western Street water pumping station. Working inside on a standby repair crew was a lot more comfortable and far less dangerous than a construction job. And taking a "city" job was a wise move for a family man. Here was long-term security and a pension after twenty years. Along with his job at the pumping station, Dad did a bit of freelance work each year. He used a few vacation days to work on construction — just enough to maintain his membership in the pipefitter's union and keep his union pension growing.

Dad said he dropped out of grade school to earn money for his family. But some of the childhood learning experiences he described struck me as pretty traumatic. When he struggled with reading or arithmetic his father boxed him in the ear. I think this gave him a warped impression of the learning process. It made me wonder if Dad wasn't looking for an opportunity to leave school early. I think his youthful entry into the workforce helped give him a practical hands-on approach to things. If something wore out or broke, Dad's first thought was to fix it. Who needs a repairman?

Our pop encouraged the enterprising spirit in all of us boys. He liked to see us out finding small jobs around the neighborhood — mowing lawns, shoveling walks or delivering papers — whatever it took to earn a little money. Maybe he overemphasized the value of work for his kids, but Dad worked hard when he was a kid. He wasn't introduced to organized sports as a youth, and having missed high school, he'd never played on an athletic team. No wonder he saw after-school jobs as the way to keep his boys occupied and out of trouble. Besides, he believed that jobs would help instill a sense of responsibility in us.

Do it right the first time

"If you're going to do something, do it right," Dad insisted. And to help us adhere to this maxim he showed us how to hold a broom, how to whisk a dirty sidewalk with brisk, side-to-side sweeps and how to replace a pane of glass. If my father saw me doing a slipshod job on some chore, he'd step in and give me a pep talk about the right way to tackle a job. After demonstrating, he'd make me do it again. "Now you're cookin' with gas," he'd say once I was on track.

"Having the right tools is ninety percent of the job," Dad told us. He believed that the handier we boys were with hammers, wrenches and saws, the better we would fare in life. He stressed that "A job isn't done until everything is cleaned up and the tools are put away." His basement tool room was adequate but unspectacular; it didn't even have a workbench. Dad kept his tools in a box-like wooden bin that was a cross between a coffin and a dresser drawer. Every tool was in there somewhere, but finding the right one could take a bit of digging. Lighting came from a sixty-watt bulb dangling from an overhead cord.

You help, you learn

Watching Dad fix things around our two-flat was an education. He repaired everything — faucets, light switches, gutters — you name it. He often recruited one of us boys to help him fix a leaky faucet or a broken window. I was the designated helper after my underhand toss sent a football through the big kitchen window. I had just intended to land the ball on the back porch.

Inside our flat, roughhousing kids sometimes left a wall in need of patching. Dad showed us how to mix Spackle powder and water to the right consistency. He used a putty knife to scoop some up. But before applying it, he took a sip of water and squirted it into the hole. This made the plaster stick better, he said. Messy but memorable.

Collecting bottles

If I found an empty pop bottle in the alley I could take it to the A&P and get the two-cent deposit back. In fact, empty bottles could really pay if I looked for them in earnest. As a young kid I pulled a coaster wagon up the alley with hopes of making a whole buck. I knocked on back doors, bugging neighbor ladies to see if they had any unwanted bottles. Their responses varied from kindly smiles and cases of empties to frowns and remarks that kids shouldn't go around begging. It was a windfall when some nice woman with a porch full of quart-size Canfield bottles told me to take them all. They were worth a nickel apiece.

The iridescent Chevy

Why the heck is Dad's car parked in front of the house, I asked myself. It was a weekday and Dad always drove to work. I'd seen him walk out the door carrying his lunch pail an hour earlier. When I asked Mom she said some guy at work owed Dad a ride and was paying him back. It was early June and I was happy to be out of fourth grade. In this buoyant mood I got the inspiration to shine Dad's green '51 Chevy. It would be a surprise. Heck, it would surprise Mom, too. I'd just go ahead and do it.

I headed down to Dad's basement tool room and searched the shelves for some kind of polish. Fumbling through cans of grease, kerosene, paint and varnish, I finally found a can labeled: PENETRATING OIL. To my uneducated eye this looked like pretty good stuff. *Yeah, this should do the job,* I figured. I grabbed a rag and hurried through the gangway to the front curb, where Dad's car was sitting unsuspectingly.

Loading my rag with a few squirts, I applied the oil, rubbing with small circular movements as I'd seen Dad do. The cloth in my hand blackened up quickly with dirt, so I had to get more rags from the basement. In the laundry room I bumped into Mom. "What are you up to?" she asked. When I told her, she shook her head, informing me that a car gets washed before it gets polished. But gee, the hood and one fender were already done. I begged her to let me finish the job. Raising her eyebrows, she said: "OK, but throw those oily rags in the garbage when you're done."

Undaunted, I went out front and kept shining. Doing the roof was tough — I really had to stretch. But in a half hour the whole job was done. Stepping back to admire my work, I was surprised at the way Dad's car shined. The circular patterns I'd used to apply the oil now looked like little rainbows. Not exactly what I had in mind when I started, but nice in a way. Dad's Chevy was completely covered with iridescent scales — like a big fish. Oh well, I'd done my best and I was tired. After dumping the oily rags I put the penetrating oil back in the tool room.

Dad didn't get home from work until after supper that night. I had just scrubbed off the soot from my car-polishing efforts and was exiting the bathroom. Voices drifted from the kitchen: "What happened to the car?" "Joe shined it." "Joe? What the hell? What did he put on it?" "I don't know, but he worked real hard. He wanted to surprise you." I heard more mumbling then subdued laughter from both of my parents.

My feelings were mixed. I was glad that I'd tried to do something nice for Dad, but I felt stupid about rubbing the wrong stuff on his car. Then I worried that I might have done some damage. The next night Dad got home at his normal time. Finding me on the balcony after supper, he thanked me for polishing his car, but told me that penetrating oil worked better for loosening rusty bolts. He said we could polish the car together on the weekend — and use Simoniz.

The Dunworth's grass

One summer I got a weekly job mowing the grass for the Dunworths, who lived on our block. The Dunworth boy, Eugene, was a year or two younger than me. Everyone called him "Skippy." His mom told me that he played Little League baseball. Skippy was never around when I cut the lawn — I figured he was at some park practicing. *He must be good*, I imagined. While my legs strained to push the mower, my mind pictured Skippy in his Little League uniform slugging homeruns and fielding fly balls. Go Skippy!

His sister Dyann was one of Margaret Mary's best friends. A happy chatty kid, she was over at our house a lot. I often passed Marg and Dyann on the sidewalk, where they roller-skated, jumped rope and played hopscotch. Dyann took dance lessons from her mother, who taught dance for a living. She was one of many parish kids who performed in the Minstrel Show staged each year in the high school auditorium.

Like most of the other parkways on our block, the Dunworth's produced an anemic crop of grass, thanks to the heavy shade of mature trees. And it was lumpy, so the mower always scalped it in places, leaving black spots. These I disguised with strategic sprinklings of grass clippings.

After cutting and raking the grass I tidied up the edges with hand clippers, then trimmed the bushes with a pair of big hedge shears. The first time I attacked the bushes, working the heavy handles in and out really blistered my hands. When Mrs. Dunworth saw them she was quite upset and showed me where I could find a pair of garden gloves in the basement.

As I pushed the mower across the Dunworth's yard one steamy afternoon, I was surprised to see Dyann approaching. She stopped and handed me a tall glass. Ah, ice-cold lemonade! I gulped it down as she watched, smiling. Dyann seemed delighted that I found her summer cooler so refreshing. I felt grateful and contented for the rest of the day. On subsequent grass-cutting jobs for the Dunworths I kept wondering when Dyann would appear with more lemonade but, alas, it was not to be.

The shovel brothers

For Jim and me, a good snowfall was money in the bank. If the white stuff came down on a school day we went straight home from school, shoveled our own walk and took off to make a few bucks clearing snow for other neighborhood folks. We had to move fast — before Mrs. Quinn phoned from across the street, asking for someone to shovel her snow. She was a nice old widow, but from my kid's perspective she had a poor grasp of private enterprise. After I'd shoveled her front walk, front porch and steps, gangway, first and second floor back porches, rear stairs and landing, she paid me one whole quarter. *Better to move fast and make some real dough,* I told myself.

Heading out at 3:45 Jim and I could really clean up by suppertime. Some two-flat owners would pay us a whole dollar for shoveling front and back. Really generous folks might even give us a buck each. Arriving home from an after-school shoveling mission, we'd be late for dinner, but there was little to fear. Dad gave us a pass because we'd been out earning money, gaining real-world experience. We might even get out of doing the dishes and be sent to bed early.

The dish drill

When supper was over we kids cleared our plates from the table and brought them to the sink. Three or four of us went to work on kitchen chores. One kid swept the floor, while others on dish duty headed for the long porcelain sink. The dishwasher had a helper or two who dried the plates and glasses and took them into the pantry. When I was a little squirt dishwashing chores went to Joan or Jim, both older than me.

There were occasional mishaps. Carrying a tall wobbling pile of plates and bowls to the pantry was risky. One faulty step could make it topple and crash to the floor. Luckily, we used dinnerware made of thick Melamine plastic and unbreakable aluminum glasses. When I was eleven we began alternating washer/dryer chores — one night I'd wash, the next night I'd dry. When my dishtowel got heavy and water soaked I liked to twirl it up tight and snap the dishwasher in the butt.

When I was in high school Dad bought a dishwashing machine. We kids thought it was terrific at first, but the novelty wore off quickly. All the pre-rinsing, loading and unloading was a pain, adding time to the task of getting the dishes washed, dried and back on the pantry shelves.

Painting lessons

With so many kids knocking around the house, bumping into walls and leaving handprints, there was always a room in need of fresh paint. So when we boys were old enough to handle brushes and rollers, Dad conscripted us for painting duty, reminding us that "Many hands make light work."

He demonstrated how to load the roller, how to paint trim with a small brush and how to use a cardboard shirt backing from the laundry as a guide for painting a nice straight line. To get us started Dad showed us where the tarps were in the basement and how to lay them out to protect the floor. He showed us how to use his extension plank. Pulling on each end, Jim and I could stretch it, doubling its length. When we set the extended plank between two ladders it gave us a platform to stand on when we painted ceilings.

By the time we older boys were in high school we knew the drill. Dad just had to tell us which room needed painting. He'd bring home some cans of latex paint and we'd take it from there. Of course, Mom, the compulsive cleaner, insisted that we wash the walls before applying any paint.

Bedrooms were likely candidates for a fresh coat of paint. Or it was time to recoat the dining room ceiling. Painting really wasn't that bad — we tuned into WLS radio or loaded a stack of 45s onto the phonograph. Listening to Bobby Rydell, Connie Francis and Frankie Avalon helped us pass the time. We wore old clothes and paper hats from the paint store. Walls were easy; ceilings were a pain in the neck — literally. It hurt to keep my head cocked back while rolling paint onto the ceiling. And the splattering roller gave me a rude raspberry in the face, leaving hundreds of tiny dots.

Sanitized for your protection

The bathroom was a monster cleaning job. All that mopping, scrubbing, rinsing, polishing — aargh! I'd start with the sink and faucets and finish up by washing the old-fashioned bathroom window with its bumpy translucent pattern of tiny web-like fans.

Comet Cleanser did a good job on the tub, sink and toilet. That toilet was no fun. Mom's standards required scouring the inside, then wiping down the outside with Climaline and finally rinsing it with a wet sponge. But by far, the toughest job was our big claw-foot tub. Nine Murphy bathers could give the inside an unholy halo. I climbed into the tub and scrubbed for all I was worth. When I climbed back out the muscles in my arm were burning.

Next I swabbed the floor of small hexagonal tiles with Spic and Span and hot water. This task required a trip to the broom closet on the back porch. In winter the mop and bucket became one frozen unit. Lifting the mop brought the bucket along with it. Returning to the bathroom, I set the bucket into the tub and turned the hot water on full blast to thaw the mop's frozen gray tentacles.

Of course, with six other kids in the house, interruptions could add half an hour to my bathroom chores. Somebody always had to go. "Aren't you done yet? I gotta go!" "I won't bother you, I just havta pee!" "Get out for one minute, will ya — I need to take a dump!" Sometimes I locked the door so nobody could get in until I was finished.

On one occasion Jim wanted in ASAP. "Just a minute!" I yelled. He came back seconds later, pounding on the door and shouting. "You're playing with yourself! There's no doubt about it — you're playing with yourself!" "Right!" I told him. "Go downstairs to the commode in the basement if you have to go so bad."

Major weekend chores

Saturday morning was prime time for chores. Meager weekday jobs paled in comparison to the big outdoor tasks that kicked off the weekend. Porches and sidewalks needed sweeping, the grass was due for cutting or leaves had to be raked. What's more, Dad was home, so there was extra pressure to get up, do your chores and make sure you did them right.

For a year or two I handled sweeping jobs. Starting with the second-floor porch, I worked my way down the back stairs all the way to the sidewalk, getting the landing and first-floor porch on the way. Once on terra firma, I whisked the back sidewalk. Looking through the gangway between our house and the one next door I saw light at the end of the tunnel. Just sweep out to the front, do the porch, the steps and the sidewalk, then freedom!

I liked to get my chores done early — that way most of the day was still ahead of me. I could call Keating or O'Leary. Maybe I'd walk to Glider's Hobby Shop or ride my bike over to Halsted and do wide circles on the asphalt behind the CTA bus barn.

Pushing sawdust

One job that could really louse up a Saturday was sweeping the basement floor. It was dark and depressing in the cellar, even on a sunny day. Dad liked to give me this brooming exercise when he was nearby fixing the washing machine or the boiler. He was right there to tell me what I was doing wrong.

I had to wet a big bucket of sawdust and throw handfuls of it onto the floor — from the laundry room to the front storerooms, then sweep it all up. If I didn't do it right, sawdust left on the concrete would tell on me. I started with a big push broom and finished up with a regular broom. It was easy enough to sweep the dirt into a dustpan if someone were holding it for me. But sweeping with one hand and working the dustpan with the other was an art. When I mastered this task I knew I was getting good. In fact, I wished that I could demonstrate my skill to the kids in my class.

Good old coal

Our coal bin was a smelly dirty place. Fine grit seeped from beneath its wooden walls, outlining them in black on the basement floor. Coal deliveries poured in right through a window. The black chunks came from a truck parked out front, and rumbled through the gangway on a conveyor that took a ninety-degree turn at the window. With their oversized shovels the deliverymen directed the flow toward the back corner of the bin. It piled up on the floor till the room was about half full.

That coal fueled our old-fashioned furnace with its heavy, cast-iron door. Luckily, we didn't have to shovel coal directly into it. Our stoker handled that job. It was a big steel box with an auger inside that screw-fed coal into the furnace. Once the stoker was filled it would supply the furnace for a few days. Dad told us boys what a luxury it was to have a stoker. It saved us from running down to the basement to feed the furnace late at night or early in the morning.

When Jim and I were old enough to wield shovels we were recruited for stoking duty. Mom reminded us on freezing-cold mornings, "Your father wants you to fill the stoker when you get home from school." It was a pain in the ass, but if Jim and I did it together it wasn't too bad.

Despite the gracious living delivered by our stoker, burned-up coal turned into cinders (or "clinkers" as some folks called them) that had to be removed from the furnace. Dad did this, dragging these jagged red-hot embers through the furnace door into five-gallon steel buckets. The glowing cinders had an unearthly appearance, like asteroids from some distant galaxy.

After they'd cooled Dad carried the cinders out to the alley. But first he dumped a shovelful of the very small ones into a cardboard box that went into the car trunk. Cinders came in handy if we got stuck in ice or slush. Dad tossed handfuls of them in front of the rear tires. Then, when he stepped on the gas, we ground our way free.

Mom's laundry labors

Dad bought Mom a big Norge washing machine and a Hamilton gas dryer to lighten the drudgery of laundry duty. Each of these workhorses sat on concrete blocks that raised them eight or ten inches above the basement floor. I imagined that their purpose was to keep Mom from being electrocuted if water flooded the laundry room.

The heavy-duty Norge performed heroically, but month after month of family-sized loads took their toll. Occasional breakdowns forced Dad to make speedy repairs. He might come home on a weeknight expecting to relax with the paper and be greeted with news of the disabled washing machine.

After supper Dad went downstairs to assess the damage. He could usually get the machine up and running, but occasionally the repairs required a new belt or gasket. If the big drum sprung a leak he had to remove a dozen bolts and take off the back plate to replace a giant gasket. Sitting on the cold concrete floor one winter night, he looked up at me and said: "If I don't put every one of these bolts on just perfect, this thing will start leaking all over again." This made the homework waiting for me upstairs seem like fun. I wished there really were a "lonely repairman," like the guy on TV, who'd jump at the chance to come over and help Dad.

Martha's Christmas creations

Two holiday seasons in a row, Martha asked us kids to help her sell the Christmas items that she made. I thought my aunt was crafting these things for fun, but years later I realized that she and Uncle Lee had been in tough financial straits and needed extra money to make ends meet.

On her sewing machine Martha turned out a batch of frilly little aprons sporting bright Christmas designs like poinsettias, jingle bells and Santa faces. I took a box of them into a big apartment building on 79th Street and went right to work. When a lady answered my knock at her door I showed her the three-dollar aprons. To my delight, she bought one instantly. I continued down the hall, knocking on doors. It was astonishing — almost every woman who saw the aprons bought one. I was sold out in less than an hour.

The next holiday season Martha crafted mini Christmas trees using crinoline rings. Priced at four bucks apiece, they moved just as quickly as the aprons. Again my clever aunt had come up with the right product at the right price at the right time. A good lesson in basic marketing.

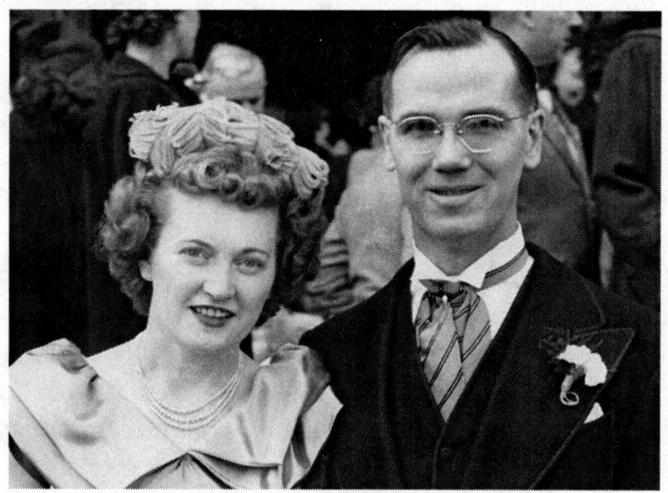

Martha and Lee at Theresa's wedding, 1949

Helping at Lee's shop

From time to time Martha phoned our house, asking if a few of us kids could help out at Lee's print shop. Her calls could come on a school night, giving us very short notice. Lee would have a job with a tight deadline. He printed brochures for local churches, schools and businesses. These booklets had to be "gathered" before being stapled and trimmed. That's where we Murphy kids came in. Gathering involved assembling the printed sheets in the proper order.

Lee picked us up and drove us to his shop on south Vincennes Avenue, where stacks of paper sat waiting on both sides of a long table. We helpers picked up pages from each stack, placing the first sheet on top of the next, and so forth — until we reached the last pile. Round and round the table we went, collecting set after set of printed sheets and stacking them into neat piles.

Martha guided each set of gathered sheets onto a machine that folded them in half. Then, using a foot pedal, she punched in two or three staples. Next Lee placed stacks of stapled brochures into a big cutter and locked them down tight. He pushed a button and WHOOSH, a heavy steel blade slid down and across, trimming the thick piles as if they were butter.

Before driving us home our aunt and uncle took us out to dinner at a local restaurant. Sometimes Lee handed us small rewards as well. When we were very young he gave us little Disney cartoon characters that he'd molded in lead. When we were older he handed us real lines of type hot off his typesetting machine. It was thrilling to hold a warm slug of metal in my hand that read:

YHPRUM EOJ

a mirror image of my name in raised capital letters.

The heart of the shop

Lee named his print shop O'Brien's Linotype because an old-fashioned Linotype machine was the backbone of the operation. This typesetting monster was a miraculous assembly of myriad clicking clacking parts. Sitting at the keyboard Lee typed every word that would be printed.

Each letter began as an engraved image on a little piece of brass, called a mat. As Lee typed, mats fell out of an overhead magazine, and made their way down through the huge machine to form lines of type. When he pulled a lever, a row of mats met molten lead, forming a line of metal type. The raised letters looked like those on a manual typewriter.

But in trying to compete with print shops that used modern "offset" presses, Lee was fighting a losing battle. Offset printing was cleaner and less labor-intensive than his method. It used photo-generated type transferred to a flexible aluminum plate that was wrapped around a cylindrical printing drum. There was no bulky

Linotype machine or molded metal type; no lead slugs to assemble or heavy type forms to lift.

Smooth quiet offset printing was cheaper and faster than my uncle's letterpress method — cheaper for the printer and the customer. Lee struggled for decades before calling it quits and closing down his shop. It took him years to sell off his old-fashioned equipment a little at a time — mostly to small town newspapers that were still using Linotype machines.

Auburn Food & Liquor

I learned a lot in my senior year at Leo — not so much from school as from my after-school job at Auburn Food & Liquor, a busy grocery store near my house. There was always plenty to do at Auburn and the quirky characters who worked there kept things interesting. My shift usually began with deliveries. Boxed grocery orders were lined up and waiting near the front door when I walked in. I'd load two or three of them into the delivery bike's deep wire basket, then push the bike off its kickstand and pedal away, hoping to earn some decent tips.

There might be two or three rounds of deliveries to make before I could tend to my store duties. I learned to patrol the aisles, checking for stock that needed replenishing. Extra canned goods were stashed beneath the shelves on the floor, concealed by removable baseboards. In the rear of the store a big cooler with glass doors gave customers access to beer and pop. Adjacent to the cooler a thriving butcher shop sold cuts of meat as well as fresh bakery goods. Way in back, behind the store proper, a little man washed and cleaned veggies before displaying them in the produce section. Some crazy things happened at Auburn Food & Liquor, which I'll talk about later.

Chapter 7

Jack

"Come on kids — we're goin' to the park!"
— Jack

My big brother Jack was the king of fun. When my toddler brain first recognized him he was in his late teens. Jack was very upbeat. He had a crisp, take-charge manner, due in part to his primary education at Bishop Quarter Military Academy. Our free-spirited older brother took us younger brothers to playground, the Museum of Science and Industry and Chicago's lakefront. Actually, Jack was our half brother. His mom passed away in the Thirties, losing a long battle with tuberculosis. A few years later, when Dad remarried, Jack automatically became the oldest Murphy kid.

Jack loved to be out and about. He looked sharp leaving the house on Saturday night to pick up his date. I remember crisp blazers, shiny silk ties and the smell of Old Spice cologne. Sometimes Jack took me with him when he ran errands. He joked around with the barber and the shoemaker. Jack liked people and they liked him. When he went to the cleaners to get his slacks pressed the lady at the counter gave him express service. She let me walk behind the curtain into the back, so I could watch Jack's pants being pressed. A sweaty little man pulled the top half of the presser down, causing plumes of white steam to shoot out, hissing like some angry dragon. It scared the hell out of me.

Assorted adventures

I always had a good time with Jack. I remember being spellbound when he took me to the show to see *Treasure Island*. And I recall a summer morning when he drove Jim and me to Jackson Park. We watched two older kids who were flying a model airplane. One of them started its tiny gas-powered engine, then ran to grab a little handle that controlled the plane's flight. At the end of invisible lines his helper ran a few steps with the small craft and tossed it skyward. Round and round it went, circling the pilot, who made it climb, dive and loop. Watching these aerial maneuvers was exciting. What's more, I loved the whine of the engine and the smell of the gas fumes.

Other excursions were more dangerous. One crisp fall day Jack took Jim and me to see Lake Michigan, about two miles east of our house. The three of us walked across the big boulders stretching out from the shore. These uneven rocks, jutting six or eight feet out of the water, were separated by gaps wide and narrow — from a few inches to a couple of feet. The larger openings looked black and forbidding. It was scary jumping from rock to rock with waves slapping against them and getting our legs wet. Teenage Jack was foolhardy to take us little kids on this adventure. He was a daredevil but he sure was fun!

One Saturday morning Jack decided to give me a big surprise. Knowing I was cowboy crazy, he took me to a local toy store that had a big display of cap pistols on the wall. "Pick any gun you want," he told me. Wow! Was I dreaming? "Go ahead, pick any one you want," he insisted with good-natured urgency. All kinds of nifty six-shooters were on display, but I was taken with the sleek lines and green handle of a compact automatic pistol. "That one!" I said. "The one with the green handle!"

Jack didn't argue. He bought me the gun I wanted, plus a box of caps. It felt like Christmas morning. When we got home I scrounged in the basement and found a beat-up holster from somebody's old cowboy outfit. My .45 automatic didn't fit into it very well, but I didn't care. I had the gun I wanted. It used a roll of caps that gave me fifty shots. Kids packing six-shooters got a lousy six shots before they had to reload. Meanwhile, I could walk right up and blast them at close range over and over with my potent automatic.

Discovering Jack's stuff

Jack's little 45 rpm phonograph was so simple to operate that Jim and I figured out how to use it — and we were preschoolers. When our big brother wasn't home we sometimes borrowed his record player and plugged it into a wall socket behind a living room chair.

Imagining that we were well concealed, we played our favorites from Jack's stash of records. I loved the *Twelfth Street Rag* and Don Cornell singing *It Isn't Fair.* Sometimes we listened to a jazzy song called *Slippin' Around.* A female voice sang the lyrics, "Slippin' around, afraid we might be found..." We were enjoying this tune one afternoon when Mom suddenly appeared. Snatching the record from the turntable, she told us that it was a "bad" song. I wondered why Jack would bring a record like that home, and hoped he wasn't in trouble with Mom because of Jim and me.

Anything involving Jack was pure magic. He wore a cool square wristwatch with an expandable band and brought fun stuff home from his dates. I loved the hat from Joker Joe's with a big red feather sticking out of it. One New Year's Day Jack walked in with a bag full of colorful hats, horns and noisemakers. My favorite was the one that made a grinding sound when I twirled it.

Jack wore wide silk ties bedecked with bold geometric shapes and big flashy paisleys. Fooling around in his room one day, I picked up a tie from the bed, flipped it over and opened the fat end. Holy smoke! There was a lady in there! She was wearing a skimpy bikini and a big smile. I loved her pose — kneeling, she held both hands behind her head so her elbows stuck out like wings. Gee — Jack's stuff was full of surprises.

Big brother to the rescue

Jack showed up when I needed him. At age four I was allowed to ride my tricycle around the corner to the alley and back. But following an adventurous impulse one afternoon, I crossed the street, heading up the next block. After making a turn or two I was completely lost. Panicking, I came to a stop and started crying. I'm not sure how long I sat there, but eventually Jack showed up in his car. Lifting me off my tricycle with one hand, he paddled my behind with the other, reminding me that I wasn't to cross any streets. My trike and I got a ride home.

On another occasion my curiosity nearly did me in. I had to see what Jack kept on top of the highboy in his room. Perched on a chair, I surveyed the top, finding loads of great stuff. *What's this thing?* I wondered as I picked up a little gizmo made of steel wire. It had two sharp needles with springs behind them. I couldn't resist taking such an interesting toy.

Moments later, just as I was about to stick one of the metal points into a wall socket, Jack appeared out of nowhere. Hoisting me from the floor by one arm, he applied a few swift swats to my rear end. Jack probably saved my life in the process. As it turned out, the metal device I'd swiped was a Spiffy, used for keeping the collar points on a dress shirt neat and straight.

Jack of all trades

I remember when Jack and Dad gave the back porch a fresh coat of gray. They set up scaffolding to get at the undersides of the stairs with their brushes. When Jack found me painting a toy truck with handfuls of gray paint, I had to spend the rest of the day inside. But Jack pulled some goofy stunts himself. One afternoon when he was repairing our second-storey roof, he took six-year-old Jim up there to see the view. Holding him out over the edge, he let Jim wiggle and squeal for a few moments before setting him back down. Some fun.

Mom would never admit it, but our old neighborhood (before we moved west) had a rodent problem. In fact, Dad spotted two suspicious-looking holes in the ground near our garage. Figuring they were rat holes, he decided to flush out the tenants. I watched from the porch as he stuck a running garden hose into one of the holes and held it there. Seconds later a rat flew out of the other hole. "Here comes one!" Dad shouted as it bolted for the back fence. Jack whacked it from behind with a coal shovel. Scratch one rat. Then another one tore out of the hole and dashed toward the fence. "Whop!" Jack's shovel flattened a second rat. This was exciting! Unfortunately, Mom called me into the house, thinking this was not a healthy sport for me to watch. I never learned the final rat tally or if any of them got away.

Where the heck is Jack?

I must have been about six when Jack joined the Marines. It was hard to believe that he was gone. Jim and I wrote him letters that Dad mailed for us. There were rare occasions when the doorbell rang and Jack came bounding up the front hall stairs — home to visit us in his crisp military uniform. He learned to fly airplanes in the Marines, but before long he was in the Air Force piloting KC-97 tankers on refueling missions that took him all over the globe. Then there came the summer when Jack courted Betty Gage, a girl from the neighborhood. He must have been home on extended leave, because I saw Jack and Betty together all the time. Sitting on our front porch they smiled and smooched. They walked hand-in-hand, stopping to embrace and smooch some more. *What's all this mushy stuff about?* I wondered.

In the fall Jim told me that Jack and Betty were getting married. He asked me if I wanted to chip in to buy Betty a wedding present. We pooled our cash, which totaled twenty-six cents. At the local dime store we bought a tiny bottle of cheap perfume. Knowing where Betty lived, Jim insisted that we deliver our gift to her house. So we walked over and rang the front doorbell. When Betty came to the door we handed her the perfume. Appearing to be delighted, she smiled and thanked us sincerely. Jim and I hurried home, feeling pretty pleased with ourselves. Did we know how to choose a gift or what? Jack and Betty were married in St. Columbanus church in November of 1951.

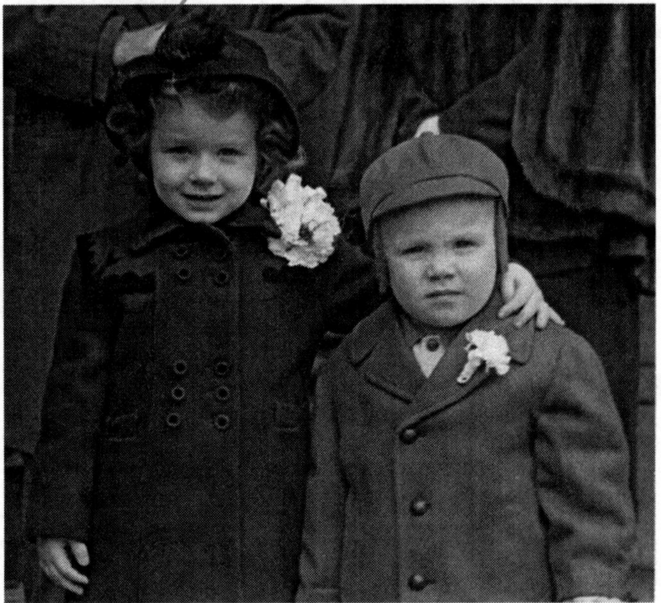

Tiny Marg and Tom brave the cold at Jack's wedding, 1951

A few weeks later our family moved west to the Auburn-Gresham area. For the next decade Jack's visits to our house included Betty and at least one new addition to their growing family. They produced ten children — eight boys and two girls. Jack always phoned on Christmas Day to wish everyone a happy holiday. Other calls from him came at odd hours, announcing the birth of the newest Murphy. I remember being awakened very early one morning by a ringing telephone. Joan answered the call. I heard "Congratulations!" then "Oh no!" in a laughing voice. I knew Jack was announcing the birth of another boy.

Airman Jack during flight training

They're here!

On visits every other summer Jack and Betty pulled up in a big station wagon filled with kids and Susie, the dog. Some of the brood stayed overnight with us, while others went to stay with various Murphy relatives. When our visitors left for home, one or two of the older boys might remain with us in Chicago for a month or so, before heading back to San Antonio via Greyhound. One summer we swapped Pat for Jack Jr. and Mike — boys number two and three.

Over the years Jack made a few surprise visits when passing through Chicago on Air Force business. One evening he came for dinner with a leather briefcase handcuffed to his wrist. He said that he was on his way to purchase a plane for the Air Force and that the bag contained official paperwork regarding the sale. Jack didn't have the keys for the cuffs. He was unable to take off his coat and had to eat using just one hand. After supper Dad drove him to Midway Airport so he could complete his mission.

On his solo visits Jack was more accessible, since there were no kids with him to keep track of. He would update us on the crew back in San Antonio and describe his current home improvement project (like Dad, Jack was always working on his house). I couldn't wait to pepper him with airplane questions — about fighters, bombers, radar, etc. One night he made an effort to explain vectors and navigation to me. I didn't have the vaguest idea of what he was talking about.

I can't forget the summer day when our whole family piled into Dad's Chevy and we rode to Meigs Field on Chicago's lakefront to watch Jack depart. Taking off in a light plane, he circled the field, rocking his wings in a good-bye gesture. Jack flew refueling missions until he'd completed twenty years of military service.

Head in the clouds

After flying from several bases in the US, Jack settled in San Antonio for good. Returning to civilian life, he kept on flying — first as a test pilot, then as a corporate pilot. His family grew to the point where six teenagers were driving cars and motor scooters. To keep this fleet fueled, he set up a fifty-gallon drum of gasoline on a stand in the back yard. I still wonder how he kept track of who used how much gas, who paid, who owed, etc. One day I asked Jack if he had a favorite airplane out of the many he'd flown over the years. "No," he said, "Some were better than others but I never found a plane that I fell in love with." Sadly, Jack's wife Betty passed away in 1993 and we lost Jack in 2003. The Air Force gave him a military send-off with a flyover and twenty-one-gun salute.

Chapter 8

Joan

"Joe, why don't you grow up?"
— Joan, 1958

Joan grew up too fast for me. I have vague recollections that we played together when I was very young. She was clever, loosening the clothesline in the back yard and pulling it low enough to stretch our little pup tent over it. One afternoon she draped blankets around all four sides of the dining room table, creating a dark little space underneath where she, Jim and I could hide out. She pointed a flashlight at us, giving our faces an eerie ghostlike pallor. Very spooky. And Joan sometimes took me with her to the to the dime store or cleaners. But by the time I was nine she was a teenager and light-years ahead of me in every way.

Holy crisis

An explosive encounter with Joan erupted one morning when I found a terrific pencil drawing of Jesus lying on her bed. Our cousin Jim, who was studying at the Art Institute of Chicago, had done the sketch as a favor to her. At age six I didn't know this. Fascinated by the drawing, I was inspired to add some color. So I got my crayons and started going over the heavier lines in red.

Suddenly Joan walked into the room and shrieked: "You ruined it! You ruined it!" She tore the paper from my hand and I ran for cover. Hiding in the bathroom I could hear her crying and telling Mom how I had wrecked the picture she was planning to show in religion class. Somehow I managed to sneak off to school unnoticed. But when I got home Joan had some choice words for me. She warned me never, ever to go near her room again. Ever! "Do you hear me?"

Experience taught me to give Joan plenty of room. I was better off observing her from a distance. Besides, her routine was years beyond my understanding. When I was in first grade learning to read (See David. See Ann. See David run...) my big sister was reading music and listening to shows on the radio. Joan got to do grownup things like being a bridesmaid for Mom's sisters — first when Martha got married in May of 1949 and then when Theresa was wed in November.

At Martha's wedding, 1949 (l to r) Front row: Dan, Jim, Joe. Back row: Dad holding Marg, Joan, Cousin Mike

My astonishing older sister

I was in awe of Joan and all the things she did. She played more and more difficult pieces in piano recitals year after year, adding to her cache of medals; she sang with her girlfriends in the parish Minstrel Show; she went ice-skating at the lagoon near St. George's Hospital. In a vague childish way I sensed that she had her act together. I marveled at the way she managed to get what she wanted.

Starting in seventh grade Joan hung out with a gaggle of girlfriends — Gerry Lucy, Eleanor Scolum and Arlene Buckley to name a few. They were all very bubbly and seemed to start every sentence with "Oh, kid!" And they loved to yak on the phone, so when Joan was home she received and returned plenty of calls. With high school came even more calls — from both girls and boys.

Our telephone sat on a recessed shelf in the hall between the kitchen and the dining room. Joan made and received calls here, which was a pain in the ass for us younger kids. Sitting on the floor she was clogging up a major traffic artery. We complained that she was hogging the hall, blocking our way to and from the kitchen. Parking in that spot was asking for trouble. Luckily, Dad came up with a solution — a trim Princess phone in Joan's room. It gave her privacy and let her blab to her heart's content. Even better, she wasn't blocking the path to our pantry snacks, so we didn't care if she talked till Doomsday. Still, I wondered why anyone would want to spend more than a minute or two on the phone.

What we brothers were doing didn't much interest Joan. However, she took notice if we were up to something unusual. One summer we older boys built a push car out of boards and buggy wheels. Joan helped us come up with a name for our little vehicle, and even helped us paint it. I'll talk more about that little project later, but the fact that our big sister took time to help us with our car made us extra proud of it. After that summer Joan rarely had a spare moment. High school, part-time jobs, dances and 45 rpm singles from George's Record Shop gobbled up her time.

Dressed for success

Joan chose to attend Mercy High School, a Catholic girls' school a few miles east of our neighborhood, taught by the Sisters of Mercy. Her uniform was a navy blue jacket, matching pleated skirt and saddle shoes. Joan liked to look good, so she ironed her own blouses and skirts. And every so often she hand-washed a batch of sweaters in Woolite. She spread them out to dry on towels covering the dining room table. I enjoyed the nice perfumed smell that Woolite gave them as I moved on to do my homework elsewhere.

Throughout her high school years Joan was always going to some dance or other. She looked like a princess in the puffy Cinderella dresses of the day. I remember her in pink, green and blue gowns — the pastels were my favorites. They made me think of Glinda, the Good Witch of the North, in *The Wizard of Oz*. And no matter what the color of her dress, Joan's dark red hair always looked fantastic.

Although she owned a few puffy dresses, Joan occasionally borrowed one. In fact, she loaned out dresses and borrowed some from friends with similar dimensions. It was a nice arrangement, but it would have collapsed without crinolines. Those buoyant springy underskirts were a mainstay of Joan's wardrobe. They furnished the oomph that gave her dresses their amazing inflated look.

Left unchecked, a few crinolines could take over an entire closet. But Joan shrunk each one down to size by pulling it into an old nylon stocking, so it looked like a giant sausage (or maybe a small torpedo). It was fun to peek into her closet just to see that row of compressed crinolines hanging against the wall, patiently waiting to explode open for the next big dance.

Joan stored her shoes in a long pocketed holder that hung on the back of her closet door. There were several pairs of high-heel "pumps" — identical in shape, but sporting different hues — navy, brown, black, green, red... White pumps were versatile. They could take on the color of a particular gown through the magic of shoe dye from an applicator bottle. Walking by Joan's room I might catch a glimpse of her standing in front of the mirror touching up an eyebrow before her date arrived.

Joan smiles sweetly as a high school senior

Kids keep out!

Looking into the girls' room was OK, but that sector was off-limits for boys. My only excuse for entering was to perform some official chore, like cleaning the mirrors or dusting the floor. The top of Joan's dresser seemed like the surface of another planet — covered with bottles of perfume and nail polish, jars of face cream, combs, brushes, hair curlers, bobby pins, nail files and tweezers.

The ever-present smell of nail polish remover made me nauseous, so I didn't stay too long. But it was fun to steal a glance at the bed. Along with Marg's stuffed animals and Joan's candy bar wrappers, I might see a program from a high school musical, a little booklet, called a "bid," from a formal dance or a fancy swizzle stick from some nightspot. Arriving home late from a Friday night date, Joan brushed her teeth and quietly slipped into bed next to Margaret Mary. A few hours later Marg would be up and doing while Joan caught up on her sack time.

From rags to rage

One frosty Saturday morning while Joan was snoozing I took her new 78 rpm record, *Rags to Riches,* by Tony Bennett, and played it on our small Admiral phonograph. I was sure the volume was too low for her to hear with the bedroom door shut. But sure enough, Joan woke up, charged into the dining room and demanded that I hand over the record.

I took it off the turntable and jokingly warned her not to come closer or I'd break it over my knee. She took a step and I raised my knee a bit higher than I intended to, snapping the brittle disc in two. I dropped the pieces and ran. Joan was furious, but in her pajamas she couldn't chase me out into the freezing cold. Somehow I escaped punishment for this little misdeed, but it made Joan more vigilant and vocal when it came to brothers messing with her stuff.

Basement bashes

In the summer between eighth grade and her first year of high school Joan threw a party for her friends in our unspectacular unfinished basement. Wow — this was a big deal. Getting the place ready for this event was a major project, so Dad conscripted Jim and me as laborers. For starters, we cleared the floor and crammed miscellaneous junk into storerooms. Next, we whitewashed the walls and ceiling — the old basement looked like a winter wonderland. We finished up by applying green paint to the window trim and a few old benches. On the night of the party Joan made sure that Mom and Dad kept us kids upstairs and out of sight.

A few years later, when she was a junior at Mercy, Joan volunteered our basement as the dressing room for "Hell Night," the initiation ceremony for Delta Omicron, the sorority she was pledging. When the big night arrived, sixteen girls (pledges and their pledge mothers) found their way to our house and headed for the basement. The pledges had to dress up in silly costumes before riding downtown on the "El" train to panhandle on the sidewalks. I was told to stay upstairs out of the way, but before the group departed I crept down the back stairs and took a peek into a basement window.

Joan looked surreal dressed as a long white cigarette, with her hair standing straight up and painted red on top to create a flame effect. The girl done up as Christine Jorgensen wore an outfit that was black on one side and white on the other — with only one breast. And the pledge dressed as a booger was covered with macaroni dyed black, blue and green. Disgusting, but pretty funny, I thought.

Moving right along

All through high school Joan was on the go, go, go. At home she didn't have a moment to spare. I never noticed her doing homework. She got her studying and assignments done somehow, somewhere — maybe at school or on the CTA. One of the few times I saw her working on a school project was when she made a big display, gluing little pipe cleaner people with round wooden heads onto a piece of poster board.

Joan had plenty of dates throughout high school — all pleasant, well-groomed guys who met Mom and Dad with a smile and a hearty "Happy to meet you!" Bob and Eddie and Frank all took their turns sitting in the parlor beaming clean-cut friendliness. We younger kids took time out from TV watching to pepper them with kid questions about where they were taking Joan or what brand of aftershave they used.

Constantly coming and going, Joan navigated around Mom with little interference and few confrontations. But on one occasion I unwittingly got her into trouble. While cleaning the carpet runner on the stairs leading to the front vestibule I noticed a bulge in one of the risers. Probing behind the carpet, I found a fresh pack of

Chesterfields. *Hey, what's this?* I wondered. Without hesitating I brought the cigarettes to Mom. She looked perplexed as she took them from me. I never thought about this again until decades later, when Joan told me that she'd stashed the pack about ten minutes before I found it, and had to make up some baloney that Mom would buy. This must have tested Joan's bluffing skills to the limit.

My older sister sometimes seemed like lodger who was renting a room in our house. She was restless at home, always having a reason for escaping. Yet there were times when I could get close enough to her for a friendly chat. If she were baking cookies or ironing late at night I might tell her that the kitchen smelled funny because I'd been there after school gluing a model airplane together. And Joan might give me pointers on what kind of clothes I should wear if I wanted to look sharp. It felt good when Joan slowed down at Christmas to reconnect the family. And come Easter Eve, she supervised us older siblings as we colored eggs for Tom and Pat, who still believed in the Easter Bunny. Joan knew how to handle the special waxy dye that gave eggs a multicolored marbled look. And I remember the Easter when she set one egg aside until all the others were dyed. Then she told us helpers to dump all the different cups of color into a pot. We dropped that last egg into the mixture and waited. When Joan fished it out its color was olive drab — as if it had been dyed to meet US Army specs.

Joan and Jean

Sometimes Joan could be really hilarious. On a Sunday afternoon in January, when I was a high school sophomore, John Sullivan and I were playing Electric Football in the dining room. (It was too cold outside to toss a football around.) Dan was on hand to help me with strategy.

Sullivan asked us whether our sister's name was Joan or Jean. Dan replied that we had twin sisters — Joan *and* Jean. Joan heard all this — her bedroom was nearby and the door was open. As she passed through the dining room a few minutes later, John stopped her, asking: "Hey, is your name Joan or Jean?" "I'm Joan," she answered. "But Jean is home if you want to meet her." "Yeah, sure," John answered, wearing a sarcastic grin. Joan insisted that she was indeed Joan, adding, "Jean's around somewhere — she might be taking a nap. If I see her I'll tell her want to meet her."

We continued our Electric Football contest as Joan walked toward the kitchen. I didn't know that she had exited the house via the back door and run downstairs. She scooted through the gangway to the front, where she reentered the house. Meanwhile, Sully and I kept our eyes glued to the metal football field. Our game moved slowly because both of us had to set up all our little men before each play. Then, at the flick of a switch, the field vibrated, scattering the players haphazardly in every direction.

After we'd run a few more plays Joan entered the dining room wearing a different outfit and with her hair in a ponytail. Dan and I greeted her as "Jean" and introduced her to Sully. Looking pretty confused, he asked: "Is your name really Jean?" "That's what they tell me," Joan answered, laughing. Again she exited through the kitchen, scurried through the gangway and came in the front way. Then, while Sullivan was absorbed in setting up his players, Joan slipped back into her room.

A few minutes later she emerged, dressed and coiffed as Joan. Approaching Sullivan, she asked, "Have you met Jean yet?" "Yeah, I did!" he answered. Before he could utter another syllable, Joan was gone. Once more she left through back and reentered through the front, stealing back into her room to change.

When she appeared again dressed as Jean, John blurted, "Hey, you're Jean, ain't ya?" "Yep, last time I checked!" "Well, your sister Joan is lookin' for ya!" "Thanks — I'll keep an eye out for her," Joan said, heading toward the kitchen. John commented that our twin sisters looked a lot alike, but after meeting them both, he'd be able to tell them apart if he saw them together. Unfortunately, that opportunity never presented itself. Dan and I waited several weeks before telling John that there was no Jean.

Battle of the zzzs

Although Joan liked to sleep in on Saturday, we younger kids were unsympathetic to her wishes. Saturday morning was prime TV time, with shows like *Space Patrol, Wild Bill Hickock* and *Captain Midnight.* I thought they all sounded better with the volume turned way up. Too bad there was just one wall separating Joan's room from the living room. She complained to Mom, who ordered us to "Turn that thing down!" We obeyed, but Joan might have to register a second or third complaint before the volume was low enough for her liking.

The phonograph in the dining room (right outside Joan's room) was another sleep killer. Jim, who was an early riser, might decide to put on an LP reflecting his latest fixation — perhaps the sound track to *Oklahoma* or some Hungarian folk songs. Or Dan might stack a few 45s by Connie Francis onto the turntable. Morning music from the dining room would evoke shouts from Joan: "Turn off that music, I'm trying to sleep!" If we ignored her she got Mom or Dad involved.

By far, the nastiest assault on our big sister's sleep came from Jim and me. Something possessed Jim to buy a brass bugle, which he practiced on until he could play several calls. Not to be outdone, I mastered a few calls as well. Then, to protest against Joan's lazy sleeping habits, one of us would crack open her bedroom door, stick the horn in and blow *Reveille,* while the other one sang, "You gotta get up, you gotta get up, you gotta get up in the morning!" This would jolt Joan out of her sleep and catapult her toward us with murder in her eyes.

If she caught up with me, I grabbed her hands to protect myself. With our fingers interlocked and our arms arching above us we tussled, twisting from side to side as she told me what a rotten brat I was. Soon Mom was on the scene to separate us like a referee, and take the bugle. When Dad got home he'd hide it someplace, but little Pat would find it in short order. Meanwhile, I nursed the gouges on the backs of my hands from Joan's long witchy nails.

The promising pianist

Joan stuck with her piano lessons into high school. Her music teacher at Mercy, Sister Theresa, thought that my sister was a gifted musician. In fact, this nun sometimes pulled her out of regular classes and moved her to a practice room (there were ten of these rooms spanning one side of the school). Here Joan and other select pianists played the same pieces over and over. Time invested here could pay off in a first place medal at one of the musical competitions held regularly at Catholic high schools throughout Chicago.

Joan was a junior when Sister Theresa suggested that she take an extra piano lesson each week. Joan talked it over with Mom and Dad and they sent word back to the music nun that the added lesson would be too expensive. However, the resourceful Sister Theresa offered a solution — she could get Joan an after-school job at Mercy Hospital to finance her music instruction. So Joan started taking the extra lesson and working in the medical records department at the hospital.

It was here where Joan met a guy named Miles. He had recently left the seminary and planned to enter Stritch Medical School in the fall. Joan and Miles chatted often but didn't start dating for several months. I was in eighth grade when Miles first picked up Joan at our house. Wow — this was the guy who was going to be a doctor! The guy who was so handsome! When Miles arrived I was in the kitchen passionately shining my shoes for the occasion. By the time I finished, he and Joan had left.

Bridesmaid Joan and fiancé Miles at Rita Reed's wedding

Off to college

By the time Joan entered college she was dating Miles exclusively. Most of her girlfriends married soon after high school and faded from the scene, but Joan found more friends at Mundelein, a Catholic women's college on the North Side. She commuted to School on the "El," traveling north from 63rd & Halsted all the way downtown, through the subway, then back up onto the elevated tracks to the Sheridan Road stop near the end of the line. It was a time-consuming twenty-mile jaunt.

A full-time student, Joan worked her way through college from freshman year right up until graduation. She kept her hospital job through second year, getting home late at night via the CTA. Then she found a job downtown three nights a week taking telephone reservations for Trans World Airlines (TWA). Quitting time was eleven p.m., so Joan didn't make it home until after midnight. I admired her grit and stamina.

Sometimes late at night I could hear the smack-thwack of Joan working at our manual Underwood typewriter. If I got up to investigate, the aroma of brewing coffee would lead me to the kitchen. I'd find Joan sitting at the table churning out a paper — probably for one of her two majors, English Lit or Education. When I was a senior in high school and working late at Auburn Food & Liquor, I often bumped into Joan when I got home. She might even get to bed before me if I had to study for a test the next day.

Joan often asked me to bring her a couple of poppy seed rolls from the store. My cousin Mike, who worked with me there, got a kick out of this routine. As a joke, he had a local bakery make two gargantuan poppy seed rolls — each as big as a birthday cake. He stuffed them into a large grocery bag, which he handed to Joan one night. "What the heck?" she asked, removing one of the monster rolls. Then she laughed as loose seeds cascaded onto the kitchen floor. Mike laughed harder than she did. Those miraculous loaves fed the multitude at our house for the next week. Soon after that humorous event all three of us had graduated — Joan from Mundelein College, Mike from Mount Carmel High School and me from Leo.

Caring for the doctor

Joan taught fourth and fifth grade classes in the Chicago public schools for two years before she and Miles got married. Completing his internship, he was awarded a fellowship to Mayo Clinic. So the newlyweds moved to Rochester, Minnesota until 1966, when Uncle Sam came calling. Now with a darling baby girl, they were off to Atlanta for a two-year stretch with the Army. Returning to Chicagoland, they settled in the northern suburbs. Miles practiced internal medicine while Joan studied interior design and joined with a lady partner to form a successful business. Meanwhile, two more lovely daughters came along. Miles retired several years ago and Joan now limits her design work to a few select clients.

Chapter 9

How sweet it was

"The milk chocolate melts in your mouth, not in your hands."
Fifties ad slogan for M&M's

Dad had a sweet tooth. The groceries he brought home usually included a cake or pie or some kind of cookies. He was partial to marshmallow cookies with a vanilla wafer bottom. They came packaged in clear plastic with cardboard dividers separating one cookie from another. Dad bought several varieties of these confectionary cookies, including pink and white ones with coconut sprinkled on top. But his favorites were chocolate-coated crowns with a red cherry-flavored center.

When Mom served these super cookies for dessert everyone got two. There was never a single cookie left. But Dad liked a touch of sweetness in his lunch pail as well, so he sometimes brought home an extra bag of cookies that Mom would hide in the pantry. Dan always found them — he had an uncanny ability to sniff out hidden treats. Finding a bag of cookies, he'd filch a few, then have to "fess up" when Mom confronted him. Dan was such a repeat offender that she dubbed him "The Cookie Snatcher."

When Dad sliced up a pie or cake from the store it always seemed that the pieces were too small. If he came home with a cake from Widen's bakery it was cause for celebration. Everything they made was wonderful. On Saturday mornings I liked to stop in and treat myself to a bismarck or an éclair. Widen's sold terrific Danish or "rolls" as we called them. A dozen cost less than a buck.

Saturdays could end on a sweet note as well. While everyone was watching *Gunsmoke* or *Your Hit Parade* Dad sometimes broke out a giant Hershey Bar, giving each of us a square or two. Once in a while he'd bring us chunks of mysterious sponge candy. It looked like the tan sponge he used for washing windows and tasted something like cotton candy.

When Easter arrived we enjoyed bags of chocolates from Fannie Mae. On his way home from work on Good Friday Dad stopped at their candy kitchens, purchasing two or three bags of "seconds." These slightly misshapen bonbons tasted just as good as the prettier ones that got packaged up.

Everyone in the family gave up candy for Lent so we were itching to enjoy some again — especially the chocolate variety. That six-week season of penance ended at midnight on Holy Saturday. When the clock struck twelve we older kids were still awake, watching *The Robe* or some other religious epic on TV. Time to savor a puckered cherry center or lopsided lemon cream before heading off to bed.

I recall Easters when stuffing my face with sweets gave me a scorching heartburn. Luckily, my younger siblings didn't have this problem. After finding the colored eggs that were hidden around the house they went straight for the jellybeans and chocolate bunnies in their baskets. Eating the real Easter eggs could wait.

Saturday candy

All of us kids were nuts about chocolate thanks, in part, to Uncle Mike. When we were young he often visited on Saturday mornings, toting a bag of chocolate bars — big, ten-cent bars like Mounds, Almond Joy and Mars Bars. There was one called 7-UP that included seven different flavors covered with dark chocolate. I always saved my favorite part (the square of orange jelly) for last. Another chocolate bar from Mike had rows of little chambers holding orange, raspberry and lime fillings. Classy candy for a kid.

Mike liked the big easy chair in our living room. As he seated himself and greeted Mom we kids gathered round. Mike always propped the youngest Murphy on his knee before handing out the goodies. We all thanked him, then he and Mom had a nice long chat. Mike updated her on our Doyle relatives in Gary, Indiana or told her about his latest trip. A pipefitter by trade, he often drifted westward in winter to work on construction jobs in warmer climes. California was his favorite destination.

Mike called little Margaret Mary "Biddy" as he bounced her on his knee. He was kind of a nice guy's tough guy, or maybe a tough guy's nice guy. If he spotted one of us kids doing something out of line, he'd call us on it in an irritated voice. Mike had served with the Marines in the Philippines before becoming a union pipefitter. He was immune to the fear of heights that spooked other fitters. In fact, he seemed to prefer working at the top of tall structures.

Uncle Mike battles a sailfish in the Gulf

A kinder sweeter era

Acquiring a taste for quality confections was part of my primary education. In first grade the row of kids in my class that contributed the most to the missions was sometimes rewarded with chocolates. Our nun would walk down the winning row with a box of bonbons, letting each kid select one. These fabulous candies could have been from one of many Chicago confectioners. Fannie Mae, Cupid, Andes and Dutch Mill were all going strong.

I heard radio commercials for chocolates with lines like, "Oh you wonderful man — you brought me Dutch Mill chocolates!" Another confectioner ended their radio commercials with a singing tag, "Johnston, Johnston, the candy that's made with love!" On TV nerdy comic actor, Arnold Stang, hawked the nickel Chunky. "What a chunk a chocolate!" he slurred admiringly. Radio spots for the marshmallowy Whiz bar were buttoned with, "Whiz, the best tasting candy bar there is!"

In the Fifties folks gave chocolates as Christmas gifts, and a box or two usually found their way into our house. We kids thought this kind of candy was very sophisticated. On Christmas morn we found hard candy, along with nuts and an orange, in our stockings. That pearlescent hard candy in a jar was OK, but by age nine I would have traded my stocking for a few assorted chocolates from Fannie Mae. To make us feel grateful Dad reminded us that the only thing he got for Christmas as a kid was an orange. But times had changed. When everyone had returned from Christmas mass and things had settled down, Mom passed around a box of chocolates she'd received from Dad or Uncle Mike.

The aisle of dreams

Occasionally, Mom sent me up to the corner A&P for something she needed fast, like a loaf of Silvercup bread — aisle one. But that aisle could really slow me down because just beyond the bread lie a vast and varied assortment of candy bars. The array was so extensive that I had to avert my eyes or lose ten minutes pondering all the different choices.

Even when I had time, selecting the right candy bar was bewildering. Bars were sold individually — not packaged in bundles of six or twelve, the way they are today. I'd find everything from Hershey bars to Bonomo's Turkish Taffy to Walnettos (little caramels with walnuts, wrapped in waxed paper). There was Baby Ruth, Powerhouse, Snickers, Three Musketeers, Milky Way, Fifth Avenue, O Henry!, Forever Yours, Zero, Butterfinger and more — all just a nickel.

Five cents purchased a candy treat to match the mood of the moment. There were hard tangy Lifesavers, fluffy-soft Mallo Cups and chewy Tootsie Rolls. Hershey sold three kinds of chocolate bars — a flat milk chocolate bar that broke into squares, milk chocolate with almonds and a dark semisweet bar.

Some candy bars were crunchy. Heath Bars were butter toffee covered with milk chocolate. Butterfingers and Clark Bars also fell into the crunchy category.

Loads of so-called "candy bars" came in oddball shapes. A Mason Mint was a flat disc the size of a coaster. Brach's made a mint bar with two oval patties. And Chunky was a squat ingot of milk chocolate with raisins and nuts. Kraft caramels were individually wrapped in plastic and came in a five-pack. Bullseyes also came five to a pack. They were caramel and a sugary filling wound up together like a cake roll.

Chocolate-covered Raisenets were boxed. So were Milk Duds (round slugs of caramel covered with milk chocolate). Welch's Mints came in a box as well. They were soft mint pellets coated with dark chocolate. I liked their high chocolate-to-mint ratio. Licorice Nibs were hard little drums that came in an orange-colored box with a clear window. Goobers (chocolate coated peanuts) and M&M's were packaged in little bags.

Chuckles were good — the five different-flavored pieces were really big flattened gumdrops. I always ate the fruit flavors first, leaving licorice for last. I did the same with gummy Mason Dots, avoiding the black, licorice-flavored ones as long as I could. A Switzer's licorice bar was two shiny black extrusions that peeled apart. They looked like the rubber glued to the door molding of Dad's Chevy. Necco Wafers were hard pastel coins about the size of a quarter. Their flavors, like their colors, were pale.

Bit-O-Honey was pretty tough going and Mr. Peanut from Planter's (peanuts glued together with sticky sweet stuff) was rock hard. Another jaw-busting bar was Bonomo's Turkish Taffy. Whacking it against something hard broke it into small but jagged pieces. The Charleston Chew bar (white gummy nougat covered with chocolate) gave my jaw muscles a workout. Hardest of all was the long narrow Slo-Poke sucker. It was a slab of caramel on a stick. This sucker was so hard, it might have been forged by a heavy industrial punch press.

A few super bars like Mounds, Almond Joy and the Mars Bar cost a whole dime. Those ten-cent bars were something special, but the toothaches they gave me were just like the ones I got from chewing on cheaper candy bars.

From Black Jack to Bazooka Joe

Chewing gum took a healthy bite out of the candy section. Wrigley brands were right up front — Spearmint, Doublemint and Juicy Fruit were popular then as now. TV spots for Doublemint showed semi-beautiful girl twins doing nothing in particular while voices sang the jingle — "Double your pleasure, double your fun with Doublemint, Doublemint, Doublemint gum!"

Other chewing choices included Beech-Nut, Clove, Teaberry, licorice-flavored Black Jack and Beeman's Pepsin Chewing Gum, which supposedly aided digestion. Dentyne Gum claimed to be good for teeth but it was too heavy with cinnamon for my taste. Peppermint-flavored Chiclets were white lozenges. They looked like a mouthful of movie star teeth smiling from behind the clear window of their box.

Dark green Clorets allegedly fought bad breath, but their strong mint flavor hurt my tongue. One of their early TV spots struck me as hilarious. The voice-over announcer boasted that clinical tests supported Clorets' breath-freshening claims. The screen showed a woman on one side of a partition blowing into a tube. On the other side, a man in a white lab coat sniffed her breath. He looked very serious as he jotted down his findings on a pad of paper. This commercial made my whole family rock with laughter.

Bright pink bubble gum sold like crazy. Dubble Bubble, little pink drum-shaped pieces, came in a five-pack. So did Bazooka bubble gum. Each thick flat piece had a tiny Bazooka Joe comic strip wrapped around it. Of course, the same selection of gum described here could be found stuck to the undersides of stools and counters at neighborhood drug stores.

Chapter 10

Jim

"What if cats could bark?"
— Jim, age six

Jim and I played together as far back as my memory will stretch. A natural builder, he showed me how to make things. I remember assembling big cardboard cutouts of Disney cartoon critters with Jim and standing them up on the living room floor. I must have been three years old. Jim taught me how to build houses out of Lincoln Logs, coaching me on construction details. After this period my memories of him are spotty until we moved to Peoria Street. But when we first arrived in our new neighborhood Jim and I explored the unfamiliar turf together.

On a cold Sunday afternoon in December we walked up to the A&P at the end of our block and sat on the parkway bordering the sidewalk. It was just sandy dirt covered with little pebbles, but those tiny stones fascinated Jim. He scooped some off the ground and gave me an up-close look, pointing out their different shapes and hues. I was captivated. The two of us sat there carefully picking up pebbles that struck our fancy and putting them into a cookie tin that Jim had brought with him. When the darkening sky turned all the pebbles gray Jim and I knew it was time to quit. We went home with our treasure, stashed it in a very special place and promptly forgot all about it.

Those pebbles were typical of Jim's discoveries. As a young kid he looked down at the sidewalk as he walked. This bothered Mom. "Hold your head up — look straight ahead," she told him. "I like to look down," he answered. "I find things." And Jim pelted Mom and Dad with questions: "Why do White Castle hamburger patties have holes in them?" "Why do white snow piles turn black?" "Why does everybody say 'Achoo' when they sneeze?"

Planting a tree

One Saturday in the spring Jim picked up a maple seed off the front sidewalk. He told me that he was going to plant it and a big tree would grow from it. I asked if I could help and got his OK. Jim said we'd have to dig a hole, so we went down to the basement and got two coal shovels.

My brother thought the dirt strip in the gangway between our house and Mrs. Olsen's place next door could use a tree, so that's where we dug. Jim kept the seed in his pants pocket while we hollowed out a hole about a foot deep. Two workmen repairing Mrs. Olsen's windows were just finishing up. As they passed us carrying their ladder, one of them asked us what we were up to. "We're planting a maple tree," Jim proudly announced. Then he asked, "Do you think this hole is big enough?" One guy answered, "Nope, you need to dig deeper." His friend concurred: "The deeper the hole, the taller your tree will grow." Both men urged us cheerfully to "keep digging" as they walked toward their truck.

Jim and I dug until our hole was three feet deep. It was getting dark and the dirt we'd unearthed was spilling onto the sidewalk. Standing in the hole with his chest at ground level, Jim decided that we'd gone down far enough. He climbed out and removed the seed from his pocket. Then, leaning over the hole, he dropped it in. We watched it whirl its way to the bottom. While we were filling in the soil Mom called us for dinner. "Be there in a minute," I shouted, shoveling faster. When Dad called us five minutes later we dropped our shovels.

At supper Mom asked what had been holding us up. We told her about the maple seed and how we had to dig a real deep hole so it would grow into a tall tree. "Who told you that?" Dad asked, wearing a quizzical smirk. "The men who fixed Mrs. Olsen's windows," I answered. Dad laughed. So did Mom. I was confused.

"What's so funny?" Jim wanted know. "Those guys were playing a joke on you," Dad said. "You plant a little seed like that in an inch of dirt!" Still laughing, Mom added: "They were pulling your leg!" Jim and I were shocked. We found it hard to believe that grownups could play such a mean joke on a couple of kids. The experience assaulted our blind faith in big people. Tired and a bit disillusioned, we went to bed early. Jim and I finished filling in the hole after church the next day.

Fort Rusnak

One fall afternoon Jim and I were returning from school when we spotted a huge wooden crate in the alley behind Rusnak Furniture. This was too good to pass up. Hurrying home, we got our coaster wagon and wheeled the big box to our backyard gate. It was too large to pass through the opening so we got some help lifting and pushing it over the fence into the yard.

We dragged the crate across the grass onto the sidewalk at the foot of the back stairs. It was roomy enough to hold two or three kids. One side, which must have been the lid, was gone, so that became the bottom. With a crow bar from the basement we removed a few slats to make an entrance. Jim and I enjoyed the feeling that this wooden hut was our very own fort.

Candy tasted better when we ate it in our fort. And it was a great place to store things — cap guns, flashlights, comic books, Band-Aids — anything that would support our fantasy of being self-sufficient. The trouble was, we had no privacy. Sitting near the foot of the back stairs our fort was in everybody's way. Tearing down the back stairs, Dan, Tom and Jim Bradley all collided with it. These unavoidable impacts knocked our shack across the sidewalk, scattering all our provisions. Mom had trouble with the fort as well. Carrying a heaping basket of laundry to the basement, she nearly tripped over it.

After a week of this Dad gave us some bad news: "You kids gotta move that crate — it's gettin' in everybody's way." Unfortunately, Jim and I didn't act soon enough, and a few days later our fort disappeared without a trace. Even worse, its precious contents were gone. Jim and I complained bitterly to Mom, but she deferred to Dad, who said, "You don't leave junk sitting around where people can trip over it." He paused then added, "Maybe the next time I tell you to do something you'll obey." A day or two later our fort's supplies were back in their former places — Band-Aids in the medicine chest, flashlights in the kitchen junk drawer, etc.

Passing the pain

At school Jim sometimes appeared to be off in his own world. This prompted teasing from classmates — something that he couldn't handle. I could see that being made fun of really hurt Jim. He sometimes came home teary-eyed, telling Mom that kids were calling him names. She did her best to soothe his angst, but it wasn't enough. Gradually, however, Jim found a way to ease his pain. He began to transfer the teasing he had to endure into teasing he could dish out — to his younger siblings.

Jim made up derogatory nicknames for all of us. I was "Headcur," because of my recurring headaches. Dan was "Daspler," a nonsense name that managed to get his goat. Margaret Mary was "ULT," short for "Ugly Liar Thief." Jim called Tom "Bulldozer," mocking his remarkable stubbornness. Only little Pat got an affectionate name, "The Scooter."

Jim was unable to tease Joan, who was two years his senior. I never saw him make an attempt. But we younger kids were easy prey. When I wasn't looking Jim would sneak up and whisper some nonsense word like "Inksprink" into my ear. He also made a variety of shrieking noises, as well as grunting, groaning, whistling and clucking sounds that were very irritating.

Jim's intense aerial event

As long as he was building something Jim was in a good mood, and he always finished what he started. After I'd made a few lightweight "flying" model planes, Jim said he wanted to take a crack at building one. So we walked to Glider's Hobby Shop and bought two similar airplane kits that required cutting out the parts before gluing them together.

I found making one of these fragile birds pretty demanding. The airplane body and wings had to be built in skeleton form and then covered with tissue paper. Jim and I started working on our planes at the same time. But while I labored, slowly cutting out the parts and gingerly applying the tissue skin, Jim breezed through the process, finishing his plane days before I completed mine. Exiting the kitchen with his flight-ready airplane, he invited Dan and me to come out to the porch and watch. Then, standing at the railing, he struck a match to the plane and tossed it. A bright fireball consumed the craft as it swooped from the second floor porch to the alley, crashing into our garbage can and disintegrating. Jim was delighted. Gleeful! I enjoyed the show too, wishing we had another airplane to immolate (but not the one I was building).

Into the woods

Jim was not the most coordinated kid on the block. He looked clumsy throwing a ball and worse trying to catch one. So I was surprised when he stayed after school one day to take baton-twirling lessons. He came home disappointed, telling Mom that he felt funny about joining the baton group. "I can't be in a class where I'm the only boy with a bunch of girls," he complained. A few months later, Jim asked Mom and Dad if he could join the Boy Scouts. And thinking this would be good for him, they gave their permission.

Soon Jim was attending meetings on Friday nights at the grammar school hall dressed in his scout uniform and armed with his official Boy Scout Manual. He memorized the Boy Scout oath: "On my honor I will do my best..." He learned how to a start fires without using matches, how to cook food by the campfire and how to find edible flora in the forest.

Before long Jim could name the different kinds of trees growing on our block and tie all kinds of clever knots. When summer came he went off to Camp Owasippe in Michigan with other scouts from his troop. Jim loved the canoeing, the long hikes and even the grub. Dad drove the whole family up to visit him on the weekend. He was having the time of his life. Laughing, he told me that some kids his age were crying for their mommies on their first night at camp.

Upwardly mobile

On summer nights while we lay on the balcony looking up at the stars, Jim talked about taking long bike rides to places like Gary, Indiana, where we had cousins. Jim couldn't wait to be away on some sortie to parts unknown. At home he liked to climb the front of the house to reach the balcony. But our two-flat was kid stuff. He soon took to scaling the commercial buildings around 79th & Halsted. His biggest challenge was the tall water tank on top of the

Capitol Theater. It was housed within a cage of curved girders that formed a fancy dome.

That impressive structure was clearly visible from our back porch. For several weeks Jim kept telling me that he wanted to climb the ladder leading to the top of the water tower. I warned him that it was dangerous and tried to talk him out of it but his mind was made up. I started looking east to check the water tank when I exited the kitchen door. Then one day about a week after cautioning Jim, I spotted a tiny silhouette ascending the ladder at the side of the tank. Jim? Possibly, but more likely it was a workman performing some routine task. After supper that night I asked Jim if he'd climbed the Capitol water tank that afternoon. He smiled with a devilish grin that confirmed my suspicions.

Big bang at Snake Valley

When Jim was in his early teens he made a startling discovery in the alley one winter morning. He found an old Army ammo clip stuffed with a dozen live .45 caliber bullets. Of course, Jim had to fire them off, and it didn't take him long to figure out how to do it. As he told me years later, he fashioned a "mini-canon" using junk from the basement. He took a length of 3/8" pipe and wrapped both ends of it with strong metal bands that extended from the pipe for about a foot. Hammered into the ground, these extensions would anchor his gun.

Then, on a snowy winter afternoon, he took this device over to Snake Valley to see if it would work. By tapping a nail into the back of each bullet, he fired them, one-by-one, into a railroad embankment. Jim said he heard the bullets ricocheting off concrete and saw their tracks in the snow. The spent shells were all flayed out because the pipe he used for a barrel was a bit too big in diameter. I told Jim that he was lucky he didn't kill himself or somebody else. He agreed.

"Laugh your troubles away..."

On a sunny morning in July, Uncle Paul from Oklahoma phoned our house to see if Jim and I were ready to head for Riverview, the famous amusement park. While visiting Murphy relatives in the Chicago area, Paul and his kids were staying with our Aunt Helen, who lived just a few miles from our house. Paul asked Jim and me to meet him at Helen's place and he'd drive us from there. We hopped a northbound bus to 63rd and boarded the "El" train. A few stops later we debarked and walked a short distance to Aunt Helen's house.

Paul and our cousins, Jim and Mary Ellen, met us at the door. Our uncle's kids were about the same age as my brother and me. Even better, they were friendly and fun-loving. We all piled into Paul's car and motored to the "world's largest amusement park."

Once we got past Riverview's front gate it was total sensory overload — colorful flags and calliope music; kids with balloons and cotton candy; folks toting big stuffed animals on their backs; the sounds of giant gears clicking and steel wheels screeching against rails. And so many smells intermingled in the air: hot dogs and axle grease; cotton candy and wet canvas; cigarette smoke and suntan lotion. The mix was intoxicating.

Hold on tight

The park boasted six roller coasters, starting with the mild-mannered Greyhound. We tried that ride first and lucky me — I got to sit next to Mary Ellen, who was a doll. This coaster gave us a long ride with lots of dips but none of the steep, gut-grabbing drops or sharp curves we'd get on the Bobs. That coaster was notorious for its fast rough ride. But on the Greyhound we could keep our seats and buy another ticket. So we rode a second and a third time.

Next we checked out The Rotor, a rotating drum the size of a large room, that pressed riders against the wall as the floor dropped out, leaving them plastered to the wall. I'd heard from a kid at school that if someone lost their lunch on this ride, it splattered all over everybody. Luckily nobody got that sick, although The Rotor made me pretty queasy. Then Mary Ellen spotted the Flying Turns and couldn't pass them up. The cars on this coaster were like bobsleds, speeding through the twisting, tube-like course — rolling high up into the banked turns and back down again. Fun!

As the sun sank on the horizon, Riverview lit up like a thousand Christmas trees. Uncle Paul said it was time to head home. But first we walked through Aladdin's Castle, a big fun house with floors that moved and tall curved mirrors that made our heads look three feet tall. What a day! I was still glowing with delight when Uncle Paul dropped Jim and me off at home. I'd completely forgotten that I was in serious trouble. The previous day someone had stolen Dan's bike after I'd left it unattended. Suddenly I feared that Dad would take me to the woodshed for this blunder without delay. But I avoided an immediate confrontation because everyone was asleep when Jim and I got home.

The Music Man

On a positive note, Jim tried his hand at several musical instruments during his teen years. First he surprised us with a shiny new bugle, which he let me toy with. Next, inspired by the Hungarian gypsy music he'd grown to love, Jim bought a used violin and started fiddling with it. He made raucous screeching sounds for a week or two before trying something different. Jim traded in his violin and came home with a trombone. Playing with the slide, he produced a range of rousing flatulent noises. But, thank God, he soon tired of that instrument and sold it.

This, however, did not end Jim's musical career. He later fell in love with the cimbalom, a stringed instrument popular throughout Eastern Europe. He purchased a huge Hungarian concert cimbalom with a range of four octaves. When two deliverymen arrived at the back door with this humongous hunk of oak Mom was beside herself. Where would this monstrosity fit in her house? Thinking fast, she decided that the dining room would have to be its temporary home.

The cimbalom graced that room for a year, occupying more floor space than the buffet. Sitting at this exotic device Jim created notes by bouncing two curved wooden sticks off the thick forest of strings. To everyone's surprise, he really stuck with the cimbalom. And after a month or so he was sounding pretty good. Eureka! Jim had finally found his instrument. With practice he mastered some pleasant Hungarian tunes. Everyone thought the cimbalom made a very nice sound. Still, Mom kept pressuring Jim to get rid of it. She was thrilled when he sold it to an ethnic restaurant.

Jim taps out a lively tune on the cimbalom

Taking off for Jack's

One grade ahead of me in school, Jim started at Leo High School in '56, the year their varsity football team won the City Championship. He made the honor roll and earned a letter in track. Jim seemed to be doing just fine. With the fall of '57 approaching he was all set to become a sophomore and I was ready to start my freshman year. But first we took a long-anticipated bus trip to visit our brother Jack and his family in Chicopee Falls, Massachusetts.

We'd saved enough money from our paper routes to buy bus tickets to Springfield, Massachusetts. The *Tribune* found two kids to handle our routes for a week. Jim and I were primed for adventure when Dad drove us to the Greyhound station downtown. He made sure we got on the right bus, and watched as our motor coach rolled out of the underground depot. We were on our way, burrowing through the curves of Lower Wacker Drive, which were illuminated from above by eerie green lights.

Somewhere in Indiana we stopped for supper at a roadside diner. There was still a little daylight left as Jim and I stepped from the bus. We sat at the counter and a pretty young waitress asked me what I wanted. I looked at the grease-stained menu a little too long for her liking. "Oh, make up your mind!" she screamed in a bitchy voice. Totally shocked, I blurted out the first thing my eyes could focus on. What was this? Waitresses were sweet and polite. Never had I run into a nasty one.

When I got my order it was meatloaf. *Meatloaf?* I asked myself. *Did I order meatloaf? I hate meatloaf!* Too scared to change my selection, I chewed a piece of the gummy slab on my plate as Jim ate heartily. We didn't tip our waitress. Not that we were trying to stiff her — we just thought that tipping was something older folks had to do. Back in our seats, Jim and I watched the sun melt into the horizon as the bus pulled out. We drifted off and slept all the way through Ohio — until our coach pulled into a huge terminal for a rest stop somewhere in New York State. Rest stop? This was more like a rude awakening. I had been resting just fine.

Temptation station

We walked into the cavernous station and used the facilities. Then, as Jim went off exploring, I approached a lifelike fortune-teller enclosed in a glass box. She was beautiful and brightly illuminated, projecting her silent, glaring charm into the darkness. I felt like I was living an episode of *The Twilight Zone.*

Jim was nowhere in sight so I drifted over to the newsstand, attracted by its neon glow. Greeting me was a rack full of racy men's magazines with names like *Pic, Vue, Gem* and *Nugget.* Wow! Those covers had the subtlety of brass knuckles. I'd never come up against a whole wall of erotic stimulation. *Better not pick anything off the rack or hang around too long,* I figured. Some righteous adult (probably a policeman) would be sure to descend on me and give me a good talking to. Heck, Jim might catch me and then tell Mom and Dad when we got home.

The staring newsstand attendant rattled me, so I grabbed a candy bar and handed him a nickel. Jim appeared out of the darkness and we walked to the bus. Taking our seats, we noticed that the paper pillows we started out with in Chicago were gone. Moments later a female bus employee walked by renting little pillows for a quarter — probably the same ones she'd just swiped from our seats. We passed on the pillows.

Our trusty Greyhound coach trundled into the night, quickly jostling me to sleep. When I woke up Jim said that while I slept he heard the guy behind us telling his girlfriend that he couldn't wait to give her a blowjob. This sounded like something really dirty, so I fantasized about what might be involved in performing a blowjob on a girl. Where did the guy blow? Into her ear? Down her blouse? Into her panties? Did he use some exotic device, like a fancy bean blower? It wasn't long before I learned the surprising answers to all these questions. And today I'm still puzzled about the strange couple that rode behind us all those decades ago. Maybe Jim heard a girl with a deep voice talking to a guy with a high one. Or maybe those folks behind us were into some form of gender bending.

Flying high with Jack

After twenty-two hours on the road our bus reached Springfield, Massachusetts. Jack was waiting at the terminal to pick us up. It was great to see him again. Ushering us into his station wagon, he introduced us to little two-year-old Ellen Therese, the youngest of his growing family. Sitting alone in the rear seat with the windows open, her long golden curls flew wild in the wind as we rode to Chicopee Falls. At Jack's place our sister-in-law, Betty, greeted us with hugs and kisses. Jack introduced us to Dennis, Jack Jr. and Mike, aged five, four and three. We ate dinner and then hit the sack early. The next morning we'd be up at six a.m. and bound for Westover Air Force Base with our big brother.

Jack was generous with his time. He took us out to the busy flight line, where F-86 jet fighters were landing — popping their drag chutes right in front of us. Wow — this was more than I'd hoped for. With Jack in the lead we climbed up into the cockpit of his big KC-97 for a brief rundown on some of the instruments and controls. Next we took a peek inside a B-25 bomber — the plane Billy Mitchell and his group flew on their famous raid over Tokyo in World War II.

Over the next week Jim and I sat with real Air Force personnel in training classes about theory of flight, survival tactics for downed airmen and how jet engines work. We saw parachutes ready to be repacked, with their silky cords stretched out full length on incredibly long tables. Jack told us that to ensure quality, a chute was periodically pulled from a packer's inventory and he had to make a jump with it. I thought that would definitely keep a guy on the ball.

Jack even arranged for Jim and me to "fly" in a Link Trainer — a stubby simulated cockpit not much bigger than a kid's rocket ride at the mall. A technician closed the canopy and I was flying blind, using only instruments. I had no idea where I was going, but it was fun. The results of my flight were not promising. I'd crashed twice and flown through a mountain range. Jim did better on his Link flight, although he flew through that mountain like I did.

On the weekend Jack taught Jim and me how to drive his Italian Vespa scooter up and down the street where he lived. Seated on his lap I slowly got the hang of working the accelerator, clutch and brakes. Jack kept the scooter stashed in his plane so he wouldn't be stuck at the airfield if he landed in some remote corner of the globe. At that time he was piloting the tanker version of the ocean-hopping Pan American Clipper. But the new jet tankers (KC-135s) would be coming soon.

Our visit to Jack's place streaked by like a Nike missile. Before we knew it Jim and I were on a Greyhound bus heading back to Chicago. When we got home we were two days late for school. The fall semester at Leo had already started. I'd missed freshman orientation and getting a locker assignment. Glee Club tryouts, mandatory for all freshmen, were over as well, but that didn't upset me greatly. Jim and I joined the student body, eager to make a good start on the year.

UFOs and beyond

We got back to our paper routes, arising to darker and darker mornings as fall muted into winter. Then one frosty a.m. Jim returned from his route trembling with excitement. He'd spotted a UFO that looked like a glowing red cigar. "It was just sitting still in the sky," he told me. "Then it turned so it just looked like a red dot, and it darted off to the east and disappeared!" Anxious to report his sighting to the *Tribune*, he called and blurted all the details. Darned if his story didn't make the next morning's paper.

Soon after his extraterrestrial sighting Jim became obsessed with France. He talked about the Eiffel Tower and the Arc de

Triomphe. He saw the movie *An American in Paris* and daydreamed about Leslie Caron singing and dancing in the City of Lights.

Then Jim's attention suddenly shifted to Oklahoma. A neighborhood gas station that sold Oklahoma brand gasoline was flanked by a billboard that spelled out OKLAHOMA in giant red letters. Jim told me that looking at that sign gave him a thrill. Enthralled by "The "Sooner State," he bought the 33 rpm soundtrack to the musical, *Oklahoma*, and sang along with it: "Oh the farmer and the cowman should be friends..."

The Sooner the better

When Mom and Dad visited our Uncle Paul in Oklahoma City early in '58, they brought a small sample of red soil back with them. We kids thought it was cool, but Jim flipped over its redness. "It's almost unbelievable!" he said to me. At this point Jim was primed and ready to take off. Then one Tuesday night after a Civil Air Patrol meeting at Foster Park, Jim informed me that he'd be taking a different route home. That was the last I saw of him for quite a while.

After a week or so Dad got a call from the police in Clinton, Oklahoma. They had picked Jim up for vagrancy and were holding him. Dad arranged to have him put on a bus heading back to Chicago. However, Jim had something else in mind. He got off at Oklahoma City, cashed in his ticket and boarded a bus bound for Austin, Texas. When the Austin police phoned a few days later Dad flew down and brought his lost son home. Jim went back to Leo and stuck it out for the remainder of his sophomore year.

His third year at Leo marked a major turning point for Jim. The semester had just begun and he was taking advanced algebra. The teacher was Brother Irwin, a skinny creepy character with a lot of pent-up hostility. While facing the blackboard to work out a problem, he would sometimes spin around suddenly, dart toward a particular student and slug him (apparently thinking the kid had been goofing off). One day while quietly paying attention, Jim became the target of Irwin's attack. Getting punched in the face shocked the hell out of him. He reacted by walking out of class and exiting the building.

The next morning Dad took Jim to the office and told B Regan, the principal, what had transpired. Regan did not summon the math teacher to get his side of the story. Instead, he and Dad urged Jim to return to Leo. Jim refused. At home that afternoon he promised Mom that he would finish high school "some day."

What next?

At home Jim was restless, confused and angry. He picked on the younger kids with a vengeance and even started fistfights with Dan and me. Jim caused such incredible dissention and unhappiness for the whole family that Mom and Dad had to act. They arranged for him to receive several weeks of treatment and counseling at a Catholic hospital.

When Jim came home Dad did not try to persuade him return to Leo. Jim worked at a few dull jobs until September, when he entered Calumet High School as a junior. This public school presented a change of scene that Jim really liked. His hostile mood improved almost overnight. As always, he earned good grades, but he felt relaxed and started to enjoy school. At home he stopped teasing his siblings.

A girl Jim met at Calumet propelled him toward his next fixation. An immigrant from Hungary, she told him about her homeland and the unsuccessful '56 revolt against the Soviets. Before long Jim became captivated by anything Hungarian. In art class he painted a spectacular poster depicting a statue of Stalin toppled by the Hungarian freedom fighters – a snapshot from the uprising. He bought records of Hungarian songs and purchased the soundtrack to *Song Without End*, a movie about the life of Hungarian composer, Franz Liszt.

All of a sudden Jim was cooking us goulash for supper and serving us palacsintas (the Hungarian version of French crêpes) for dessert. It was good to see him so happy. He savored every minute of the time he spent at the public high school. Jim's most remarkable accomplishment at Calumet took place during swim class. On a bet he swam the width of the pool underwater four times, finishing blue and unconscious. Coach Zayner worked on him until a Fire Department pulmotor arrived with oxygen. After Jim pinked up he got a ride to St. George's Hospital, where he spent the night. My brother's breathtaking swim so impressed the senior class president that he told Jim it was his most memorable high school experience.

Continuing adventures

After high school Jim held a few boring jobs until the summer of '65 when he traveled to Chiapas, Mexico. He joined a group from Loyola University on a mission to rebuild structures in the town of San Christóbal de las Casas. During his visit he met a lady named Lucha, whom he married a short time later. Their union produced four sons who grew up in San Christóbal and still live there today, enjoying successful careers. Regretfully, Lucha passed away in 2006. Now remarried, Jim lives in Chicago. His plans for the future do not include travel.

Chapter 11

Dan

"You can't win, Joe — you have no strategy!"
— Dan

Although Dan was a just sixteen months younger than me I barely noticed him until I was almost five years old. I'd just flunked out of kindergarten, having failed to grasp what it was all about. After being lost in that crowd of about fifty kids it was now easier to spot my younger curly-haired brother. He was very talkative, although he pronounced words "car" and "far" like "cow" and "fow." I was used to playing with Jim, who was two years older than me. Now Dan, who usually played with our little sister, wanted to hang with us.

As soon as we moved into our new digs on Peoria Street Dan made friends with Dolores McCarthy, who lived next door. Both first graders at St. Leo Grammar School, they remained close pals until fourth grade. Then one day Dolores' Dad answered the door and told Dan that she couldn't come out. As Dan walked away, he heard the old man urging his daughter to find some girls to play with.

The thrill seeker

The glasses Dan started wearing in fourth grade made him appear wise beyond his years. But he was, in fact, a studious kid who took to independent reading early. He loved books about big jungle cats and American Indian tribes.

After school Dan watched episodes of Martin and Osa Johnson on TV. Their African exploits, filmed in the Thirties, showed them in one desperate situation after another. Luckily, they always managed to escape — sometimes via their amphibious plane waiting in a nearby river. From episode to episode Martin and Osa encountered strange tribes, rhinos, hippos, pythons, lions, tigers, cheetahs, elephants, baboons — the works. They slashed their way through thick jungles, slogged through crocodile-infested swamps and traversed barren stretches of the Serengeti Plain. Dan reveled in this stuff.

He also liked watching old movies that featured Clyde Beatty, the lion tamer/actor. And on Saturday mornings Dan tuned in to *The Buster Brown Show,* hosted by a hefty white-haired gent who called himself "Smilin' Ed McConnell." When Ed uttered the magic words, "Plunk your magic twanger, Froggy," Froggy the Gremlin, a little rubber frog, popped into view, accompanied by a loud BOING!

The show included weekly episodes of *Gunga the Elephant Boy.* Set in India, the series followed the adventures of young Gunga Ram. Location shots of elephants, big cats and other wild critters were intercut with clips of Gunga, which were filmed in California. In real life Gunga was a student at UCLA named Nino Marcel.

On Sunday *Wild Kingdom* with Marlin Perkins taught Dan more about exotic animals. He liked to talk about lions, tigers, leopards and such. Dan told me that a cheetah could run faster than the speed limit and that a leopard was so strong, it dragged its prey up into a tree to eat it. He enhanced these descriptions with animated gestures — growling, pawing and occasional pouncing. Even so, I was more entertained when Dan made his double-jointed thumbs pop in and out of their sockets.

Dan and I bet each other about which cat would win if a tiger went up against a lion or a panther tussled with a leopard. He didn't inherit his love of cats from our mother — she was not fond of cats or dogs. No pet animal was going to chew up her furniture or shed hair all over her clean house. So when Dan took it upon himself to buy a puppy at the pet shop, Mom was not thrilled. After a week or so Dad took the little doggy to work with him, where he gave it away.

Heap big adventures

Dan's fascination with American Indians was spurred by TV shows like *Broken Arrow* and *Brave Eagle.* He always sympathized with the Indians when they clashed with the US Cavalry. The white men were the bad guys in his book.

My brother studied the Sioux, Comanche, Iroquois and other tribes, but it was the Apaches with their desert lifestyle, that really struck a chord with him. Dan admired Cochise and Geronimo, Apache rebels who fought against government encroachment into their native territories. He also revered the peaceful Nez Perce tribe and their leader, Chief Joseph.

On family hikes through the Indiana State Parks Dan rushed ahead, checking out the rocky hollow around the next bend. He acquired remarkable knowledge about the geography of Illinois, the US, the continents and major cities around the globe. I thought he was bound to be an explorer.

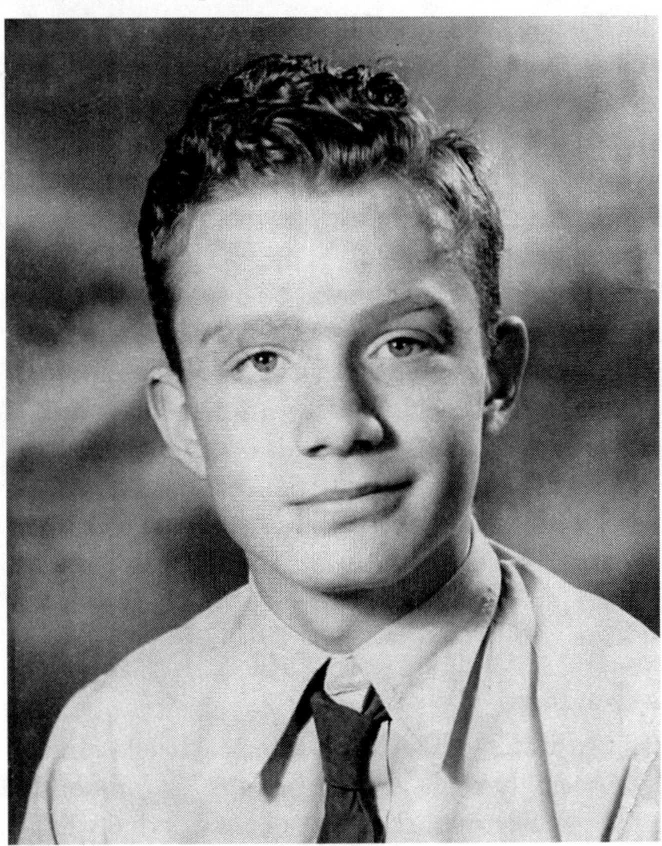

Dan in seventh grade

Onward to victory

Notre Dame football was another of Dan's passions. Before we had a TV he'd seen Mom sitting next to our tall Zenith radio on Saturday afternoons listening to Notre Dame football games. Rosary beads in hand, she prayed for victory as the Fighting Irish battled Michigan State, Purdue or Southern Cal. Dan learned early that it was a glorious day when Our Lady's school won, and a dark day when it lost.

Dan watched every game that Notre Dame game played on TV. He was devoted to the Fighting Irish. So what if the lineup was studded with names like Portilo, Pietrosante and Zajeski. Watching a game he'd be on the edge of his chair shouting, then on his feet screaming — jumping up and down with clenched fists. Notre Dame usually won, thank God, because Dan was defeated if they lost. He knew the name of every "Irish" player on the field. What's more, he could give pretty close to a play-by-play account of the last Notre Dame game. Even today he can give an accurate rundown of any ND game he ever watched.

An avid gamester, Dan enjoyed board games like *Sorry!*, *Clue* and *Monopoly*. On Christmas mornings while I was plowing into my pile of presents under the tree, Dan was reading the instructions to some game he'd received. "You wanna play this game?" he'd ask. "It looks like fun." "Later!" I'd tell him, still digging to get at my next gift. I wasn't surprised that Dan mastered chess. He played after school with kids from his class — Jerome Gerhman or Bob Weber — and sometimes with Bill Caroli, who lived across the street. Dan enjoyed the strategy involved in chess — it was a good game for him.

Birthday bummer

With Dan's twelfth birthday approaching, I tried to imagine what kind of gift he might want. *Anything relating to animals or Indians will be on target,* I figured. There were a few days left when I noticed something new in the window of Glider's Hobby Shop — a life-sized plastic model of a squirrel. It even had realistic fur! Inside the shop I looked at the kit — a cinch to make. The hardest part would be gluing on the fake fur.

When his birthday arrived I couldn't wait for Dan to unwrap my present. He opened a few others before picking it up. Then off came the wrapping paper. He looked at the box, then at me. "Are you kidding?" he asked in disbelief. "You think I'm six years old or something?" "I thought you'd like it," I answered, trying to conceal my disappointment. Dan, the animal lover, was obviously after bigger game.

The sleep slayer

With only three bedrooms in our flat to accommodate nine inhabitants, Dan and Tom had to sleep on a hide-a-bed in the den. Tom turned in at a decent hour but Dan dallied. I didn't envy either one of them trying to sleep next to the front hall and right around the corner from the living room, where Mom watched Jack Paar at night. Jim and I slept in the back bedroom, pretty well insulated from noise. Unfortunately, pajamas for all us boys were kept in the back bedroom dresser.

A wall switch near the door lit the ceiling light fixture. After Jim and I had said our prayers and closed our eyes Dan would enter, flick on the light and snap us right out of our sleep. "Get out," we'd shout. "Get out and stay out!" Dan would answer, "I forgot something" or "There's something in here I need." Over and over we told him to get his stuff out of the room earlier. Again and again we warned him not to blast us out of our sleep.

As we got older Dan's bedtime habits got nastier. He'd click on the ceiling light two or even three times on some nights. My responses to Dan's intrusions got cruder and nastier without affecting him in the least. "Get out now!" "Get the hell out!" "Get the *bleep* out!" All were equally ineffective. It could be eleven o'clock and Dan would come in and start looking for something. I don't know when he finally got to sleep, but it was late. On some mornings he shared tidbits from the *Tonight Show* that he'd heard coming from the TV in the living room.

The Infuriator

Dan definitely had a talent for pissing me off. On one occasion when he really got me steamed, I chased him up the back stairs to the second floor. But he was fast enough to get inside and lock the kitchen door, so I couldn't get at him. I was so mad that I punched in the door's big window, sending a shower of broken glass onto the floor inside.

A few years later, when we were both in high school, I spotted Dan standing in the living room wearing a pair of chinos that I'd just bought for myself. He was holding a glass of milk in one hand and adjusting the TV with the other. Immediately I saw a big scuff mark and a rip on the front of my pants. "You swiped my pants and wrecked them!" I shouted. Dan just turned to me with a casual smirk on his face. I took a swing at him that missed, but in ducking, he swirled milk in a circular pattern over half the room.

A kinder gentler Dan

Despite the fact that he could get under my skin, Dan was an upbeat kid and an eager volunteer. When Sister Ellen Angela was recruiting altar boys, Dan answered the call. He came home with some serious Latin to memorize: *"Ad Deum qui laetificat juventutum meum. Quia tu es, Deus fortitudo mea..."* Dan had to learn the mass inside out — when to kneel, when to stand, when to move the heavy mass book (the missal) from one side of the altar to the other.

Altar boys also had to ring a cluster of bells during the offertory and bring water and wine to the priest in little capped bottles called cruets. All the details to remember and execute at the right moment scared me. With so many chances to screw up in front of a church full of people, I shied away from altar boy duty.

Dan's commitment impressed me. He practiced his Latin faithfully and attended after-school altar boy meetings regularly. Within a few weeks he was on the altar wearing a black cassock and white surplice. There was Dan ringing the bells, standing and kneeling at the right moments. We folks in the pews took our standing and kneeling cues from the altar boys.

It amazed me to see Dan getting up at six a.m. because he was never an early riser. But now he was rolling out of bed and scurrying over to St. Leo Church to serve mass. I didn't see Dan on the altar very often because he was usually needed at the church and I normally went to mass at the high school chapel up the block.

Stood up at the altar

One Sunday morning after finishing my paper route I went to a late mass at the chapel. Son of a gun! There was Dan up on the altar. But something was amiss — he was the only altar boy in sight! Uh-oh — somebody had overslept, leaving Dan with double duty. He did just fine until the consecration, when he took both cruets (water and wine) up to the altar without first removing their caps.

When Father Mollen walked up with the chalice Dan realized that he wasn't prepared to pour anything. He hesitated, then stuck one cruet under his left arm and removed the cap. Then he retrieved the cruet from beneath his arm. Holding the open cruet and its cap in one hand and the uncapped cruet in the other, Dan looked stumped. He couldn't decide what to do next. It was hilarious! I didn't know whether to laugh or cry.

The sympathetic priest took everything from Dan and set it on the altar so they could sort things out. After communion was distributed, Dan managed one more spectacular goof by kicking the altar bells across the marble floor. Their jingle-jangling racket must have awakened anyone who had dozed off during mass. When Dan got home he was very embarrassed and equally annoyed that his co-server pulled a no-show. He said that Sister Ellen Angela would be pretty angry at this kid. Wasn't it a sacrilege to leave a fellow altar boy in the lurch? Well, at the very least it was poor form.

Molloy madness

The cruets episode didn't faze Dan. He told me it was nothing compared to the time our esteemed pastor, Patrick J. Molloy (who was now a monsignor), was joined on the altar by a visiting monsignor from another state. This kindly old cleric popped in unexpectedly, taking Molloy by surprise. In the sacristy behind the altar the visiting churchman had a friendly chat with the altar boys, which delayed Dan in setting out an extra set of cruets for him.

Breaking away to see what else might be needed on the altar, he passed Molloy, who cracked him across the face, shouting, "Cruets — where are the cruets?" This kind of berserk behavior was typical of Molloy. After mass the departing monsignor stopped Dan and his co-server in the sacristy. Handing them each a quarter he said consolingly, "Don't feel bad — he's always been that way."

The big picture

Despite his misadventures, Dan stuck with the altar boys well into eighth grade. He could whine about things but Dan was optimistic and always looking forward to something — the next "free day" from school, the start of football season or some big event that was hitting town.

When it came to family, Dan knew the name of every uncle, aunt and cousin on Mom's side of the family — the side we stayed in touch with. But he kept track of who was who on Dad's side as well. These were folks we saw only at weddings and funerals. Uninhibited, Dan walked right up to Murphy uncles and cousins, introduced himself and chatted freely with them. He reminded me that we had cousins living in Northern Ireland. Dan's historical perspective included our ancestors and where they came from. He studied Irish history going back to the English conquests in the 16th century and Cromwell's despicable treatment of the Irish in the 17th century.

Travels with Dan

With each passing year Dan became more cosmopolitan. Before he'd finished grammar school he was taking solo sightseeing trips around Chicago on the CTA. Loving big events, he was energized by crowds of people. One Friday night in eighth grade he decided to see the Barnum and Bailey Circus playing at the Amphitheater near the old stockyards. Knowing Mom and Dad would nix this outing if he asked to go, he slipped out of the house and hopped a northbound bus to the show. Dan said the big top was terrific, with horses and elephants, clowns and trapeze artists. An elephant stepped on a pretty bareback rider right in front of him. I never knew anything about this exploit until Dan told me four decades later.

The summer before he entered high school Dan discovered the Treasure Chest Arcade downtown on Randolph Street. The place was a maze of clinking pinball machines and clattering mechanical games with flashing colored lights. Way in the back there was a small recording booth where it only cost a quarter to cut a record. Dan made a flimsy little disc and played it on our phonograph at home. Holy cow — there was Dan's voice singing. It was barely audible but still very exciting! I couldn't wait to check out this recording place.

A few days later Dan, Jim and I rode the "El" downtown together. Debarking at Washington, we climbed the subway stairs to the sidewalk and hiked one whole block to the big noisy arcade. All three of us squeezed into the dark booth to see how much goofy noise we could make in thirty seconds. We cut half a dozen little records, singing whatever came into our minds. Then Jim recorded some of his bizarre sound effects. A week later our Murphy trio, plus little brother Tom, went downtown to cut more records.

This trip was great fun, but the biggest kick for Dan, Jim and me was just being downtown on Randolph. The blinking neon and brightly lit marquees on both sides of the street were intoxicating. The United Artists, Oriental and Woods theaters were all thriving. Looking up we saw what was playing: Charlton Heston in *Ben Hur*; Jimmy Stewart and Kim Novak in *Vertigo*. We stopped to get a hamburger and were floored by the price. Better to hold off and get our money's worth at Wimpy's Grill on 80th & Halsted. At home everyone got a laugh out of the flimsy records. Too bad they wore out after just a few plays on the turntable.

JFK all the way

When John F. Kennedy announced his candidacy for president in 1960 something inside Dan caught fire. Primed by Mom and Dad's Democratic ideals he became a dedicated campaign worker, even stuffing Democratic handbills into the newspapers he delivered. Right before the election he hopped a ride with Martha and Lee to Midway Airport. They went to greet JFK on his arrival in Chicago for a campaign rally. Dan got within a few feet of Kennedy, hoping to shake his hand, but a large, fast-moving woman cut him off. This disappointment didn't dampen his spirit, however. With the election just a few days away it was a big thrill to get so close to the future president.

Walking the talk

Energized by people, Dan loved crowds. The more folks the merrier. He enjoyed listening to the stories people told, especially stories from immigrants who described the obstacles they had overcome. After college he tried sales work for a brief period before finding a job that he loved. Dan went to work for the State of Illinois, placing job seekers with Chicago area employers. Over the next thirty years he worked mainly in "Job Development," interviewing thousands of applicants from all over the country and the world. Dan found this work personally rewarding — no wonder he was so good at it. Now retired, he enjoys travel, a large book collection and, of course, Notre Dame football.

Chapter 12

Neighborhood places

"Have you seen the Frank's charge card?"
— Mom

Our neighborhood was mostly blocks of brick two-flats and bungalows shaded by tall trees — elms, maples and oaks. But there was a very urban feeling to the surroundings. Right at the end of our block 79th Street cut through. A major east-west transportation artery on the South Side, it was always busy. Any time I walked up the block I saw cars and trucks whizzing by. CTA buses stopped to pick up passengers at the corner. On Saturday mornings the street buzzed with shoppers. There were so many stores and they were all thriving. People stocked up on groceries at the A&P and bought pastries at Widen's Bakery. Things were humming — everything clicked. I got a jolt of energy from the lively scene.

Leo High School

Right at the northwest corner of our block stood Leo High School, a Catholic institution of higher learning staffed by the venerable Christian Brothers of Ireland. As a kid I saw high school students on my block in the spring. At lunchtime they were out stretching their legs or sitting along the sidewalk. For the most part they were pretty friendly. One of them was Pat O'Brien, who lived across the alley from us. My brothers and I occasionally talked to him and his friends. Pat was a nice kid who played touch football with us when we were a few years older.

On some mornings, while we were getting dressed for school or wolfing down breakfast, we heard the Leo marching band practicing. Usually the drums came through first, then the chorus of other instruments. The music got louder and louder. If I went out onto the front balcony I'd see the band, dressed in regular school clothes, marching down Peoria Street playing the Leo fight song. Sprouting goose bumps, I felt as though I were watching the victorious American Army marching into Paris.

Walking east

It was fun to walk east along 79th Street. Rusnak Furniture had great window displays depicting well-appointed parlors and dining rooms. And the windows of Frank's Department Store reflected the passing seasons with modest style. Across 79th Street people were entering or leaving Woolworth's. The newsstand at 79th & Halsted was a beehive. Droves of people, on foot and in cars, stopped there to buy newspapers. The guy on duty worked at warp speed. I always gave him exact change and got out of the way fast. Magazine racks held everything from comic books to *Look* and *Life* to *Popular Mechanics.* A great selection, but browsing on that bustling corner was too much like tap dancing. Looking north I'd see the big stone Mutual National Bank, where my savings account had been growing since fourth grade. To the south the Capitol Theater's huge sign and marquee stood out prominently.

Dueling dime stores

In grammar school we Murphy kids went home for lunch; our house was just a few blocks from St. Leo. But on a freezing-cold day I liked to cut through our two neighborhood dime stores, Kresge's and Woolworth's. They helped take the sting out of the frigid trek home.

Kresge's was on 78th & Halsted; Woolworth's was half a block south, bordering 79th. Both stores had long diner-like counters with stools where shoppers could get a Coke, hot dog or piece of pie. An elderly lady on duty served drinks like Green River and Cherry Coke. She pushed a metal plunger, forcing the syrup into a glass (or cone-shaped paper cup in a metal holder). Then she pulled a lever that released a narrow stream of fizz water. A quick stir with a spoon and it was ready to be sipped.

A kid's eye view

When I was eight the dime store counters met me at eye level. I got a close-up look at everything — little plastic spacemen with clear removable helmets, glitzy bracelets and necklaces, rows of open lipsticks in dozens of gaudy hues, toy soldiers, cap guns, squirt guns, yo-yos, spools of colored thread, red rubber balls, plastic Pez dispensers — all manner of shiny colorful stuff. Lincoln Log sets, rubber dolls, baseball bats and *Monopoly* games all went by in a blur. A Hohner Marine Band harmonica, made of wood and metal with real brass reeds, cost all of fifty-nine cents. Packed inside a hinged paper box, it was wrapped in waxed paper printed with instructions for playing *Old Folks at Home.*

Woolworth's roasted nuts, storing them in a huge glass display case with a top window that was tilted on an angle. This large sheet of glass was always loose, so I could easily slide it up a bit — far enough to filch a few cashews.

The pet department sold chirping parakeets and twittering canaries. Little pet turtles wore brightly painted shells sporting floral decals. Kids could pick out goldfish from a tank and carry them home in little white cartons like the ones from the Chinese take-out joint.

Some things at the dime store were only a dime, like the kid's rocket ride at Kresge's. A little tyke sat inside for a minute or two while the ship dipped, rocked and growled like an upset stomach. A few steps away stood a photo booth that took four pictures for a quarter. A bunch of kids crowded into the booth and everyone got into the picture. The photos they went home with showed every face wearing a silly expression and jutting into the frame from a different angle. These cheap photos from the Fifties held up well over the decades. In fact, they seem to be some of the best-loved shots in people's photo albums.

In each of the dime stores one whole counter was devoted to school supplies: three-ring binders, loose-leaf paper, wooden rulers, big art gum erasers the color of brown sugar, pencil sharpeners, protractors for measuring angles, and compasses for making circles. And the coveted Parker fountain pen was proudly displayed. It had a filling lever on the side and a metal cap with a clip that looked like gold.

The Capitol Theater

The Capitol near 80th & Halsted was a true movie palace. Built in 1925, its interior was adorned with touches of Greek and Roman art. The walls were bedecked with classic reliefs and the lobby floor was an elaborate mosaic. Lights on the aisle seats of each row spilled golden rays onto the carpeting. The ceiling was a spectacular night sky dotted with hundreds of twinkling stars. As kid I was flabbergasted looking up at it for the first time.

It cost a quarter for kids under thirteen to enter the Capitol, where a double feature was always in progress. We Murphy boys often arrived halfway through one movie and stayed until we were caught up. "This is where we came in," one of us would say. Half a minute later we'd be outside adjusting our eyes to the daylight on Halsted Street.

Two bits for a double feature at the Capitol was a good deal, but when I delivered the *Chicago American* (extinct since1962) I got in free on Friday nights using my carrier's pass. This little privilege made me feel important. I'll never forget the time it got me in to see *Love Is a Many-Splendored Thing*, a romance with Jennifer Jones and William Holden that swept me away.

Teenage couples loved to make out in the balcony. Sometimes my brothers and I went up there if the first floor was crowded. On one occasion we sat next to a pair of lovebirds smooching the afternoon away. The guy was wearing his high school letter jacket and couldn't tell that we were loading up his elbow with popcorn, empty candy boxes and sticks from our fudgesicles. We laughed hysterically when, releasing his girlfriend, he sent our debris spilling all over the place. The duo left us with tender wishes expressed in a volley of four-letter words.

I am rewarded

If one of us kids had been especially well behaved, Mom and Dad might take us to the show at night. What a big-time, grown-up thrill. One evening I got to go with them to see a movie starring Rhonda Fleming. She aroused feelings that took my ten-year-old body by surprise. Afterwards we went to a local drugstore and I had my first strawberry soda.

On another occasion I went with Dad to the Capitol where he put on quite a show. When he sat down his seat broke with a resounding "BLAM!" We moved across the aisle, where he tried another seat with the same result: BLAM! *Geeze, this is embarrassing,* I thought. On the third try, Dad gingerly eased his tush into a seat without breaking it. The experience made me think that my father must be pretty overweight. In reality he was just an average-sized guy. On subsequent visits to the Capitol I found more broken seats, and chalked them up to lousy maintenance.

The Capitol Annex Restaurant stood next door to the show. It was a good place to stop for a hot turkey sandwich, but the Muzak in that place was barely audible. I sometimes wondered if the tunes I heard were just my imagination. A heavy date for Joan was a movie at the Capitol followed by a sundae at the Annex.

The Cosmo

Right across the street from the Capitol stood a much less impressive movie house, the Cosmo. Architecturally it was nothing compared to the Capitol, but it attracted enough viewers to stay in business. My brothers and I saw *Invaders from Mars* and *The Creature from the Black Lagoon* there. Both movies made me afraid of the dark for weeks. On second thought, we might have seen *The Creature* at the Highland on 79th & Ashland about a mile west.

Nestled up to the south wall of the Cosmo, nudging its way into a parking lot, was a little popcorn hut. It was nothing more than a shed run by a wonderful lady who made the best hotdogs I've ever tasted. She put everything on them — mustard, relish, onions, tomatoes and cucumber slices. Then she finished them with a sprinkling of celery salt. She also sold buttery popcorn and penny candy, including my favorite — red gummy coins that stuck to my molars and the roof of my mouth.

Greaser central

The Green Mill, a cavernous pool hall/malt shop, sat next door to the Cosmo. This neighborhood greaser hangout had a strange forbidden-fruit attraction for me. Walking by, I couldn't resist gazing into its huge storefront window. I'd see guys playing pool and maybe someone hunched over a pinball machine. There was a long counter with about a dozen stools where nobody was ever seated.

On a sunny afternoon the place looked blank and bright. In fact, the Green Mill had a surreal appearance morning, noon or night. It gave me an eerie feeling like the one I got years later from *Nighthawks*, the Ed Hopper painting of a few lonely people sitting in a diner at night.

The Green Mill's arcade games attracted me in my pre-teen years. I stopped in a few times but never felt welcome. The smoke-filled air, blaring jukebox and not-so-friendly glances from teenage regulars made me nervous. However, I got a real kick out of the aerial gunner game one summer afternoon.

Every part of this game was metal, making it super conductive to electricity. The targets on the airplanes flying by were little steel studs. Looking into the steel gun site I tried to lock its crosshairs onto the stud while I pulled the trigger. When I hit a target and stayed on it, my score kept going up — ding-ding-ding-ding. But on one of the targets the wiring was faulty. The crosshairs locked onto it and wouldn't let go. My finger stayed frozen to the trigger as a burst of strong electric shocks jolted my forehead and shot down my spine. I was paralyzed until the plane flew out of view. This gave me an awful headache that sent me home for a nap.

Rusnak Furniture

The Rusnak building on 79th Street, mentioned earlier, was an imposing four-storey structure with a classy terra-cotta front. The freight dock in back was centered at the north end of our alley and its doors seemed to be open most of the time. Passing by, I saw neat stuff galore in the shipping room — furniture being retouched, piles of excelsior packing material, big cones of brown twine and stacks of forest-green quilted blankets for padding the furniture to be delivered. Bubble pack had yet to be invented.

Walking past the freight door one day I spotted a square pink area on one wall. As I got closer it turned out to be a naked lady. WOW! Here was one of those "dirty" calendars I'd heard about. Hanging there it tempted me day after day to take a peek and besmirch my young soul. I tried hard to ignore the pink lady. And there was a new one each month, which didn't make things any easier.

Frank's Department Store

Standing just a block east of my house, Frank's made up a sizeable chunk of the 79th Street scene. The front windows were updated to reflect the seasons. Walking along 79th one Sunday afternoon, I saw a decorator dressing one of the pale lady mannequins. He rotated her smoothly as if they were dancing. Noticing me, he smiled briefly, then turned to adjust the outfit on his plaster partner.

Franks had three floors, a mezzanine level and a basement. Cosmetics were on the first floor near the entrance. I liked the perfumy smell but could never find an excuse for loitering there. Creams and lotions were a waste of money. When I bought something for Mom, Aunt Martha or my sisters it had to be hard goods — something that would last. Such durable items were sold downstairs in the basement housewares section.

One small corner of the lower level housed a shoemaker shop. I could hear the cobbler working at the grinding and buffing wheels as I approached his nook. Over the years this little man, sporting a soiled green apron, replaced countless soles and heels for the Murphy clan. He rarely said much, but on one occasion he told me my shoes were too far gone to fix and handed them back to me. I reached over the counter and dropped them into his trash barrel.

Adjacent to the cobbler's shop a row of bikes and tricycles stood gleaming brightly. And as Christmas approached the store set up a glistening snowy backdrop for Santa Claus. Seated comfortably, the jolly old elf welcomed tots with open arms and a hearty "Ho, ho, ho!" Just steps away a big holiday train layout featured two Lionel trains.

Moving up

A mezzanine level, sandwiched between the first and second floors, housed a good-sized barbershop (there were usually three or four barbers on duty). On Saturdays Mom and Dad could leave a couple of us boys there while they shopped. Comic books, like *Superman, Spider-Man, Archie* and *Beetle Bailey* kept us quiet while we waited to get clipped.

Even better, snacks were just a few steps away on the landing. Several red-capped gumball machines held candy and nuts aplenty. Putting a nickel in the slot, I turned the round handle like a doorknob. Then, as I lifted a metal flap, a generous portion of goodies fell into my hand. Sometimes the knob on the cashew machine went completely nuts. The more times I turned it, the more cashews I got. Three or four turns was my max — I didn't want to be too greedy or get caught ripping off Frank's.

Our spring footwear fling

Right before Easter our whole family got into the car and rode one block over to Frank's for new clothes — especially new shoes. Winter was hard on footwear. Come snowy days, we kids wore galoshes — no doubt about it. But some days fooled us. With the streets clear of snow we left for school thinking that our shoes were up to the elements. Somehow the slushy puddles lingering out there slipped our minds. The worst ones formed near curbs as the snow and ice melted. They were often deep enough to engulf our shoes and ankles.

Returning home with wet cold feet, we set our soggy footwear beneath the kitchen radiator to dry. The overnight dehydrating process gave them a stiff upward curl. So we had to break in our weather-warped shoes to make them wearable — a process that was downright painful. By spring we Murphy boys were sorely in need of fresh footwear.

The shoe department at Frank's was right on the first floor, and the salesmen used old-fashioned wooden measuring sticks. While Jim and Dan were getting measured I wandered over to the foot X-ray machine that gave a fluoroscopic view of how your shoes fit. Seeing it as a toy, I enjoyed looking down at the bright green screen showing my skeleton feet. I shuffled them back and forth and wiggled my toes until Dad or the salesman told me to stop horsing around. Nobody was concerned about X-ray exposure. Who knew? While we boys were being shod, Mom might be nearby at Frank's big display of Easter candy, selecting sweets for her younger kids, who still believed in the Easter Bunny.

Robes and footballs

The second floor at Frank's sold underwear, sleepwear, notions and sporting goods. A sepia-toned photomural took up one whole wall. It showed a boy about ten years old making a model airplane. Holding a brush, he was just about to apply a dab of glue. I liked to gaze at that big picture while Mom and Dad bought socks and underwear. It had a dreamy quality that drew me into a world where everything worked out fine and Wally Cleaver might have been the kid next door. Year after year, when I went to Frank's to buy footballs, the boy was still there on the wall, his hand frozen in time and space. He still hadn't applied that dab of glue.

The lagoon

About half a mile east of Halsted, near St. George's Hospital, a chain of three lagoons meandered through the residential area. A broad border of flagstones edging the water added an elegant touch. And at the narrow spots, where one lagoon flowed into another, neighborhood streets crossed over low bridges.

Kids who fished this watery trio just called it "the lagoon." The only boats in sight were toy sailboats and speedboats powered by tiny electric motors. My brothers and I enjoyed fishing from the shoreline using cut-up worms for bait and the smallest of hooks. Lying on our stomachs, we dropped our lines into the shallow water and waited. Little bluegills and crappie quickly went for the bait. They were too small to keep but what did we know? Our catch went home with us, swimming in a coffee can. We snagged crayfish by letting the hooked worm sit on the bottom, just a foot below the surface. Sooner or later one of those ugly little guys grabbed the bait. Then we pulled straight up.

In winter the lagoon was an ice-skating mecca. Moms and dads were there with kids big and small. Couples glided along arm in arm. Folks skated from lagoon to lagoon, ducking as they passed under the arched stone bridges. Fifty-gallon steel drums protruded from the ice here and there, compliments of the Chicago Department of Streets and Sanitation. Supposedly they helped the water freeze.

Jim and I liked the frozen lagoon. We bundled up with sweaters under our coats and wore scarves, mittens and stocking caps. Unfortunately, I didn't have skates that fit. The hand-me-downs I used were way too large, so I bulked up my feet with several pairs of socks. The loose fit and my weak ankles made the skate blades flair out to the sides. I was skating half on metal and half on leather; Jim was doing a little better. At least were moving and enjoying ourselves. Some older kids made fancy circles and skated backwards. A few teenage boys with hockey sticks slapped a puck around.

Glider's

Glider's Bicycle & Hobby Shop was tucked into the front of a large apartment building a few blocks west of my house on 79th Street. There were two doors — one for the bike shop, run by Old Man Glider, the grouch, and another for the hobby shop, tended by Mrs. Glider, who had a much sweeter disposition than her hubby.

I liked the smell of new rubber in the bike shop but didn't linger there. The vibes from Mr. G. were hostile. And next door in the hobby shop I could enjoy the fragrant smell of balsa wood. The scent emanated from a bin near the entrance that held three-foot lengths of this aromatic wood. I bought sheets and sometimes blocks of balsa for pet projects, like carving little cars or boats.

An array of aircraft assembled by local modelers hung from the ceiling, suspended by threads. There were fighters, bombers, light planes, military transports and helicopters. I loved the big Cessna with its tidy red-and-white paint job. If I were in the apartment building around suppertime collecting for my paper route, I'd gaze through the front window to admire that plane. The glint of the setting sun on its wings gave me a magical high.

Mallatt's

Even though kids referred to Mallatt's as "Moldy's," they loved this small variety store on 79th Street near Morgan. It was stocked with candy bars, pop, potato chips, baseball cards, paper kites, crayons, paste, glue, comic books, ping-pong balls and yo-yos. Grownups could purchase cigarettes, cigars, newspapers, magazines, lighters, sunglasses, batteries and such. Old Man Mallatt, a grump, was always in the place. When I was a third grader he refused to give me the two-cent deposit on a pop bottle I found in the street. "I don't buy bottles!" he told me sternly. Over the years he didn't get much friendlier.

Despite this, I remained a regular customer — especially in the summer. I stopped there after finishing my paper route on steamy afternoons. Yorking down an ice-cold Coke felt wonderful for the first few seconds. Cocking my head back, I finished half the bottle in a few rhythmic gulps. The ice-cold effervescence felt great throttling down my throat. But immediately I got a spectacular pain in my forehead that nearly knocked me over. And it hung on for a full minute. This reminded me that I couldn't chug ice-cold Coke like the folks in TV commercials did.

The pop at Mallatt's was stored in an old-fashioned red cooler with *Coca-Cola* painted on the front. Lifting the hinged top revealed rows of colorful bottle caps. The bulge near the mouth of each bottle allowed it to hang between metal rails with the rest of the bottle suspended in icy-cold water. Choices included the standard Coke, Pepsi and 7-up, along with more exotic drinks like ginger ale, cream soda and Kayo, a strange chocolate concoction with a cartoon rendering of Moon Mullins on the bottle.

Dropping a dime into the machine, I made my selection and slid the bottle to the end of the track. Next, a ninety-degree turn and a gentle push guided it into the escape hatch. Then a good yank pulled it up through the loosened metal jaws. Success! The opener on the face of the cooler was handy. When I snapped off the bottle cap it fell into a built-in receptacle. Cold white smoke wafted from my bottle.

Good-bye Good Humor

Our home on Peoria Street was only a block away from a big Good Humor ice cream barn on 79th Street. Scores of trucks and leg-propelled carts poured out of the place all day in the summer. They were loaded with Creamsicles, Fudgesicles, Strawberry Shortcake Bars, and other fanciful ice cream creations. Many featured an outer coating of nuts, coconut or crumbs with something special in the center. The tricycle vendors pedaled down the street on sultry afternoons, jingling the bells on their handlebars. Hearing them, we kids scrambled to dig up some cash. We checked our pockets, begged Mom for change, even scrounged for coins beneath the cushions of the living room furniture.

The trucks were usually out later, chiming a few notes over and over. Audible for blocks, they gave us plenty of advance notice. I preferred evening encounters with the Good Humor man. Without the hot sun beating down on my ice cream, it didn't melt and drip so much.

One summer when I was ten or eleven, the Good Humor barn caught fire and burned down. Several trucks were destroyed and countless ice cream treats melted into warm pudding. The Chicago Fire Department hosed everything down thoroughly. In the morning milky water flowed down Peoria Street. By mid-afternoon the summer sun had given it the smell of baby barf. The brick front of the burned-out building was left standing, but firemen knocked out all of the tall front windows. Then a crew came along and nailed plywood sheets over the openings.

The next day I rode my bike through the alley to view the damage from the rear. I could see scorched trucks inside. An older kid who lived nearby showed me a big silver star he'd pried off the hood of a Good Humor truck with a crowbar. What happened next was definitely no fun, but I'll get to that later.

Saint Sabina's

St. Sabina was a neighboring Catholic parish only half a mile west of St. Leo territory along 79th Street. The school hall came in handy for all kinds of activities. On Saturday afternoons kids went roller-skating there. Wearing rented skates with wooden wheels, scores of youngsters went round and round in circles to the tune of pop songs played over the PA system.

On Sunday nights Sabina's gym hosted high school socials. These weekly dances drew teens from all over the South Side. A live band played sets between half-hour stretches of pop tunes that were pumped through a set of big speakers. Occasional fistfights broke out, adding a dash of excitement to the evening. Alcohol lubricated some teenage boys who might have loosened up better with a few dance lessons.

All through high school Sullivan and O'Leary, my touch football opponents, tried to talk me into going to the Sabina socials. I kept telling them I didn't have a suit. They kept telling me I didn't need one. I eventually made it to Sabina's, but by that time I was out of high school.

Chapter 13

The time of our lives

"God give me patience and resignation."
— Mom

We Murphys occupied the second floor of our brick two-flat on Peoria Street for thirteen and a half years. When we left in the summer of 1965 it seemed that eons had passed since we'd moved in. Looking back, I wondered what we'd done to use up that long stretch of time. I thought we'd watched too much TV, especially when cold weather made plopping in front of our black-and-white set seem like the natural thing to do. Frosty Saturday afternoons found two or three of us Murphy boys lying on the living room floor watching old cowboy movies. After seeing us reclining on the carpet so often, our uncle Mike dubbed us "The Horizontal Brothers."

Cowboy movies

Weathered westerns from Chicago TV stations starred straight-shooting buckaroos like Johnny Mack Brown and Bob Steele. These old black-and-white flicks had a bleached out look — like they'd been shot under a bright, blazing-hot sun. I wondered why cowboys wore dark clothes in that kind of weather. Watching them made me sweat. And when a posse arrived in front of the local saloon, all the dust their horses kicked up made me cough. I felt like going to the kitchen for a cold glass of water. Too many westerns had the same ending. The cowboy hero rides into the sunset with his male sidekick while some sweet young thing watches longingly from the corral gate. My gut told me there was something odd about those hombres.

Western fantasies

As a young kid I was fascinated by all the hardware that cowboys wore: shiny six-shooters with pearly-white handles, nifty gun belts stuffed with bullets, jangling spurs... It was the glitzy stuff in those shabby-looking westerns that caught my eye. I loved to watch the hero load cartridges into his six-gun or rifle. I could feel the heft of those real brass bullets in my hand. They were so unlike the cheap wooden ones that came with toy gun-and-holster sets. I couldn't fathom why those toy bullets were painted lipstick red.

The hand-me-down gun belt I inherited didn't have a single cartridge in it. Unruffled, I rummaged through the kitchen junk drawer and scrounged up two or three gold-plated caps from retired fountain pens. I thought these fake bullets looked better than none all. Still, I daydreamed about being the complete cowboy — with twin blue-steel revolvers, chaps, spurs — even the big white hat.

Tom Corbett, Space Cadet

This low-budget serial was my first exposure to science fiction. The show's theme music, a brisk military march, got my seven-year-old blood up at the start of each episode. Tom and his crewmates, Astro and Manning, were intense guys who survived one intergalactic scrape after another. Their space cadet shirts featured a puffy triangular collar patch highlighted with studs — a real eye-grabber on our black-and-white TV. Tom's spacecraft was roomy but dingy, resembling a well-used locker room. Its saving grace was a dramatic round window through which Tom gazed at the stars. I knew by the determined set of his jaw that Tom Corbett, Space Cadet, would maintain order throughout the universe.

Flash Gordon

The adventures of Flash Gordon were fun to watch after school. Science fiction was a great escape, and every episode of Flash and his pals left me hanging. Danger, excitement, silver ray guns and light paths to walk on kept me riveted to our TV set. I loved the rocket ships; they looked like flying Electrolux vacuum cleaners and sounded like cement mixers.

Ming the Merciless, ruler of the planet Mongo, appeared on a huge TV screen now and then trying to scare Flash and Dr.

Zarkov, but Flash never flinched. Once he went up against a lion and choked it to death! His skinny blonde girlfriend, Dale Arden, always fainted when things got tough. What good was she? On the other hand, Ming's daughter, Princess Aura (much foxier than Dale), was constantly risking her neck to help Flash. Why didn't he dump Dale for the Princess? What was wrong with that boy's head?

Live from Chicago

We loved to watch *Kukla, Fran and Ollie* with the motherly Fran Allison up front talking to little roundheaded Kukla, Ollie the dragon and a cast of other loveable characters. Puppet wizard Burr Tillstrom stayed out of view, giving his little characters voices and movement. This warm gentle show gave me a feeling that all was right with the world.

Elmer the Elephant was another terrific show. Elmer was a person inside an elephant costume (head and trunk) looking out of a stall at the camera. Sitting to one side was John Conrad dressed as a ringmaster. He knew how to talk to Elmer and the TV audience at the same time. When Elmer knocked Conrad's hat off he got flustered in a funny, good-natured way. Conrad knew how to play to the camera for laughs. Sometimes Elmer rang a little bell hanging at the side of his stall. Their antics and interaction were well timed and very entertaining.

There were lunchtime shows for kids, too. *Uncle Johnny Coons* was a popular one. Johnny talked to the camera and played old *Our Gang* movies. I thought it strange that he ate lunch every day on the show. And why did he make such a big deal out of what he was eating? He explained that his sandwich was made on bread from the Jewel Food Store. And he sometimes had Yummy brand ice cream (made by Jewel) for dessert. Dessert after lunch? No wonder he was fat.

The most entertaining noontime character of all was Dick "Two Ton" Baker. This roly-poly character really knew how to joke around and enjoy himself. Even better, he played the piano like a champ and sang along to the music. He also did the TV ads for Riverview amusement park, delivering the message with good-natured gusto: "Laugh your troubles away at mad merry Riverview!"

Summer TV

In summer we kids got to watch the daytime TV shows we couldn't view during the school year. On weekday mornings François Pope, the famous chef, looked good in crisp black and white. Lively classical music accompanied the opening. Then François appeared, giving a rundown on the day's menu. Assisted by his sons, Frank and Bob, he whipped up an array of delectable entrées. Beef or pork, fish or fowl, François delivered. He turned lowly spuds into heavenly creations; he even made asparagus look good.

I loved watching François and his boys make sauces. The camera looked straight down on them as they sautéed ingredients, shaking in some sherry or tossing in a pinch of salt or spice. Watching them make desserts was fantastic — they folded in meringue and beat things with whisks. They made a wooden spoon hitting a crockery bowl sound good. "Now students, I want you to notice how nice that looks," François said proudly as he finished some fancy dinner presentation or dessert.

Rainy days were good for watching game shows on television, but something in my gut rebelled against resorting to TV at ten or eleven in the morning. If the weather was dark and soggy we boys might head for the basement and play ping-pong. Sometimes on rainy days I'd build a model airplane or set up our electric train. Reading a book was the farthest thing from my mind.

Storming the beach

There were special summer days when Mom spent the afternoon frying chicken and making potato salad. Even better, she stirred up a gallon of strong dark iced tea, well sugared and tangy with lots of fresh lemon juice. She mixed it in a huge oval roasting pan, tossing in the lemon rinds for good measure. Finally, she poured it into a big thermos jug with a push-button spigot on the front. As soon as Dad got home from work everyone piled into the car and we headed for Rainbow Beach at 79th Street and Lake Michigan. We kids had our swimsuits on so we wouldn't have to change. All of us were pretty young at the time.

When we reached the lake Mom and Dad picked a spot on the grassy park leading to the beach. Here they spread a couple of army blankets for a quick family picnic. Eager to hit the beach, we kids wolfed down our food and bolted for the water.

Splashing near the shore was fun but we couldn't go out too far — none of us knew how to swim. Fully clothed, Mom and Dad watched us from a blanket spread on the sand. The sky darkened as they sat there trying to keep track of us. Soon every kid on the beach had the same black silhouette. Time to call us in.

I was eight or nine when Dad brought along some fat automotive inner tubes on one of our twilight beach trips. He stopped at a gas station on the way and filled them with air. Near the shore I settled into one of the tubes and hand-paddled a good way out. As the waves rocked my tube, I heard Mom and Dad calling, telling me to come back in. All the shouting convinced me that I must be in big trouble. Then I noticed how dark the sky was and I couldn't see any tubes or swimmers near me.

Panicking, I gripped my inner tube for dear life. Too scared to paddle toward shore, I wondered if I'd drift out and drown in the deep dark lake. Then, what luck! A lifeguard splashed out of nowhere and pushed me to the shore. But even worse for Mom and Dad, Jim pulled the exact same stunt, floating out until a lifeguard caught him and nudged him ashore. That was the first and last time we took inner tubes to the beach.

The 25 Cartoons

Twice a year the Capitol Theater played *The 25 Cartoons.* For a quarter kids could see enough of Bugs Bunny, Daffy Duck and the Road Runner to hold them for months (until the next *25 Cartoons* show).

With one of my brothers (and maybe Jim Bradley) I got in line at 8:30 a.m. When the show started at nine the seats were filled to the top row of the balcony. This cartoon fest was just for kids — no parents around to control our rowdiness or limit the amount of popcorn and candy we ingested. We blew our money on boxes of Jujubes, Mason Dots or Slo Poke suckers — all great for promoting tooth decay and ripping the fillings out of young teeth.

When the screen lit up with the big WB (Warner Brothers) logo and the Looney Tunes music started, hundreds of kids screamed with delight. The cartoons were totally predictable — Elmer Fudd,

Yosemite Sam and Sylvester the Cat always got clobbered. They ran off cliffs and fell hundreds of feet. Safes fell on them and cannons blasted them at point-blank range. But they bounced right back a second later, fully recovered and ready for more. Bugs Bunny and Tweety Bird were the brains of the cartoon critters, consistently getting away with murder. I wondered which one would come out on top if they were both in the same cartoon.

All during the show we filled our faces with junk, washing it down with pop from the vending machine in the lobby. You'd put a dime in the machine, then select *Ice* or *No Ice* and the flavor: Coke, Cherry Coke, Green River — whatever. If you pressed Coke you'd walk away with a paper cup of fizz water that tasted sort of like Coke, but with traces of orange, cherry or some other flavor.

The show was a riot of loud laughs. It was fun to take your empty Dots or Lemonheads box and blow through it, making a sissified duck sound. Kids kept walking up and down the aisles throughout the show, heading to the concession stand or the washrooms. A drawing for prizes followed the cartoons. Kids holding lucky ticket stubs won some pretty neat stuff. First prize was something big, like a Schwinn bike loaded with accessories. Second prize might be a portable radio. There were plenty of smaller prizes too, like Duncan yo-yos and popular board games.

On our way to one of these cartoon marathons Jim Bradley and I bought a two-pound box of Brach's chocolate covered cherries at the A&P. We pigged out on them until the box was empty. But all that sugar caught up with me on the way home — my throat felt like it had been sandblasted and I had a flaming heartburn. Even worse, the bright noonday sun aggravated the headache I got from staring at the screen. Bradley, on the other hand, felt fine. "Hey Joe," he asked, "you wanna stop at Wimpy's for a hamburger?"

The following year when I came home from the cartoon fest without my scarf, Mom sent me back to get it. "A good wool scarf like that costs money," she told me as I left the house. At the Capitol an usher led me to an alcove in the lobby and opened a door to a small closet. Inside, on the floor, sat a cardboard box heaped with sweaters, mittens and stocking caps. Rummaging through the pile,

I even dug up a yo-yo and some rosary beads. Everything but my scarf.

Piano pecking

Mom loved the piano and Dad loved to hear her play, so he gave her a Baldwin spinet soon after they were married. She could play any kind of music but her harried schedule didn't allow much time for tickling the ivories. Even so, Mom occasionally sat down and played a tune from memory before some minor household emergency interrupted.

As a kid I enjoyed pecking out tunes on the keyboard — songs like the *Notre Dame Victory March*, the *Twelfth Street Rag* or pieces that Joan or Marg were practicing at the time. One day I noticed sheet music for the tune, *Cherry Pink (and Apple Blossom White)*, on the piano. When Joan played it for me I liked the melody and Latin cha-cha beat. With one finger I plunked out this tune over and over until shouting voices from another room told me to give it a rest. Others, seated at the dining room table, were doing their homework and I was disturbing them. End of music session. But I'd be back a day or two later toying with one tune or another.

Jim tinkered with the piano as well, but he used both hands and pounded out harsh-sounding chords. Everything he played was fast and choppy, like a military march. His music was punishing to my ears and it amazed me when he claimed to be playing several different songs. They all sounded the same to me. But what the heck, he was having fun and letting off steam. Jim's face got redder and redder as he hit the keys — and when he reached the finale he was smiling gleefully. Mom didn't discourage musical dabbling by us boys, but piano lessons were reserved for her girls.

Mea culpa, mea culpa...

Common gray slush packed into a sphere was a dense deadly missile. Making a ball out of slush was easy enough, but the stuff soaked through my cotton gloves and froze my hands. One winter afternoon I was slinging slush at passing vehicles when I saw Nancy Murphy across the street walking toward her house. I'd never even met Nancy, though I knew her sister Peggy and liked her a lot. But since Nancy was a few years older than me I saw her as fair game. I tossed the slushy glob in a high arc that quickly descended. “Plush!” Right on Nancy’s babushka! Before she could turn to see me I ran into the gangway and out of sight. Then I felt like a chickenhearted puke. *What did Nancy ever do to me to deserve that?* I asked myself. *We have the same last name. She might even be a distant cousin.*

The perennial pigeons

The business district around 79th & Halsted was home to flocks of dull gray pigeons. Scores of these unspectacular birds were drawn like magnets to the sidewalks. They congregated in front of the bigger buildings, strutting around, pecking at nothing in particular. A few birds sported black-striped shoulders or random flecks of white, showing a touch of style.

I noticed other pigeons with a blurred brown and white color scheme, like an out-of-focus sepia-toned photo. Rarest of all was a pure white pigeon. Seeing one of these reminded me of the Holy Ghost (now known to Catholics as the Holy Spirit). Our Baltimore Catechism showed an illustration of the “Immaculate Conception,” in which a pure white dove appears to the Virgin Mary.

Pigeons liked to gather in front of the Mutual National Bank and Frank’s Department Store, but the Capitol Theater was pigeon paradise. Its multi-level roof provided countless nooks and crannies for breeding. Meanwhile, folks on the ground used names like “flying rats” and “shit bombers” to describe the ubiquitous birds. The ornate water tower on top of the building furnished penthouse lodging for a few birds – maybe those at the top of the pecking order.

Looking east from our back porch I could see the Capitol water tower clearly. Surrounded by fancy ironwork, it resembled the dome on the capitol building in Washington, D C. Cutting through its maze of decorative girders, a ladder led to the top. Jim felt an irresistible urge to ascend that ladder. Dan and I were content to climb up to the Capitol’s roof for a bird’s-eye view of 79th & Halsted. Below us a matinee audience was watching John Wayne or Alan Ladd. And no way could the ushers find us with their flashlights. What a kick. Jim, however, was seeking bigger risks and thrills.

My pigeon passenger

There was plenty to see on the Capitol roof. Countless nests filled the recesses near the fire escapes and along the brick abutments separating roof sections. One summer afternoon I hung back while Jim climbed to a higher level. I was surprised to see a pigeon waddling toward me, totally unfazed by my presence. When I picked up the bird it made no effort to flee. How about that!

Setting it on my shoulder, I descended. And incredibly, the bird was still riding with me when I reached the ground. For several days I walked around the neighborhood shouldering my faithful pigeon. I kept it in a cardboard box on the back porch. Then one morning the box was empty. I figured my pet's little bird brain had come to its senses, directing it back to the Capitol roof.

Bombs away!

The worst spot in the neighborhood for catching a pigeon splat was the sidewalk on Green Street bordering Frank's Department Store. We locals were careful to avoid that motley stretch of cement. But an unsuspecting visitor to Frank's could get a nasty surprise. As a teenager I caught a big white glob on my forehead one day. Rushing to my after-school job at Frank's, I forgot to skirt the drop zone. Then a few years later, preoccupied with a school dance that night, I dropped my guard and collected a sizeable blob on my jacket. I didn't notice it until Mrs. Hughes, our neighborhood florist, pointed it out when I went to pick up a corsage for my date.

Sink or swim

During the summer between my fifth and sixth grades our folks sent Jim, Dan and me to the Calumet High School pool for swimming lessons. There must have been a hundred boys, aged eight to twelve — all stark naked (no swimsuits allowed). Learning started in the shallow end of the pool with Mr. Zayner. He was Calumet's football coach, and was probably picking up some extra cash teaching summer swim lessons.

With two lifeguard assistants, it was Zayner's job to make swimmers out of us. The lifeguards were there mainly to make sure we took showers and didn't horse around. Before entering the pool every kid got the dirt ball test from a lifeguard. He rubbed his thumb a few times against your ankle. If this produced little gray balls, you had to take another shower.

Zayner's teaching strategy was simple. He made us jump in the shallow end of the pool and try to swim from one side to the other, then back. Five or six kids raced against each other in each heat. I watched how the other kids did it, then gave it a shot when my turn came. Our group of beginners went through this drill for a week or two without anyone drowning. At that point Zayner took some of us down to the deep end and told us to jump in. He stood by with a long pole to fish out kids who struggled.

Unfortunately, I was a bit tardy in arriving and didn't hear all of the coach's instructions. I watched one kid jump in and flail his way over to the ladder on the side of the pool. Hoping to hear the coach better, I edged my way along the side of the pool until I was right behind him. He turned and gave me a stern look — just like the look that Dad gave me if I didn't obey him on the double. Reading Zayner wrong, I jumped into the deep water. And sunk like a rock. I thought I'd keep going down for all eternity when, finally, my body reversed directions. As my head broke through the surface I grabbed the pole extended into the water. The coach pulled me out, shouting, "What's the matter with you? Wait till I tell you to jump! Now you go back to the shallow water until you can learn how to listen!" So I walked down to the group that was still trying to swim across the pool and got in line.

I turned around and there was Dan standing right behind me. What the heck? No time to talk — I had to jump into the water and swim. On the way home Jim told me that after seeing my performance at the deep end, Dan asked Mr. Zayner if he could go back to the shallow water. Despite all this, Dan and I were soon sent back to the deep end. And a week or two later all three of us Murphy boys had swum the entire length of the pool, earning official Red Cross beginner swimmer cards.

Chapter 14

Marg

"Why can't I go? All my friends are going!"
— Margaret Mary

"What a beautiful child!" "What a darling!" "Isn't she adorable?" Everyone thought that Margaret Mary was a doll and I happened to agree. She was just a tot when Jim and I put her in our coaster wagon one spring day and surrounded her with blossoms from the bridal wreath bush in the yard. We pulled her around in a circle calling her "Señorita Beaquita." Little Marg took this nonsense in stride, smiling and cute as ever. At night she liked to cuddle up on the couch with our mother, drifting off to sleep as Mom lie there watching *What's My Line?* or *The Price is Right.*

While she was a still a preschooler Jim and I put together a show starring Marg, who appeared once again as "Señorita Beauquita." For this basement production we strung up an army blanket as a backdrop. Margaret Mary stepped in front of it and sang whatever came into her head. Then Jim and I presented a lame science fiction skit and that was the show. Our audience — a few kids who lived up the block — gave us a polite round of applause. We took the blanket down, folded it and put it back in the hall closet.

Before she started grammar school Marg played Dan's soap opera game with him and Dolores, who lived next door. The three of them threw lines at each other, keeping the story going. Decades later, when I took classes in improvisational theater, it struck me that they were doing improv as little kids. There must be an urge to perform running through my family that's been squelched by the common sense goal of finding a secure job.

When Margaret Mary started at St. Leo Grammar School she looked adorable in her little navy blue jumper. She and her friend, Dyann Dunworth, who lived on our block, were in the same class, so they didn't have to face the first day of school all alone. But before long, newfound friends were visiting our house, including Nancy Doll, who lived on Sangamon, a block west of us.

The brown-flecked sidewalk running up our block was the playground where Marg and her friends jumped rope, practiced hopscotch and roller-skated. I was amazed at how easily my little sister skated on that rough surface. She forged ahead fearlessly making quick, turnabout stops with no problem. Like most kids back then, she wore steel skates that tightened to her shoes with a key. The pebbled concrete resisted anything that rolled, so kids couldn't coast very far. It looked like labor-intensive fun to me. Those steel skate wheels hitting the sidewalk sounded like someone with a bad cough.

Making the grade

Grammar school was no great challenge for Margaret Mary. Her report cards always showed E for excellent in arithmetic, English and spelling, which she liked. History and geography left her cold. These were the "boring" subjects, she said. Marg enjoyed music. She took piano lessons from Sister Mary Florence starting in first grade. She practiced regularly and played all her pieces well. Year after year Mom was proud of her daughter's recital performances in the school hall.

I went to Marg's second-grade recital, where she played Polonaise. She was introduced, walked to the piano and ripped through the piece so quickly that I couldn't help laughing while the folks around me applauded. In fifth grade Marg took baton lessons at school, doing the twirling and tossing exercises with ease. At the baton recital she counted the cadence for the group — "One, two, three, four..." Things other girls needed lessons for came naturally to her — cartwheels, tumbling, whatever.

Margaret Mary, age nine, at the piano

At home Margaret Mary did her homework, practiced her music and watched TV. There were minor squabbles with brothers over who got to see what programs, but Mom settled them quickly, shaming us boys with choice words on how we should treat our little sister.

Special occasions like birthdays and holidays made Margaret Mary glow. She was radiant blowing out her birthday candles. And she was a vision in white posing in her First Communion dress as Dad snapped her picture in front of the house.

Marg was thrilled when Santa brought her a little battery-powered sewing machine that worked just like Mom's big Singer. And she loved the mini cooking set she got one Christmas, with mixes for tiny cakes and cookies. One Saturday morning Marg got up early, mixed some cookie dough and dabbed dots of it onto her pint-sized cookie sheet. She slid it into Mom's oven before going out to play. Returning hours later, she opened the oven door to find a bunch of tiny smoking black dots, permanently bonded to the metal sheet.

Neighborhood episodes

Not wanting to be left behind, Marg tagged along when we boys went skating at the lagoon near St. George's Hospital. She had to wear Joan's hockey-style skates, which were way too big for her, but extra wool stockings bulked up her feet. She tied the laces snugly and was up gliding across the ice. Marg even went along with us one day when we scaled the roof of the Capitol Theater. She got a kick out of the roosting pigeons and the panoramic view of Halsted Street.

Greater adventures lie ahead. One afternoon Virginia Bushnell, an eighth-grader who lived across the street, took my nine-year-old sister for a ride on the handlebars of her bike. Virginia and her friends were heading across Halsted toward Emerald Avenue. That's the last thing Marg remembered until she was back home, climbing the last few stairs up to the porch.

She'd been thrown off the bike and must have hit her head because she was in a trance. The biking girls walked Marg all the way home in her semiconscious state. Mom immediately gave her a bath and called Dad, who came home from work and took Marg to the hospital for X-rays. As a grownup she recalled how annoying it was to keep removing and replacing the bow in her hair as the technician took pictures of her head.

Dan gave Marg a scare one afternoon behind the Cosmo Theater. Walking through the alley they spotted a big steel drum spouting flames (someone was burning trash illegally). Dan picked up an old discarded broom and held it over the barrel until it caught fire. Then, trying to frighten Marg, he swung it toward her but got too close. Oops! Her coat was on fire. Screaming, she pulled it off and stomped on it. Dan jumped in to help smother the flames. Margaret Mary's hair was singed, but luckily her skin wasn't burned. Dan recalls that she ranted at him all the way home. Marg couldn't hide the damage to her hair or the muddy coat with the crispy collar. I forget what Dan's punishment was for pulling this stupid stunt, but I thought he got off easy.

As I walked home from school at lunchtime one day I noticed that Margaret Mary and Dyann Dunworth were right behind me. They started giggling about something, so I turned and asked what was so funny. To my chagrin, they said it was the way my feet went out to the side as I walked. Maybe that was amusing to them, but I didn't like being laughed at. Not a bit. What could I do could do about the way my feet hit the sidewalk?

A few days later, while lying in bed reading, I looked at my feet. Wow — they were splayed way out to either side. When Marg came in to do some dusting, I got an idea. *Maybe if I turn my feet inward and she sits on them it will help them to point straight ahead.* I asked her if she would foot-sit me for a quarter. She accepted my offer. So with my feet in a pigeon-toed position I said "Ready!" Marg sat on my feet for a few minutes — until the pain was killing me. "OK, that's enough," I yelped. My little sister went off to spend her quarter. I got up and took a few steps, staring at my feet. They were still flaring out the same as ever, and my ankles hurt like hell.

Hey, this will knock you out!

I still feel guilty about the time I made Marg pass out. I told her about a stunt Jim Dunbar had pulled on me that made me lose consciousness. I said that if she'd take ten deep breaths and hold the last one, I could give her a bear hug that would make her faint. Surprisingly, she went along with me. We were near the hall radiator just outside the living room. Dad was in his chair reading the paper and didn't notice what we were up to.

Marg took ten deep breaths. I gave her a hug. She went limp and slipped from my grip. As she slid to the floor, her head hit the radiator. She was lying on the carpet unconscious with blood streaming down her cheek. "Wake up, Wake up!" I shouted. Dad jumped out of his chair and sat Marg up against the wall. Moments later, after she'd come to, he helped her to the bathroom and covered her cut with a Band-Aid. Then he turned and asked me what had happened. As I explained he grew furious. He asked me who had taught me the bear-hug maneuver and I told him. "Don't you never try that on anybody again! You hear me?" Dad's anger scrambled his words a bit, but his message was clear. And luckily, Marg's cut healed with just a tiny scar.

Singing and dancing

In fifth grade Margaret Mary asked if she could take Irish step dancing at school. Pat Roach, the leader of a local dance troupe, was giving group lessons in the school auditorium. Mom and Dad approved. They even bought records of hornpipes and reels to help Marg practice at home. Her dancing attire was a plaid skirt, a white blouse and thick-heeled black leather shoes. She danced like a champ and really enjoyed the lessons. What's more, the records she danced to at home awakened the Irish spirit in the whole Murphy clan. But lively as it was, that kind of dancing struck me as awfully severe. Marg had to stand arrow-straight with her arms held stiffly at her sides, like a soldier at attention.

After a few performances Pat Roach came over to the house for a chat with Mom and Dad. He asked if their daughter could join his traveling dance troupe that gave weekend performances in numerous cities throughout the year. They told him that all the traveling would take their young daughter too far away too often. Soon afterward Marg said good-bye to Irish dancing, returning to her normal, action-packed routine.

For two years my little sister sang in the girls' grammar school choir. In eighth grade she stood in the back row, right in the center, with the other "strong" voices. Unfortunately, choir provided the perfect social setting. And that Murphy girl talked too much to suit Sister Mary Cecil, the no-nonsense choir nun. She showed her disapproval by moving Marg down one row — a slap on the wrist that had no effect my sister's (or the choir's) performance.

The Nine Fridays

All through grammar school Marg was determined to complete the "Nine Fridays." This involved going to mass and communion on the first Friday of each month for nine months in a row. Marg's nun gave strong hints that making the Nine Fridays would elevate one's stature in heaven. Inspired by this prospect, Marg got up early on First Fridays, abstained from breakfast and attended early mass at the church, accompanied by whichever brother was on the Nine Fridays track at the time. "It was fun," she told me decades later. "I never finished all nine Fridays, but I loved going to Lohner's Bakery after mass. They had the greatest little chocolate donuts — and milk!"

Free home demonstration

Kids in the upper grades at St. Leo sold some pricey religious items to support the missions. One that really stood out was an illuminated statue of the Virgin Mary. Marg's seventh-grade nun owned one of these luminous beauties and loaned it out on a regular basis. Each kid in her class got to keep it for a few days, so the statue eventually found its way to our house.

I fell in love with the radiant virgin at first sight. She was a foot high with a cord that plugged into a wall socket. The statue glowed, surrounding itself with a soft aura. Even better, the base unscrewed, and inside was an oversized rosary. Mom was so taken with the plastic Mary that she bought one straightaway. And when I found a matching plug-in Jesus in a neighborhood store a month later, we kids chipped in and bought it for Mom. The twin statues graced the top of our Baldwin spinet for years, one glowing at each end.

Sleeping over

Like most girls, Margaret Mary loved slumber parties. When her girlfriends came to our house for an overnight they spread blankets on the living room floor, then gabbed and giggled into the wee hours. Unfortunately, they were within earshot of Dan and Tom, who were on the hide-a-bed in the den trying to get some sleep.

Pajama parties were pretty controlled in our second-floor flat, but Marg confessed that overnights at other girls' houses were much livelier. Yvonne Fitzpatrick's slumber party was wild. And at Kathy O'Brien's overnight, the whole group of six girls in pajamas went AWOL at four a.m., stealing over to the house of some boy in their class. They rang the doorbell, panicked and scrambled back to the O'Brien's place.

Marg dressed for her grammar school graduation – June, 1961

Fun on the run

Margaret Mary was no homebody. She loved to be off somewhere away from the house. In this respect she was more of a thrill seeker than Joan. Marg made sure she went on the grammar school trip to the circus each year. Missing out on anything fun left her feeling cheated. So if her girlfriends were going someplace Marg made sure she was going too.

Whenever Mom tried to curtail one of Marg's social activities a heated confrontation ensued. Her overbooked dance card was often the cause of screaming, yelling and crying. Unlike her older sister, Margaret Mary argued and insisted; shouted and sobbed. It seemed to me that she thrived on conflict, but at least she was honest. There was no excuse-making or sneaking out. It was a rare occasion when Dad disciplined Marg. But when, in eighth grade, she came to supper wearing lipstick, he grabbed a wet washrag and wiped it off her face.

Margaret Mary got prettier every year. It was no surprise that boys were attracted to her. This worried Mom, who wanted her daughter to focus on schoolwork and music. One day a boy in Marg's eighth-grade class had the gall to walk her home from school. Our own Tom, who hadn't quite reached his teens, felt honor bound to report this to Mom (always headstrong, he was going though a righteous period). I can't recall Mom's reaction to the news from Tom, but Marg's after-school escort did not walk her home again.

When Margaret Mary was an eighth grader I was a senior in high school. My upbringing told me that she was too young for boys but I could see why guys liked her. She was attractive. And what did I know about dating? Zilch! When a few of my classmates asked me about my sister I was embarrassed. How did they even know I had a sister? Despite our parents' disapproval, Marg was learning how to use makeup — especially eyeliner. In fact, during her early teens she sometimes stood in front of a mirror for an hour or more doing her lashes over and over. At about the same time she developed a compulsion for checking to make sure all the doors were locked at night.

Growing girlfriends

Toward the end of her grammar school days Marg was bringing girlfriends galore over to our house. I had no complaints about this. If I were doing my homework at the kitchen table she might stop with Pat or Pam or whoever on her way to the back door. I liked talking to the girls, even though they were four years younger than me and not yet in high school. They were looking better and better to me every time I saw them, but they were verboten — that four-year age gap was a vast impassible chasm.

I got my high school class ring in junior year. It was gold with a big red garnet. I was proud of it. I could see myself wearing that ring decades later. One side of it showed the mighty Leo Lion. The other side sported a crest, encircled by the Leo High School motto: FACTA NON VERBA. The Latin words mean DEEDS NOT WORDS. I wore my ring for a few weeks before it disappeared. *Where the heck is it?* I wondered, after looking all over the house. I asked everyone to keep an eye out for it, hoping it would turn up. But after a month or so my hopes of recovering it faded and I eventually forgot about the ring. However, I remember clearly that Marg and one of her girlfriends liked to play with it. I still suspect that it traveled outside the house where it got lost.

Free dance lessons

When Margaret Mary was still in grammar school she taught Dan and me how to bebop. Next to touch football, this was the most fun I had through my high school years. At that time rock and roll was simple, happy and musical. The lyrics were silly but they were crisp and clear. We could hear and understand them. Songs like *Blueberry Hill* by Fats Domino and *Calendar Girl* by Neil Sedaka were great fun.

When a couple of us felt the urge to dance, we carried the phonograph into the kitchen and moved the table out of the way, clearing a good-sized patch of linoleum to practice on. Marg, the natural dancer, showed us how to keep the beat and spin our partner without elbowing her in the head. I couldn't have found a better teacher or dance partner.

Marg was graceful, energetic and amazingly flexible. Together we perfected a maneuver where we stood back-to-back and I flipped her over my shoulders so she landed on her feet facing me. We kept right on bebopping. She was tireless, dancing to Sam Cooke's *Wonderful World* or *Diana* by Paul Anka. Marg loved Bobby Darin singing *Dream Lover* and Frankie Avalon crooning *Venus* (both cha-chas). Dan teased her, babbling the lyrics to *Venus* in a baby-talk imitation of Frankie Avalon. But Marg came back at him with a trembling voice that spoofed his beloved Connie Francis singing *Where The Boys Are.*

Cousin Mike makes the scene

I was a high school senior when Uncle Connie, Aunt Vivian and Cousin Mike got an apartment a mile west of us. Soon Mike was visiting our house regularly. I helped him get a job at Auburn Food & Liquor on Halsted. We were both stock boys but Mike had his driver's license. So while I hauled groceries on a clunky delivery bike he made deliveries using the store owner's station wagon.

I was seeing a lot of Mike at work and more of him at home. He came over all the time. Mike liked sitting in the kitchen and chatting, especially with Margaret Mary. When I left the table to do my homework in another room, Mike lingered, chitchatting with my sister. It didn't dawn on me that he had a mad crush on her until

Dan commented, "Mike sure spends a lot of time talking to Marg." The scene had sure changed. Two or three years earlier Mike and I were building model cars propelled by CO_2 gas and racing them on the sidewalk. Now our interests were shifting toward full-sized cars and full-sized girls who might want to go for a ride.

Still making magic

Margaret Mary had a steady boyfriend throughout high school. She commuted to college and then taught primary education in Chicago's south suburban schools. One day, as she was ushering her kids into the classroom, she caught the attention of Bob Thomas, who had just given a talk at the school. At that time Bob was kicking field goals for the Chicago Bears. He started dating my sister and they married a year later, settling west of Chicago. Marg earned a Master's Degree and Bob became a judge. Their three children are now grown up, graduated from college and doing well.

Chapter 15

Freewheeling

"Get a bicycle. You will not regret it. If you live."
— Mark Twain

We had too much time to while away in the summer — three whole months. I suppose that if we Murphy brothers had been red-blooded all-American boys, we would have been out playing baseball from morn till night. But most of us were nearsighted and had trouble tracking such a small, fast moving object. I didn't like getting beaned when somebody threw a ball to me. The embarrassment hurt worse than the impact.

The twin Schwinns

Recalling how much fun it was to swipe Joan's bike when I was six, I longed to own one. Unfortunately, her little two-wheeler was long gone. And Jim, itching to explore the world beyond our neighborhood, craved a bicycle even more than I did. That's why we were both tickled pink with the red Schwinn bikes we got for Christmas in 1954.

As soon as the snow melted we were out riding around the block — and itching to travel farther. Little by little, Mom and Dad trusted us to go for longer and longer jaunts. Our cycling exploits gave us freedom and independence. When spring came with daylight savings time I loved going for a quick bike ride before dark. I pumped my legs until my thighs burned, then stood on the pedals and enjoyed the breeze cooling my face and arms. It was exhilarating — I could jump on my bike and be a mile away from home in minutes. And the better the weather, the farther I wanted to go. Jim felt the same way, so we kept pushing the envelope of our cycling boundaries. By the time summer arrived we were exploring turf miles away in every direction. It was an education cruising through unfamiliar neighborhoods with different kinds of houses.

East always struck me as the direction of promise. State Street ("that great street" as the song boasts) was just eight blocks east of Hasted. Turning left at State I could pedal my way to the heart of downtown — a mere ten miles north. And though I never made that trek, cycling to State Street gave me an adventuresome high. Jim and I sometimes pedaled miles east of State, past exotic-sounding boulevards like Cottage Grove and Stony Island. We paid a few surprise visits to aunts and uncles who lived near the lake.

On some summer days there was no trace of Jim or his bike. He rose early and disappeared on a solo cycling expedition, not getting back home until after supper. Jim caught hell from Dad for worrying Mom all day, but he felt the thrill of exploring outweighed the punishment. As we lay in bed he told me about the amazing things he'd seen — refineries with tall towers spouting flames into the sky and colossal storage tanks with stairways winding up their sides.

Sprucing up your wheels

A kid up the block showed me how to give my bike a motorized sound. All it took was a long "wiener" balloon from Mallatt's store and a breath or two of air. After tying both ends of the balloon to my bike's front fork I pushed it into the spokes. As they moved by the balloon, the spokes made a dull thudding sound that mimicked a car motor. Clipping a playing card to your front fork created a crisper sound — more like a motorcycle.

I envied kids who had fancy accessories adorning their bikes. When Bill Caroli, who lived across the street, got a bike speedometer for his birthday I felt pangs of envy. But what I craved most was a sleek carrier with a glitzy reflector covering my rear fender. And I wouldn't have turned down some colored plastic streamers for my handlebar grips.

Perhaps the sexiest accessory of all was a horn pod that fit between the twin crossbars of a Schwinn bike. Its bulging curves were stylish in a sensuous automotive way. Pressing the silver button in the middle produced a nasal buzzing sound. Another neat accessory was the generator-powered rear light. Its pickup wheel spinning against the rear tire delivered electric juice to the tiny bulb.

Then there was the bike siren — loud, obnoxious and fun. Driven by the front tire, the faster it turned, the louder it screamed. With one of these on my bike I disturbed the calm of summer days and nights on my block for weeks — until I got tired of hearing the noise myself.

Bicycle maintenance

Soon after Jim and I got our new bikes Dad showed us how to clean our coaster brakes — a formidable task for kids. We had to remove the rear wheel and take the brakes completely apart. There were dozens of parts so we paid close attention. Dad soaked the parts in kerosene, then wiped them clean and packed them with fresh grease, before sliding them back into the wheel hub. I was only eleven years old and Jim was twelve, but Dad explained the process clearly and we learned. After that, Jim and I cleaned our brakes periodically, sometimes helping each other. It always made them work better. Dad was a good teacher and (amazingly) he trusted us to handle kerosene, the same stuff that fuels jet engines!

Jim's toboggan slide ride

I came home one Saturday afternoon in the fall to learn that Jim had just returned from the hospital. He'd taken a nasty spill out at Dan Ryan Woods, a Cook County forest preserve west of our neighborhood. Always a thrill seeker, Jim viewed the steep toboggan slides as a challenge. Riding down on a bike meant picking up speed while bouncing over wooden beams the size of railroad ties.

Starting from the high ridge where toboggans began their descent, Jim rode the bumpy run all the way down, miraculously reaching the bottom in one piece. Then, emboldened by his success, he headed down a steeper slide.

Years later Jim told me that the last thing he remembered before waking up was seeing his bike flying through the air above him. A kindly lady employed by the county carried him into a service shed, where she looked after him until an ambulance arrived. Dad brought Jim home from the hospital covered with bandages. His flying bike adventure rewarded him with scuffs and bruises aplenty but, miraculously, Jim didn't break anything. Like his neck.

It's gone!

"Wanna go swimmin' at Gage Park?" Jim's invitation was irresistible. I was building a model airplane in the basement but swimming struck me as a better way to beat the heat. After tying my suit and towel in place behind my bike seat I noticed that the front tire was flat. I told Dan I was in a jam and he let me borrow his bike.

Jim and I pedaled seven miles to Gage Park at 55th & Western. Once there, I realized that I'd left my lock and chain attached to my bike at home. With one chain between us, Jim and I didn't think of using it to lock both bicycles. Jim leaned his bike against one side of a tree, securing it with his lock and chain. I rested Dan's bike against the opposite side. We headed for the cool blue pool.

The water was so packed with kids that nobody could swim. But it was fun just splashing around. I looked through the chain-link fence once or twice — Dan's bike was still there. Then a whistle blew and a loud megaphone voice shouted, "Everyone out of the water!" A boy had hit his head on the diving board, knocking himself unconscious. Park employees crowded around the deep end of the pool where they'd pulled him from the water. I couldn't see much, but within a few minutes a crew of firemen arrived with a stretcher and carried the kid away.

When the whistle blew again everyone jumped back into the pool. We were having fun diving under water, trying to do handstands amidst a forest of legs. The chlorine smelled good to me. Its exotic scent conjured up visions of Esther Williams diving into a circle of shapely water nymphs. All too soon the afternoon swim session was over. Dried off and dressed I felt calm and refreshed. Jim and I left the locker room and turned to get our bikes when a horrific reality confronted me: Dan's bike was gone! "IT'S GONE!" I shrieked, looking at Jim. "It's gone," he echoed in a calm, resigned voice.

Panic slugged me hard in the gut. I told Jim some kid had just taken the bike for a joyride and would bring it right back. He assured me that Dan's bike was gone for good. After a few moments of dazed numbness I got the idea to tell a policeman about my plight. And what luck — there was one right at the corner, directing kids across the street.

I approached him in the middle of the crosswalk with my pathetic plea, "Somebody stole my bike!" He didn't even look down at me. I said it again, "Hey, somebody stole my bike!" Still no response. *Is this guy deaf?* I wondered. I tried a third time, using new words that might sound more urgent, "Some kid just stole my bike!" Finally he looked down at me and said, "Sorry, kid — there's nothing I can do about it."

I rode home straddling the rear fender of Jim's bike and clutching the back of his seat. I begged him not to say anything about the stolen bike. When we reached 79th & Peoria, Jim turned into the alley, pedaling toward our house. Before we got far Dan shot out of a neighbor's back yard and ran toward us. "You wouldn't believe it!" he shouted as Jim hit the brakes. "The biggest rat I ever saw — it musta been this long!" He was holding his hands a foot and a half apart.

Catching his breath after the rat report, Dan asked about his bike. It was hard to do but I told him that someone had stolen it. "Real funny — where is it?" Dan demanded. He didn't believe me. Jim chimed in, "Somebody stole it while we were swimming!" "I'm sorry," I pleaded. "I'll get you a new bike." As Dan realized that this was no joke his face reddened. "You lost my bike?" He screamed. "Somebody stole it," I insisted. "Didn't you lock it up?" "We couldn't lock it — Joe forgot his chain." Thanks Jim.

Dan looked at me wearing an injured puzzled expression. "You lost my bike! You have to get me a new one!" I agreed with him. "You can use mine!" I offered. Dan stalked off toward our house, and looking back at me he shouted, "Dad will make you buy me a new bike!" Luckily, Dad got home a bit late that night. And I hit the sack early to make sure he didn't see me. It was not a good time to be in the doghouse. Jim and I were scheduled for an outing with our Uncle Paul from Oklahoma and his kids the very next day. We were going with them for day of fun at Riverview.

I couldn't dodge Dad for long. The night after my Riverview romp he asked me about the outing at supper. I reported that everyone had loads of fun. "Good," he said, adding that he wanted to see me later. Uh-oh! When the dishes were done I walked into the living room. Dad set the newspaper he was reading on his lap and took me to task regarding the stolen bike. He didn't hit me. Instead, he said I'd have to give him money from my paper route each week until I'd covered the cost of a new bike for Dan — just what I expected. The payback took months. And Dan was happy to get a new bike long before I'd handed my last installment to Dad.

One-speed fun

Almost every bike rolling through the Fifties had one speed and a coaster brake. Schwinn was the big wheel in bikes, although there were other good brands around, like Monarch, Huffy and Columbia — all made in the USA. Bike tires were fat and forgiving. They let kids ride over rugged terrain and up and down curbs. Approaching a steep curb, I'd stand and pull up on my handlebars to help the front wheel jump from the street to the sidewalk.

European bikes with skinny tires, multiple speeds and hand brakes were an oddity. I saw a few of them when Dad and I went bike browsing at Mages, the giant sporting goods store downtown. But in the neighborhood, seeing a "racer," as we called that kind of bike, was a rare event. What kind of wimp would want one of those scrawny things, anyway?

The first time I saw a "racer" in action was at an organized bicycle race. One summer night Dad took Dan and me over to Shewbridge Field (Leo High School's home turf in the fall) to watch a pack of sweaty cyclists circling a wooden track. It was a big bowl-shaped affair, banked at the corners. The surface was wood ribs an inch wide spaced about a half inch apart. Looking like spokes fanning out from the center of the track, they met the bike tires at a right angle.

Over and over the bikers whooshed by us. One guy who came out of the race stopped and asked us if we were enjoying ourselves. We said we were having a great time, which brought a smile to his sweat-drenched face. He told us that these fast racing bikes were built without brakes and that their sew-up tires were actually sewn together to completely enclose their rubber inner tubes. I thought that would make fixing a flat a major project.

Thigh-building work bikes

Some bikes earned their keep throughout the Fifties. The neighborhood Good Humor man was likely to be a teenage kid pedaling a bastardized bicycle that was a three-wheeled contraption with a big boxy compartment up front. Inside was a very cool collection of ice cream delights. Dry ice (frozen CO_2) kept the treats frozen solid — literally hard as a rock. And it was pitch black inside that freezing box, so Mr. Good Humor had to know exactly where each item was. When he opened the small square hatch on top, white smoke came pouring out. The dry ice was a novelty. If we begged hard enough we might wheedle a piece of it from the Good Humor guy. Far colder than regular ice — it really stung our hands. And it was pure white, like the thick curly smoke it made when we dropped it into water.

Another bike trundling through our neighborhood streets was the ungainly grocery delivery bike. It had a shrunk-down front wheel that made room for a deep wire basket. I often saw the kid from the Spic 'n Span deli pedaling one of these freight haulers down Peoria Street. And as I found out later, working at Auburn Food and Liquor, these heavy bikes could carry ample cargo.

Bye-bye bikes

After supper in the summer packs of boys in their young teens cruised the neighborhood streets on stripped-down bikes with no fenders. They looked like the practice squad for Hell's Angels, the infamous motorcycle gang. These guys breezed by wearing Diego tees or no shirts at all, leaning back, arms hanging loose at their sides. A couple of them might be gripping the backs of their bike seats as they pedaled. This bunch would soon be abandoning bicycles for motorized vehicles. It seemed strange to me, but as soon as boys entered high school they abruptly cast off their bikes. At that age bicycles suddenly became very uncool. It was time to be driving a car or at least something with a motor, like a Cushman scooter. No self-respecting high school boy would be caught dead pedaling a bicycle.

Chapter 16

Trains, planes and push cars

Well I might take a plane
I might take a train
But if I have to walk
I'm gonna get there just the same...
Kansas City, Wilbert Harrison, 1959

If you walked up the street where I lived in the Fifties you'd see cars with names that don't exist today. There were bulky Hudsons and svelte, low-slung Studebakers. You might find a big stately Packard or a Nash with a grill like some tough guy's gritted teeth. Kaisers and Frazers were still around too. In fact, Sears sold a car in their catalog in the early Fifties called the Allstate that was really a Henry J. made by Kaiser.

Crosley, an outfit that made radios, was turning out small cars, including a ragtop, called the Hotshot. Nash sold cute little Metropolitan convertibles made in England that still show up in TV commercials. What's more, cars back then sported snazzy two-tone color schemes — pink and black, turquoise and white, black and red.

The Lincoln Continental wore a "Continental Kit" on its rear end. The spare tire sat inside a big metal donut that rested on a shelf between the trunk and the rear bumper. The Nash Rambler was a popular family car. Some of the Rambler TV spots were animated cartoons with an announcer's voice that asked, "Does your car look like a jukebox on wheels?" Ramblers highlighted their common-sense features, like rustproofing and dual brake cylinders. They also played up their fully reclining front seats, suggesting that mom, pop and the kids could pull over (God knows where) at night, let the seats down and sleep till dawn safe and worry-free. It was a simpler more trusting time for sure.

There weren't many imports on the scene — an occasional Mercedes or Porsche from Germany or maybe a little British MG, but there wasn't a Japanese car in sight. Who could imagine a well-made car from Japan? Wasn't the stuff from that place just dime-store junk made of tin or papier-mâché?

At the same time, Harley-Davidson motorcycles were thundering down Halsted and across 79th Street. And you might see some nice cycles made by Indian as well. A kid in my grammar school class bragged about his big brother's Cushman motor scooter. Owning the top-of-the-line Cushman Eagle was very cool. Of course, anything with a motor was a quantum leap from a leg-powered bike.

Trains on our brains

As young kids Dan and I loved model trains. When he was in first grade Dan had hopes that Santa would bring him a train set for Christmas. Day after day he stopped on his way home from school to watch the electric train in a store window on Halsted. A little engine chugged along, pulling its cars through a snowy landscape. That Christmas proved to be a very special one, because we kids got a terrific train set — not from Santa, but from Joan. She earned it by selling eight subscriptions to the *Chicago Herald American* newspaper.

What a fantastic surprise! Right on our living room floor a sleek Santa Fe diesel pulled a line of colorful freight cars around an oval of track. The engine had a deep husky horn and a little man kicked a bundle out of the boxcar. We were thrilled! Then, a few years later, after Dan and I begged and prodded, Dad gave us a second train. This one was powered by a big Union Pacific steamer with eight driver wheels. Now, with two trains at our command, we tried to find a way to run them both at once.

The miracle of the switch tracks

Dan and I fantasized about switch tracks and the railroading possibilities they offered. We looked through books of track layouts for ideas on how to switch trains from one line to another. Our goal was a holiday layout that would occupy the entire floor in some room of the house. Living room? Maybe. Den? Possibly. This layout had to cover a lot of turf without tripping up family members and friends.

By fall we'd saved enough to buy a pair of switches from Harrison Wholesale on 61st & Western. I took a CTA bus that dropped me off right in front of the place — a low building with a nice terracotta front. The interior was pretty spartan — ample floor space and a few counters. At one counter customers looked at the Harrison catalog and filled out order slips. They paid at a second counter and picked up their purchases at a third counter after the items had been pulled from stock.

I filled out a slip, handed it to a clerk and paid him cash. Then I joined the folks who were waiting to receive the goods they'd paid for. After ten minutes or so my name was called, and wow! The clerk pushed a box toward me that was big enough to hold an air conditioner. But **American Flyer Trains** was printed clearly on the outside, so I figured it must be the right item.

With help from the driver I got the box and myself onto a CTA bus. A block from my house I debarked and lugged the hefty load home. As I carried it up the front hall steps Dan commented on the box's whopping size. Moments later in the kitchen we opened the carton and discovered, to our delight, that it held not one, but three sets of switch tracks. Hurray!

We reveled in our good fortune before some ethical questions came up. Should we just keep one set and return the other two? Would somebody get in trouble for giving merchandise away if we kept all three sets? Would Harrison Wholesale check their records and trace the missing switches back to us? Nah! We'd just make somebody look stupid if we pointed out the mistake. With that issue settled it was time to expand our layout plans to include six switches.

Please watch your step

I still wonder how we got away with it, but throughout the Christmas season of '57 train tracks surrounded both the living room and den. We were only able to run one train on this layout, but it was great fun. Our big steamer chugged from one room to another, rounding one corner of the heavily trafficked front hall. "Don't step on the tracks!" we warned visiting relatives and neighborhood kids.

Little tykes loved our holiday train. On their knees they watched the engine chug toward them under the sofa, headlight beaming, smoke puffing and whistle blowing. We filled the hopper car with Christmas candy and made special stops so the toddlers could grab some.

There were minor mishaps, like derailments caused by shifting furniture and tinsel falling onto the tracks. That old-fashioned lead tinsel would cause a short, stopping the train cold. The only major accident occurred on New Year's Day, when an uncle, striding into the den to greet us, kicked a few cars across the room. Luckily they hit the drapes, which minimized the damage.

The wild blue yonder

If model trains weren't enough, I got hooked on model airplanes at age ten. I built dozens of planes — plastic ones for display and balsa wood craft designed to fly. Inspiration came from knowing that my brother Jack was an Air Force pilot. And further impetus was furnished by my "artist" cousin, Jim Doyle, who sent us Murphy kids pencil drawings of World War II fighters and bombers. Aunt Martha, who maintained close contact with Jim, brought us of piles of these drawings, which were always on IBM punch cards.

Self-portrait by my artist cousin, Jim Doyle

Jack's aerophile influence on us younger brothers began back in 1950, when he gave us a toy airplane with a gas motor for Christmas. Dad knew we were years too young for this toy, so he hid it inside an old suitcase in a basement storeroom. Then, one summer afternoon, I was exploring the far reaches of the basement, motivated more by boredom than curiosity, when I discovered the suitcase. I opened it and holy cats! There was an airplane inside! It was shiny red plastic with a little gas-powered engine up front. The white propeller was painted with red tips.

I couldn't wait to show this to my brothers. "Hey," I shouted, hurrying up the back stairs with the suitcase. Jim and Dan were on the porch when I arrived and Jim Bradley was scurrying up the stairs behind me. (He could always tell when something was up.) "Wait till you see this," I said, opening the suitcase. "Wow!" shouted Bradley. In a flash he grabbed the plane and tossed it off the porch. It fell like a brick into the yard.

We screamed and shouted at Bradley, calling him "Idiot," "Moron" and worse. Then, dashing downstairs to check for damage, we found that the landing gear was busted. Accordingly, we heaped more scorn on Bradley, who took off for parts unknown.

Pat and Jim Bradley looking a bit knackered on St. Patty's Day

At supper I told Dad about finding the airplane in the suitcase. "What were you doing in that front storeroom?" he hollered. Dad was really angry — I thought he was going to belt me. "Don't ever go in that room!" he raged. "The stuff in there is private!" After a long pause he confessed, "That plane is for you kids when you're a little older. Jack gave it to you for Christmas years ago and we've been saving it." To my amazement he dropped the subject, so after a few days Jim and I wired and glued the plane's lame landing gear. It looked like it might hold.

Within a week or two we'd pooled enough money to buy a can of fuel and a dry-cell battery for starting the engine. But we also needed a pump for the can, plus wires and a clip to deliver electricity to the cylinder head. It started to dawn on me that this whole airplane routine was awfully expensive. Jim tried to start the engine, snapping the prop counterclockwise over and over. Kaplup, kaplup, kaplup...no luck. I gave it a shot and got the same results. Jim tried again. Kaplup, kaplup... We decided to check with Glider's Hobby Shop for advice.

Ground school

Talking to Mrs. Glider and some kids who were browsing in the store, we learned that you didn't just take a "ready-made" plane out of the box and fly it. The new engine had to be broken in through a laborious process involving castor oil, time and patience. Oh boy! At that point Jim and I took a break from flying models. I went back to making planes that sat on the dresser.

We returned the gas-powered dud to its suitcase hangar for quite a spell. Meanwhile, my interest shifted to the new jet fighters and the warbirds of World War II. Over the years I'd seen many of the older planes drawn on IBM cards by my cousin Jim. At work he'd salvaged used cards from the trash and sketched on them at lunchtime. When I brought a handful of his airplane sketches to school the boys in my class went berserk over them. One kid even offered to buy them.

Building character

The first wooden airplane kit I assembled taught me a lesson: READ ALL THE INSTRUCTIONS BEFORE GLUING ANY PARTS TOGETHER! After using half of a Gillette Blue Blade to cut out the parts from sheets of balsa wood, my index finger throbbed with pain. But I was making progress. I looked at the plans without paying much attention to the printed instructions.

I was going great guns gluing jigs, spars and stringers together with a passion. Oops! I suddenly discovered that jig F should have been glued in place back in step six. Now, at step ten, I couldn't fit it in without taking everything apart. Frustrated, I tried to undo things. Luckily, some pieces weren't completely dry and came undone. Other parts wouldn't yield and broke. I glued them back together, then read the assembly instructions before starting over.

The second time around I got past step ten, only to find that some parts were too weak to use. What the heck? The patterns for certain pieces were stamped on good strong wood, while others were stamped on wood that was softer than Styrofoam. I had to buy a sheet of balsa wood, trace the weak parts onto it, and then cut them out all over again.

It took me a week to assemble the plane and apply its tissue paper skin. Then I brought my finished bird over to the practice field at Calumet High School for a test flight. With the rubber-band-powered prop cranked tight, I raised my arm and launched the craft with a gentle toss. It flew straight and level for quite a distance, crashing into the front door of the school. The nose caved in and the wings popped off. It was a good flight in a bad location. I had to find a bigger field.

The soap box surprise

I thought flying models were awfully fragile compared to the rugged push cars Jim and I had made a few years earlier. I wished we had the wherewithal make some kind of self-propelled vehicle. Inspiration came one Saturday when Dad took the whole family downtown to the One Hour Movie at the Today Theater. This little cinema on Madison Street was still screening black-and-white Movietone newsreels.

One of the segments showed the annual soapbox derby held in Akron, Ohio. I loved those cars! They weren't just boards on wheels — they had three dimensions. Their young drivers actually climbed into them and gripped a steering wheel. Even better, nobody had to push them — they rolled down a long steep hill at what seemed to be incredible speeds.

The image of those sleek soapbox racers was still in my mind the next summer as I strolled along 79th Street past the burned-out Good Humor barn. I had to walk around a huge 4x8-foot sheet of plywood lying on the sidewalk. It had been covering one of the shattered front windows, but some kids had probably kicked it out just for fun. *Wait a minute,* it struck me, *This is just what I need to build a soapbox racer!*

The big wooden sheet was too unwieldy for me to haul by myself, so I recruited Jim to help me carry it home. "Man this is heavy," he complained. "How you gonna make a car out of this?" I had only the vaguest notion. "Like a big model airplane without the wings," I told him. We dragged the plywood sheet down the stairs into the basement. "Glad that's over," Jim said as he walked toward the door. Glancing back at my project, he laughed and said, "Good luck, Joe." Jim headed outside to pursue his own fantasies.

I decided to give my car a canoe-like shape, with the seat in the middle and the sides tapering to points at the front and rear. Using Dad's T-square and a carpenter pencil, I drew the car's profile on the plywood sheet. Next I dragged it onto the top of an old table so I could saw it. After cutting out both sides I made a dashboard and the back of a seat. Then I screwed these parts securely into place with the help of brackets from the hardware store.

I bent the sides together so that my car came to a point at each end. Next, I capped the ends securely with sheet aluminum — my racer was taking shape! Anxious to sit in it, I began to ease my butt into the seat. But whoa! What the...oh no...it wouldn't fit. "Shit!" I screamed. The car was too narrow, thanks to my guestimated dimensions. I was building a lousy kiddy car. Disgusted and discouraged, I abandoned my soapbox project. A week later, however, when Uncle Mike examined the plywood shell, he said I'd done a good job, even if it was a bit too small. Praise from Mike was rare, so his compliment lifted my spirits.

My silver jetliner

Visiting the hobby shop I spotted a plastic kit for the new Boeing 707 jetliner. I had to have it. After all, my brother Jack was flying the military version of this plane in the Air Force. I felt inspired to do a super job on this project. After buffing some rough edges off the parts I assembled them with loving care, making sure I didn't smear one drop of cement on the plastic.

The finished model was gorgeous. There wasn't a sloppy seam or glue smudge anywhere. Then, wanting to elevate my airliner to a higher plane, I decided to spray paint it silver. Heading to the basement around midnight, I placed my 707 on a piece of plywood, which I carefully set on a stool. Then, circling the stool, I sprayed the craft from every angle. Finally, I set the plane and its plywood base deep inside a cardboard box and carried it to the front storeroom, where we kids were not supposed to go. My silver bird would rest there safe and unmolested while the paint dried. By daybreak it would be ready for the finishing touches.

First thing the next morning I had to view my gleaming 707 — breakfast could wait. I scrambled down the back stairs and hurried through the basement to the front storeroom. I opened the door and looked down. What! Was that a... hand? Yes! The print of a big dark hand surrounded the body of my jetliner! It was Bradley! He'd struck again! The Destroyer had picked up my plane while the paint was still wet. Through what miraculous power was he able to divine its location? At what ungodly hour was he drawn to the storeroom? I was dumbfounded. There seemed to be no escape from this kid's destructive grip.

The cadets

Our trip to Jack's house and Westover Air Force Base inspired Jim and me to join the Civil Air Patrol (CAP for short). Dressed in khaki uniforms we hoofed it over to weekly meetings at Foster Park. Some of the kids in our squadron intended to enlist in the Air Force after high school. On certain weekends we went with a group of CAP folks to visit airports around Chicago. This gave us a close-up look at aircraft large and small.

One Sunday afternoon at Midway Airport Jim and I checked out the cockpit of a DC-6 airliner. The following summer we went to Civil Air Patrol camp at Chanute Air Force Base in Rantoul, Illinois. Along with cadets from other Chicago area squadrons, we flew there in a C-119 "Flying Boxcar," compliments of the Illinois Air National Guard.

I was excited to fly in this twin-tailed troop carrier of Korean War vintage. With parachutes strapped to our bottoms we cadets sat along the sides of the plane facing each other like soldiers in a John Wayne movie. One of the Guardsmen opened the jump door and invited us to take a look outside. I took my turn and knew that I'd never make it as a paratrooper. By the way, the C-119 was featured years later in *The Flight of the Phoenix,* a movie starring Jimmy Stewart as the pilot.

At Chanute AFB we lived in barracks with CAP cadets from all parts of Illinois. We got up early every morning and marched to breakfast, then to orientation classes far from our barracks. By noon the sun was broiling hot but on and on we marched — to flimsy wooden buildings whose interiors made the heat outside seem like air conditioning. Sitting and sweating, we learned about the theory of flight, airplane instruments and radar.

We made our bunks. We shined our shoes. A real Air Force drill instructor screamed at us: "Tenhut! Right face! Left face! 'Bout face! Forwaard haarch! Tada rear haarch!" We got better and better. I don't remember seeing any female cadets marching, walking or even standing around watching for that matter. Then, the day before we went home, cadets from all the barracks marched across the parade grounds in a graduation exercise, accompanied by a big Air Force band. Strutting my stuff to John Philip Sousa gave me goose bumps.

Home from camp, I began my sophomore year at Leo. I kept up with my studies and attended CAP meetings regularly. But when a certain cadet named Judy dropped out of our squadron, the thrill was gone. Suddenly I saw myself as an overage Boy Scout marching around and saluting high school kids. My interest in flying took a nosedive. A few weeks later I said good-bye to the Civil Air Patrol.

Chapter 17

Paper routes

REDS ORBIT ARTIFICIAL MOON

Chicago Tribune headline, Oct 5, 1957

From age eleven into my early teens I worked paper routes for several Chicago newspapers, including the *Chicago American,* the *Tribune,* the *Sun Times* and the *Southtown Economist.* My first route was after school delivering the *American.* I went home and changed, then biked about six blocks east to get my papers. The pick-up point was an old garage that had been converted to a depot for newspaper carriers.

A swarthy middle-aged guy we knew as "Sam" managed this place. The khaki shirt and pants he always wore were wrinkled, making him look like a disheveled Boy Scout leader. He had a black push-broom mustache and his worldly-wise expression told you there was no pulling the wool over his beady little eyes.

Sam didn't mind cussing hard if you were wasting time or folding a paper into a "glider." The illegal glider fold gave the paper the dimensions of a square potholder. It was a joy to fling a glider from my bike, but customers didn't like it. They complained that with so many folds in it the paper was hard to read.

Sam liked kids who came in, grabbed their papers and got out fast. The papers for each route were pre-counted and stacked in designated spaces on the table-high counters that lined the garage walls. I rolled my thirty-five or forty papers, stuffed them into my canvas carrier bag and hauled it outside to my bike. Setting the bag on the front fender, I pulled its carrying strap behind one handlebar grip, then stretched it across and secured it behind the other grip so the bag hung tight.

My route started about a mile west of Sam's garage. I liked the neighborhood — mostly big brick bungalows. The nicer ones had classy art-glass windows and well kept front lawns. The shrubs were trimmed with an angular precision that rivaled the work of a stonemason. Tips on this route were better than average. There was one lady in particular who always gave me a quarter. Her husband and my dad knew each other (I made a point of mentioning this the first time I collected). I thought this woman was rich, like many of her neighbors.

Despite the snob appeal of those few glamorous blocks, the highlight of my route was an enormous, three-storey apartment building at 79th & Carpenter. For the first few weeks finding where all the different customers were located in the building was a challenge. Delivering to the main entrance was just a matter of dumping some papers into the lobby. But some demanding customers wanted their papers on the back porch.

The rear of this structure was a huge U-shaped affair with a central concrete court. At first, landing a paper in the right place was difficult. I had to spot the correct porch out of that labyrinthine network of gray banisters and stairs. It took finesse to toss a folded newspaper up three stories with just enough arc to make it over the banister. Sometimes the paper bounced off a clothesline spanning the porch and fell back to the concrete court. Still, I could usually land it on the third-floor porch on my first try.

Collecting from customers in this building was an education. I'd enter the roomy front lobby, which was illuminated by a dim orange light. The floor was an expanse of small white tiles edged by an ornate border of multicolored tiles. One wall was completely covered by brass mailboxes. The buttons next to residents' names formed two long rows.

Another world

Pressing the button next to a customer's name, I waited to get "buzzed in." A resident upstairs pushed a button that made a buzzing sound in the lobby as it freed the lock on the downstairs door. Hearing that sound, I turned the knob and entered the stairwell. Just a year earlier I thought it was fun to push all the buttons and run like hell. I'd beat it out the door laughing at the long, long buzz of dozens of renters all trying to let me in. But those childish days were behind me. I was now here on official business.

A flight of stairs took me to a long, dimly lit hallway. And though the floor was carpeted, it squeaked in places as I approached a customer's dark-stained door. Behind it might be a young man or an old woman — possibly a person with a foreign accent — maybe a pleasant soul, maybe an ornery crabass.

Apartment dwellers were more likely than homeowners to have me step inside while they scraped up a few coins to pay for the paper. Several elderly folks liked to chat. Some showed me framed pictures of their deceased spouses or snapshots of their kids, who had married and moved away to distant parts of the country. Some complained about how much everything cost — rent, groceries, bus fare. Others ranted about how cold the hot water was or how hard it was to get anything fixed.

The hallways throughout this building were permeated with the smell of Cantonese cooking, which wafted its way up from the Lang Lee Chinese take-out joint on the first floor. But each apartment had its own unique scent — it could be basic boiled cabbage, exotic Italian spices or mothballs.

One apartment had such a bad odor that I dreaded knocking on the door. It always smelled like turpentine, only stronger. I wondered what could produce such a lasting lousy smell and how anyone could stay in the place longer than five minutes without running out for air. Amazingly, it didn't bother the elderly couple that lived there. What a relief it was to get back out into the hallway and savor the refreshing aroma of chow mein.

When collecting in that building I might visit Glider's Hobby Shop, which occupied part of the first floor along 79th Street. I was tempted to linger there but I had to stay on-task and get home for supper. Most of the money from customers was due each Wednesday at Sam's garage. Each of us carriers had to pay our "bill," the percentage of our collections that went to the *Chicago American.*

Inside Sam's shack I climbed two or three steps to a raised area with a counter. Standing there with Sam breathing down my neck, I carefully counted out enough coins to meet my bill. Sam rarely had anything pleasant to say. He usually made some gruff comment like, "You got a complaint yesterday from Mrs. Stackler on Aberdeen." I was happy to get the bill thing over with and get going on my route. Looking back, the whole "bill" scenario reminds me of *Oliver Twist*, where Fagin, the master pickpocket, trained his band of street-savvy young boys.

The twice-a-week Southtown

A year later I was delivering the *Southtown Economist*, which came out on Sundays and Wednesdays. Like other Southtown carriers, I picked up my papers at a gas station on 81st & Halsted. Dozens of bundles were dumped onto one corner of the pavement. Each carrier always found an extra bundle of forty papers for his route. The Southtown wanted us to deliver them to prospective customers and then try to collect. If people paid, the Southtown considered them new customers. This was called "route building."

There was one kid who picked up his extra bundle every week and deftly dumped it into a trash basket at the gas station. I needed about eighty papers to do my route, not counting the bonus bundle. This was too big a load for bicycle delivery so I used the red coaster wagon that Dad had purchased at the Hi-Lo food store years earlier.

My route took me south on Halsted and east under a viaduct into a neighborhood of small frame houses and brick bungalows. Covering about twelve blocks, that route seemed to go on forever. What a drag it was to get up on Sunday morning and pull a wagon three miles. Collecting east of Halsted broadened my real-world education. I talked to all kinds of people, made change and kept track of who paid and who didn't. Most people paid their forty-cent paper bill with coins, which sometimes included five or ten pennies.

Once in a while someone tried to pay with a ten or twenty dollar bill. I thought this was a miserable maneuver to avoid parting with a paltry forty cents. Funny thing was, if I'd been out collecting awhile I had enough nickels, dimes and quarters on me to make change for a twenty. When I informed customers of this they balked and said something like "What am I gonna do with all that change?" Some crude suggestions came to mind, but I kept them to myself.

After a Saturday morning of collecting, the front pockets of my pants were hanging heavy with change. I worried that one of them would burst a seam and coins would rain down my leg, splashing all over the sidewalk. When my weighty pockets made me walk funny it was time to head home.

Even when it made me stagger, toting all that cold cash gave me a prosperous independent feeling. It was a grown-up feeling I thought other kids didn't get. Before I reached home I might stop at Wimpy's Grill on the corner of 80th & Halsted for a cheeseburger or a piece of pie and coffee. This sorry-looking hut, with its dirty windows and yellowing walls, served what I thought was a slice of heaven — boysenberry pie. A piece cost thirty-five cents. Coffee was a dime.

The Big Time

Midway through eighth grade I was thrilled to get a *Chicago Tribune* route — right on Peoria street where I lived. It was January, 1957 and the kid who'd handled the route for the previous year had collected his Christmas tips and moved on. The hefty wad of holiday tips that carriers got was the highlight of a *Tribune* route. And there was no collecting to do. The paper hired grown-ups to handle that chore.

Still, it was no fun getting up at 5:30 a.m. in winter to deliver a hundred and twenty papers. When I pulled myself out of bed on those first January mornings it was pitch black outside and bitter cold. Nobody was stirring at that hour except the Irish Christian Brothers, who taught at Leo High School up the block. Wearing black topcoats, they were out taking their morning constitutional. The good brothers walked by briskly but silently, some of them giving me a "good morning" nod. I felt like I had joined a secret fraternity of nightwalkers. A week or two after I started my route, Jim, who was a freshman at Leo, got a Trib route from 79th to 83rd & Green, just one block east of Peoria. So we had parallel routes and started at the same time each morning, but Jim usually got home first.

The pitch-black 5:30 a.m. blues

Two strong guys from the Trib delivery branch came in a truck and dropped off our papers each morning between 4:40 and 5 a.m. They took our carts from beneath the back porch, pushed them out to the front sidewalk and loaded them up. Some mornings Jim and I found them covered by tarps that had collected an inch or two of snow. As I pushed my cart its big creaking wheels cut black stripes into the snow-white sidewalk.

I started my route by delivering to both sides of my block, then I headed down the west side of Peoria Street to 83rd. Coming back up the east side, I finished right near my house. The route was lined with brick homes — two-flats, bungalows and a few three-storey apartment buildings. Many papers had to be dropped inside the front hall, and one sadistic schmuck wanted his Trib delivered to the third floor in the rear — between the doors!

All of my customers' addresses were hand-written on thick, card-like tickets crowded around a ring that dangled from the push handle of my cart. When I got a new customer I'd find a new ticket on my ring, giving the name and address. There would also be a reminder note tucked in among my papers. I'd deliver a paper to the new customer that morning — no problem. But the next day I might forget all about them. I had no system for jogging my memory. Sure, there was a new address card on my ring, but on a biting-cold black morning, remembering to check through those cards with bare ungloved hands could easily slip my mind.

Morning daydreams

As winter yielded to spring the sun came up earlier, so I was starting my route in daylight. By this time delivering morning papers had become pretty routine. I often found myself daydreaming about Annette Funicello, my favorite Mouseketeer on *The Mickey Mouse Club.* I entertained elaborate scenarios in which I saved Annette's life.

Sometimes I rescued her from a perilous situation at Disneyland. She was a hundred feet up, dangling by one hand from a runaway Mickey or Goofy ride. I scaled the superstructure and caught her just as she began to fall. Hanging from a girder by one arm, I pulled her close to me with the other. Trembling, Annette held me tight, gazing into my eyes with love and admiration. Back on earth I had probably missed delivering a paper at this point. The next morning I might find a complaint ticket in my cart. I got so lost in my morning fantasies that the delivery branch office phoned and warned me that I'd better shape up.

Early a.m. incidents

Summer mornings brought new adventures to my route. In June an elderly lady came out of her bungalow at 6:30 a.m., complaining that I didn't stuff the paper into her mailbox correctly. She told me to fold it twice and stuff it, round end first, into the slot. I said I'd try to be neater. She called me a "smartass."

A few mornings later her husband came hulking towards me as I approached the house. Looking very angry, he demanded to know what I'd done with their mailbox! This really floored me. When I asked what he was talking about he said I'd stolen the mailbox to get back at his wife for correcting me. I couldn't convince him that I didn't take the box, and feared that he might slug me. He turned and stormed up the front steps. Glaring back at me, he shouted that he was going to report my theft to the *Tribune*. Oh boy!

One Sunday morning in July a seedy-looking, middle-aged guy in a parked car beckoned to me. I grabbed a paper from the cart and walked his way, thinking he wanted to buy one. (I usually had an extra or two.) As I approached the car he opened the door and asked me if I wanted to "go for a ride." A sick creepy feeling came over me as I babbled a few hapless words in reply — something like, "No thanks, I have to go on a picnic with my family." I went back to delivering papers without a thought of getting his license plate number or calling the cops.

Going back to sleep

As the fall mornings grew colder, I warmed up with a cup of coffee when I got home from my route, then flopped onto my bed for a while. Mom would roust me, but there wouldn't be enough time to finish my homework or even get my ducks in a row for the day ahead. Too often I'd be late for religion, my first class of the day at Leo. The teacher, Brother Sullivan, was a tall, middle-aged gent who looked far too distinguished to be teaching high school freshmen.

Sullivan maintained order with classy authority and a wry sense of humor. One morning when I arrived after the bell, he stopped his lecture and conducted a brief survey. He asked how many students took the bus to school. Several hands went up. Next, he asked which boys walked more than half a mile to Leo. A few more hands went up. The questions continued until Sullivan asked if anybody lived less than a block from school. Mine was the only hand that was raised. "Only one boy," he remarked, "our friend, Joseph Murphy! And how many boys came late to class this morning? Raise your hands!" Again, mine was the only hand that went up.

"How is it Murphy," he continued, "that you live closer than any of your classmates, yet you're always the one who's late?" Embarrassed, I blurted something about oversleeping. "Murphy," he said calmly, "I see you every morning at 5:45 delivering papers, and you can't manage to get here on time." I heard laughs from behind me. "I think we'll give you detention tonight, and I advise you to show up on time." More laughter from behind me. As he wrote me a jug slip he concluded, "Maybe you should get to bed earlier so you can stay awake in the morning!"

A month or so later, on "Parents Night," Dad went to school with me to check on my academic progress. We met with each of my teachers and discussed my so-so grades. Dad agreed that I could be doing much better in my studies. One or two of the brothers mentioned that they'd seen me delivering papers in the morning, but they didn't make an issue of it. I was relieved when Brother Sullivan didn't recommend that I give up my route.

Don't blow it now

At this point there were only five or six weeks remaining before Christmas. My plan was to keep the paper route through December, then grab my Christmas tips and quit. But as the weather grew colder, staying focused on the route got harder. In November, when I got three customer complaints in one week, the delivery branch called one night at suppertime and told me they were letting me go.

I was so upset that I just hung up the phone. When I walked back to the kitchen table Dad asked me what happened. I told him.

He jumped from his chair as if he'd just sat on a tack and rushed to the phone. Half a minute later he was talking to the branch manager. "Whattaya mean letting him go!" he shouted. "He's worked that route all year — let the kid get his Christmas tips! No...no...not until he gets his Christmas tips!" There was a long pause. Then he said "Alright" and hung up. He told me I was keeping my route but I'd have to "WAKE UP" and not get any more complaints.

I couldn't believe that I still had a job after hanging up on the boss. What's more, I was amazed at how forceful my old man could be. I was really proud of him. *If Dad can stand up for me like that,* I told myself, *I can take my route more seriously.* I suddenly became very careful about checking my tickets and not goofing up. I knew it was important to keep my route for the Christmas tips, but more than that, I wanted to show Dad that I appreciated the way he went to bat for me.

"Hi, I'm your paperboy!"

In mid-December the guys who filled our carts each morning handed Jim and me stacks of the flimsy little Christmas calendars we'd need to get our long-awaited tips. Those little four-color calendars of 1958 were nothing special — their main purpose was to bring the paperboy face-to-face with his customers, most likely for the first time. All through the year they'd been sound asleep when their paper arrived. Now, at Christmas, it was time to pay the piper.

The very day I got those calendars, I couldn't wait to hand them out. Right after supper I grabbed a thick handful and headed south on Peoria, ringing doorbells and introducing myself. Most folks gave me a buck, although I got a pair of three-dollar tips and one festive fiver. I was doing OK except for Mr. "third floor rear between the doors." He took the calendar and grumbled, "Well, don't think you're getting anything extra for delivering the paper!"

Two blocks south of my house I rang the doorbell of a second-storey flat and got buzzed in. As I climbed the stairs a charming middle-aged lady appeared on the landing and welcomed me.

"Hi Joe," she said in a warm voice. "Come on up — you must be freezing." I wondered how she knew my name. She ushered me from the hall into the parlor. Her husband was seated in a recliner watching TV. He got up and shook my hand. "Hello, young man," he uttered with a smile. "Take your coat off and have a seat."

As I sat down on the couch, his wife offered me some Christmas cookies, arranged neatly on a plate. Before I could take a bite, pops started talking about Leo football. He asked me what was wrong with this year's team. The previous season Leo had won the City Championship under coach Jim Arneberg. This year things hadn't gone so well.

Then, seating herself on the couch, his wife asked me how school was going. We chatted briefly before she rose and headed toward the hall. Looking back at me she said, "Jenny will be ready in a few minutes."

"Who's Jenny?" I asked. Turning toward me with a perplexed look, she asked, "You're Joe aren't you?" "Yeah!" I answered. "Well, Jenny's your date!" she said, emphatically. I was too surprised to answer at first, but managed to stammer: "I'm the paperboy!" "What?" she answered. "Paperboy!" her husband barked. They looked at me, then at each other and burst into laughter. "I just came here to give you a Christmas calendar," I added. Getting up to leave, I handed pops a calendar. He tried to stand but was laughing so hard that his wife had help him up. She reminded him to give me a tip and he pulled out his wallet. He handed me a buck, then added one more for good measure.

As I walked toward the door, mom called down the hall — "Jenny, Joe is leaving!" "What?" I heard as a pretty face popped out of a doorway. Pointing at me and laughing again, the lady said, "His name is Joe — we thought he was your date but he's the paper boy!" "What?" the girl said. "Oh, that's too funny!" I waved to her. Still giggling, she said "Hi, paperboy!" I told her to have fun on her date, then scurried down the stairs and out the front door.

Chapter 18

Tight spots

"Better to be safe than sorry!"
— Dad

Growing up in my family there was "never a dull moment" as Mom used to say. Just the age differences between us kids set the stage for many a conflict. As I mentioned earlier, we boys were told to stay out of Joan's room and keep the noise level down when she was sleeping,

Older kids were urged to set a good example for younger ones. If a donut or cookie was broken in two, the younger kid might complain that someone else got the "bigger half." In this case the older brother or sister should hand the larger portion to the whining brat. What's more, bigger kids were not to bully smaller weaker ones. Nor should they hog the TV or ignore younger siblings who needed help with their homework.

Thanks for keeping your sanity, Mom!

Mom hated petty fights over board games like *Monopoly* that were supposed to be fun. Dan, who always knew the rules, would quit if he thought someone was cheating. And if Jim got upset, his teasing might lead to chaos. His name-calling could snowball into a terrible scene, with all of us slinging names back and forth: "Mope!" "Liar!" "Dumb Brain!" "Thief!" Game pieces could fly — maybe even the board. Mom quelled eruptions like these and reported them to Dad when he got home.

At supper, not eating everything on your plate was asking for trouble. "Come on — take a bite," Mom would plead. "People are starving to death in China!" Dad would add. Refusal to bite the bullet and eat your broccoli could merit a few licks on the legs from Dad's belt. I preferred the belt to eating squash.

Other offenses that could lead to a licking included profanity. "Mom, Joe said s-h-i-t!" I had to convince Mom that the squealer heard me wrong or brace myself for Dad's strap. Sassing Mom or dodging chores were also grounds for getting the belt. Worse than ditching work was pulling a disappearing act. Mom's protective instincts made her worry about where we kids were at all times. Once safe at home, deserters were disciplined.

Out of the mouths of babes...

As I sat in the den one Saturday morning Pat toddled by on his way to the kitchen. Arriving, he greeted Dad with a hardy "Son of a birch!" "What?" asked Dad. "Who said those words to you?" "Joe!" he answered eagerly. "Those are bad words." Dad told him. "Don't ever say those words." Then he grumbled something that ended with "Wait'll I get that Joe!"

Before he could call me I was out the front door and down the stairs to the sidewalk. I'd probably escaped a crack in the face, but a few days later Dad took me to task about "Son of a birch!" My defense was that I was just telling Jim what a neighbor said when he found a dent in his car. Pat must have been nearby listening, but he heard the last word as "birch." My dent story was a lie that I hoped Dad would buy. After a long pause he let me off the hook with a warning not to repeat swear words in the house.

Besides my mouth I had to watch my clothes. Borrowing apparel led to trouble. Those of us wearing similar sizes were supposed to ask, not just take someone else's shirt or pants. Unchecked curiosity could cause problems too. Sometimes a younger brother would stumble upon an unfinished model that I'd hidden and smear the paint or dislodge parts that were still drying. I warned everyone about this, especially Jim Bradley, but he refused to get the message. Bradley was amazing. He could grab something and break it in a flash — before I could scream "No!" or "Stop!"

My 25-pound bow

I was walking down Halsted on the way home from school when a flash of red caught the corner of my eye. Turning to look, I saw a quiver of brightly feathered arrows in the window of Crane

Sporting Goods. Stopping to admire them, I noticed that several bows were displayed as well.

I had to get a closer look at this gear so I entered the store. The man behind the counter had a lot to say about bows, arrows and archery. I was surprised to learn that there were archery ranges around Chicago — even indoor ones where folks could play Robin Hood rain or shine.

I approached a wall covered with fancy multicolored bows, all made of shiny fiberglass. The sales clerk picked one up, cocked it and handed it to me. I could barely pull the string back an inch. "That's a powerful bow — it has forty pounds of tension," he said. And the price he quoted was a mite strong, too. Turning to leave, I told this guy that his bows were great but out of my price range. "Wait a sec," he said, "I'll be right back."

Before I could collect my schoolbooks from the counter he returned, toting a handsome wooden bow. "We don't sell many all-wood bows," he said, "but this is a very nice twenty-five pounder." He cocked it and handed it to me. The bow felt like it was made for me. I was sold, but the price was twenty bucks. I told the clerk that it would take a month of delivering papers for me to earn that much. He said that I could use the store's layaway plan, so I left bow in limbo and made weekly payments until my account was paid in full.

The day I brought my new bow home Jim and I took it to Snake Valley, where there were no other humans in sight. We shot arrow after arrow without a care, aiming at steel drums, abandoned cars and heaps of busted-up concrete. Jim peeled back a piece of tarpaper from the ground and I nailed a coiled-up garter snake.

Then, just to see how high they'd go, we fired several arrows straight into the sky. It was fun to watch them turn around and dive back to earth, plowing inches into the dirt. We had to watch carefully to make sure that an arrow didn't pierce one of our skulls.

Back home we couldn't resist trying this stunt in the back yard. Tempting fate, I shot several arrows skyward. A slight breeze made their trip back to earth unpredictable. Some bounced off the concrete alley, others dug into Mrs. Olsen's flower garden and one came down in the gangway between our house and the Schmid's place.

Since nobody witnessed our folly Jim and I were reckless enough to launch several of these rocket arrows in front of our house. They dove into parkways, bushes and front yards. Some rebounded from the sidewalk; a few hit the street. When one dented the roof of a car we called it quits.

Meanwhile, Mom was fielding phone calls from vigilant neighbors. One lady told our mother that Jim and I were a danger to everyone on the block. Another caller said that if she saw the Murphy boys with their bow and arrow again she'd call the police. Mom was mortified. I had to surrender my bow and arrows for many moons.

The baby custard incident

After school one day Mom sent me to the A&P for a few items, including a jar of baby custard for little Pat. With such a short grocery list I didn't bother with a shopping cart. Silvercup bread, lettuce, tuna...uh-oh — my arms were filling up fast. By the time I found the baby food I couldn't hold one more item, so I stuck the jar of custard into the back pocket of my pants. Up at the checkout counter I unloaded my arms onto the conveyor. A pretty high school girl started ringing up my purchases on a mechanical cash register — clickadyapadip, clickadyapadip...

She was nearly finished as the manager approached. He stopped abruptly and asked me why I had a jar of baby food in my back pocket. I told him I'd put it there and just forgot about it. My answer made him frown. He wanted to talk to one of my parents. "You'd better come with me," he said, so I followed him to his little cube of an office. I gave him my phone number when he asked for it, then waited while he called and reported the incident. Inside of five minutes Dad walked in.

"What's the problem?" he asked. The manager told him that I was trying to leave the store without paying for a jar of baby custard. Dad looked askance at the guy and asked impatiently, "Why would the kid steal a jar of baby food? Does that make sense to you?" "I don't know," the manager answered, "but he had it in his pocket." "Dad," I pleaded, "I just couldn't carry anything else in my arms." My father asked for the price of the custard — I think it was about thirty cents. He shook his head in disgust and led me from the office to the checkout counter, where he paid the embarrassed clerk. On the way home I explained everything in detail to Dad. He told me to stick with a shopping cart.

Nasty name-calling

One spring day Dan and I were walking home from school together when, somehow, he got into a verbal spat with a girl who was walking west like us, but on the opposite side of the street. They shouted back and forth at each other for two blocks. I didn't even know the girl so I stayed out of it (I still can't remember what she and Dan were squabbling about). This girl was walking with Patricia Bartkus, who was Greek and drop-dead gorgeous. I dreamed about meeting her some day.

When the shouting grew more heated, Patricia jumped in. Ugly names flew back and forth. Then Patricia crossed the line. "Your brother has a flat head!" she screamed. *What a cheap shot,* I told myself. This reference to Jim had nothing to do with the argument. In a nanosecond I shouted back: "Well, at least he's not a *"crude ethnic slur."* That shut her up fast. I had to say something really shitty. It was a point of honor.

The next day at school I was summoned to Sister Superior's office, where Mrs. Bartkus, Patricia's mother, was waiting. The head nun asked me if I had called her daughter a *"crude ethnic slur."* I knew that I couldn't argue the fine points of what I'd implied or what Patricia had inferred, so I just said, "Yes sister." I had to apologize to Mrs. B., who appeared to be properly avenged. The event was over quickly and I was sent back to class.

Our reckless roller

Through our pre-teen years Jim and I built several wheeled vehicles. The oddest of these began as a wood frame resting on a trash pile behind Rusnak Furniture. Jim decided to use it as the platform for a push car that would ride on roller skate wheels. Taking a pair of skates apart yielded four sets of wheels, which Jim and I nailed to the corners of the frame. We flipped it over and pushed it around on the basement floor. Very smooth but there was no place to sit.

The frame was just a wooden rectangle with two cross members. Luckily, a few days later, Jim came home with a seat cushion he'd found behind the Cosmo Theater. "Look at this," he said, "perfect for our car." I checked it out — thick, springy, no rips or tears — it was just what we needed. "And there's another one just like it," Jim added. Without wasting a moment we fetched the other cushion.

The rough riders

With the seats nailed in place, we carried our car from the basement to the blacktop surface of Peoria Street. Jim and I decided that the best way to ride it was to lie flat on our stomachs, as if we were swimming. Performance was disappointing right from the start. Steering this contraption was impossible — it drifted drunkenly from side to side like the pointer on a Ouija Board; it veered into curbs and rolled beneath parked cars.

There were problems with the small roller skate wheels as well. Holes in the street gobbled them up, stopping our vehicle and hurling its rider onto the blacktop or into a curb. Even the vent holes in a sewer cover could stop the car. What's more, our conveyance rode so low to the ground that pushing it gave us back and neck pains. On top of all this, our skate wheel mobile couldn't handle the rugged surface of our concrete alley. Undeterred, Jim and I tried to make improvements. We even added a stylish touch to the rear end, hammering two small pieces of sheet brass right in the center to forma rakish V, like the tail of a jet fighter.

I can't remember why, but one day we pushed our roller skate car through the bumpy alley to the open freight door behind Rusnak's. With the guys on the dock watching I felt the need to show off, so I stood the car up and attempted a belly flop. BAM! The rough concrete stopped the wheels cold, but my body slid forward. AAAUGH!!! My member was caught between the brass tail parts. I moaned in agony while Jim roared with laughter. A big black guy on the dock shouted: "What's the matter sonny, did you get yo tingaling caught?" At this, Jim laughed even harder. With tears in my eyes I slowly freed myself from the vehicle and walked home. Soon after this episode Jim and I junked our roller skate car, agreeing that it was a pain in the neck, not to mention other places.

Tetrachloride terror

One day after school John Keating followed me into the basement when I went to get my bike. Feeling playful, John started chasing me. And as luck would have it, he kicked a gallon bottle of carbon tetrachloride into the concrete wall, shattering it and sending its contents flooding onto the floor. The powerful fumes stung our lungs. Coughing and retching, we bolted for the door.

Outside, Keating said he'd better get home and beat it fast. I ran upstairs to tell Mom. She was already on the phone with Mrs. Burke, our first floor tenant. "Cleaning fluid smell? Did you open some windows? I'll tell John as soon as he gets home...wait...I'll come downstairs...be right there."

I told Mom that Keating had broken a bottle of something with an awful smell. "Wait till your father gets home," she warned, hurrying downstairs to the front hall. "What in the name of God?" she gasped as we entered the fume-filled vestibule.

My mother opened the heavy front door to let in some fresh air. I rang the Burke's bell but there was no answer. Oh God, I thought, everybody downstairs is dead! I tried the bell again. Still no answer. Then Jim Bradley came running up the front steps. He said that his whole family was on the back porch.

Fear not...

Just then Dad arrived home from work. Everyone rushed to his car to tell him about the emergency. Slamming the driver door, he mumbled something that combined curse words and saints' names. We followed him through the gangway to the back of the house.

Dad opened the basement door, ran into the laundry room and propped open a window. As he rushed back outside his face looked red with anger. *Oh boy, I'm really going to get it,* I feared. Looking back, it wasn't anger that reddened Dad's face — he was gasping for air.

Next he darted into the Burke's flat and opened more windows. Luckily, it was a mild September afternoon, so nobody was in danger of freezing. Then, as he made a second run to open more basement windows, the Burke's filed back into their flat. I laid low.

When Mom called me to supper I moved slowly to my place at her end of the table.

Dad got to the basement issue straightaway. "What were you kids doing fooling around in the basement?" he asked heatedly. I said I'd just gone in to get my bike, but Keating started chasing me. "I put that jug way back next to the wall where nobody would see it," he said, shaking his head. Miraculously, I didn't get the belt or even a crack across the face — just strict orders not to let any kids into the basement. The next day before I left for school Mom told me, "Your father hosed out the basement last night. He woke up this morning with a terrible headache."

The new two-flat

During the summer of '56 a new two-flat went up on the vacant lot across the street from our house. Its light-colored brick made it clash with the surrounding homes built of the dark brick in vogue three decades earlier. Mom and Dad warned us sternly to stay out of the unfinished house. Didn't our cousin Mike nearly get killed playing on a construction site a year earlier?

I obeyed for two whole months. Then, late in June, when the brickwork was finished and the roof was on, I had to take a look. With Jim Bradley right behind me I climbed in through a rear window and scaled a partially finished staircase to the second floor. A stretch of plywood on top of some scaffolding provided a secluded spot near the roof. There was barely enough clearance to sit. Looking around, I spotted an open duct and, of course, I had to investigate. I stuffed my arm in as far as it would go...and wow, there was something in there! I grabbed it and pulled it out. Whattaya know — an open pack of Camel cigarettes!

Heck! Some older kids had already been here. *Hey, kids aren't supposed to smoke,* I reasoned. *Maybe I'll play a trick on these guys.* I replaced the smokes into the duct. Bradley and I sat on the plywood perch for another fifteen minutes, telling each other what a great hideout we'd found. Terrific, but it was still baking hot at seven p.m. Drenched with sweat, we headed for cooler environs, climbing downstairs and back outside through a first-floor window.

I returned the next night by myself, armed with a small can of 3-In-One Oil. Up in the hideout loft I retrieved the pack of Camels from the duct and shook out all the cigarettes. Then I carefully squirted oil into each one. They looked like soggy pork sausages as I slid them back into the pack. Laughing out loud, I returned the slimy Camels to their place deep in the duct. Ha-ha — I stole out of the building like a rat. Across the street I found Jim, Dan and some neighborhood kids sitting on our front stoop. I was still laughing.

"What's so funny?" someone asked. I blurted the details of my prank to all. Everybody thought it was hilarious. But a day or two later Bradley told me that Johnny O'Donnell was looking for me and intended to kill me. Oh boy! Somebody had snitched. I wished I'd kept my dumb mouth shut about lubricating those cigarettes. O'Donnell was a big strong guy and three or four years older than me. For the rest of that summer I tried to avoid the north end of our block where the O'Donnells lived.

Chapter 19

Tom

"Look! A deer!"
— Tom

Even as a little shrimp Tom was willful and resolute. An early walker, he never really toddled. Instead, he took determined little steps, as if he knew right where he was going. Tom's earliest babblings commanded attention; he had an unusually deep voice and a determined tone. He was curious and very aware of what was going on. If something was up he wanted to be plugged in. So when we older brothers were heading to the show or the park — or even to the library, Tom tagged along.

Tom believed firmly that he and his brothers should stick together. He was ten when Martha and Lee offered to take him along on their vacation to the Ozarks. The idea of going without his brothers was so foreign to him that he nearly turned down their invitation. When Dan was invited along as well, Tom felt much better about making the trip.

Like Joan and Jim, Tom was a true redhead. His dark rust-hued hair and freckles gave him a Huck Finn appearance. He loved fishing and would have been right at home standing barefoot on a raft. Tom loved the natural environment. He was drawn like a magnet to forests, mountains, rivers and streams. Tom could hardly wait for our next family vacation so he could immerse himself the woods, surrounded by the flora and fauna he found so captivating.

Living on the edge

When the spring brought bright warm days two-year-old Tom got to play with his toys on the balcony, shaded by our big elm. Whoever was watching him took a bathroom break, leaving him unattended for a few minutes. What happened next scared the living daylights out of me.

Mom asked me to check on him, so I went out to take a look. Tom was nowhere to be seen — he'd simply disappeared. I thought with horror that he'd fallen two stories from the balcony, possibly landing on the limestone front steps. Oh God! I rushed to the railing and looked down. Everything appeared to be normal.

Then I glanced to the left. There was Tom, standing on the outer ledge about ten feet away from me. He'd crawled out through one of the spaces between the brick columns surrounding the balcony and was perched there in his playsuit facing the building. Standing on the ledge with his hands on the brickwork, he didn't look the least bit scared.

Trying to sound calm, I asked him to come back in. He paused a moment before answering, "OK, I come in now." Tom shuffled sideways to an open space and crawled back onto the balcony. Whew! My heart slid from my throat back into my chest. On Saturday Dad lined the inside of the balcony with chicken wire, blocking all the openings that might tempt an adventurous toddler.

Tom's foolery

When Tom was three or four years old one of us older kids discovered that he could be coaxed into sleepwalking. On several occasions we ordered him around the house, giving him silly tasks to perform: "Go into the dining room...take the book off the table... go out to the kitchen...throw the book in the garbage." With his eyes wide open he unflinchingly obeyed every order. It was hilarious.

Then, fearing that Mom or Dad might wake up, we guided Tom back to his bed and tucked him in for the night. Forty years later, when I reminded Tom of these sleepwalks, he said that he'd been awake and just playing along for the fun of it, so the joke was really on us older kids. I didn't believe him.

One day Tom teamed up with two older brothers to give Mom quite a shock. Jim and Dan folded up the hide-a-bed with Tom inside. They replaced the cushions before calling her into the den. When she arrived they removed the cushions, opened the bed and out popped Tom. Horrified, Mom told the pranksters never to pull that stunt again. As a grownup I can see that Tom could have been crushed or suffocated. But boys don't think that way.

The caffeine kid

At age six Tom decided to start drinking coffee with his breakfast. Mom was shocked. She told him to stop, knowing he was way too young for coffee. But Tom was a stubborn little guy — he kept right on drinking his morning coffee month after month.

As the years passed, other boys in Tom's class grew taller while he stayed short. We told him this was a result of his coffee drinking. I thought other factors could be slowing his growth as well. He slept on the hide-a-bed in the den — within earshot of the living room, where the TV droned on well after the ten o'clock news. Worst of all, his bed partner was Dan, the guy who fussed around at night, keeping those of us in bed from getting to sleep. Incidentally, Tom grew up to be the tallest of all the Murphy boys.

Like Dan, Tom became an altar boy. He memorized his Latin and practiced the required maneuvers for serving mass. Before long he was getting up early to serve mass at the church or the high school chapel. Mom thought that Tom was a born altar boy. In the delivery room before his birth she had a beautiful dream about why this child was going to be a boy. My mother attached religious significance to this experience. I always felt that she hoped Tom would find a "vocation," meaning that he'd follow a calling toward the Catholic priesthood.

True blue through and through

Tom held firmly to his Catholic beliefs; his religious faith was always very strong. When our Aunt Theresa had a brain tumor removed, six-year-old Tom gave up candy for a year with hopes that she would get well. He didn't question things that irked me, like why we had to fast before going to communion or why we were forbidden to eat meat on Friday — or why there were Holy Days of Obligation, when we had to attend mass.

Seeing how headstrong Tom could be, Jim nicknamed him "Bulldozer." This moniker must have annoyed Tom, but he was able to ignore Jim's taunts. However, Jim sometimes persisted in teasing

Tom, singing a little "Bulldozer" song he'd composed. This might elicit an angry grunt from his little brother, but not much more.

The great awakening

Throughout his first six years of grammar school Tom was a lousy student. As his grades indicated, the classroom did not thrill him. Then, in seventh grade, he suddenly became a model student. Something clicked inside his head and he decided to become smart. From that point on he was a poster boy for good study habits. He got right to his homework after school, avoiding distractions and finishing before supper. Focus and diligence paid off for Tom. At his eighth-grade graduation ceremony he was awarded a scholarship to Leo High School.

Fishing frenzy

Tom loved to fish. Throughout the summer between his fourth and fifth grades he often went angling at the lagoon near our house. In fact, it got so he was going every day. Tom had become a fishing fanatic.

Kneeling on the shore, he caught scores of little fish, using only a hook and a short piece of fishing line. No pole was needed. He came home with jars and coffee cans of water holding little fish. When I razzed him about the puny size of his catch, Tom was quick to describe the one he'd almost hooked, holding his hands ten or twelve inches apart. He was not lacking in imagination.

Before long word of Tom's fishing trips reached Johnny Highland, a pudgy kid about Tom's age, who lived up the block. Soon they were heading for the lagoon together. The Tom-and-Johnny team hauled in scores of tiny fish, all too small to eat. They wanted to keep their catch alive but cans and jars were not doing the job.

Johnny's solution was to dump his fish into the aboveground swimming pool in his back yard. This did not thrill his teenage sisters, blonde twins who enjoyed the pool on hot summer afternoons. But despite their objections, Johnny kept pouring fish into the pool. And as the summer wore on, more and more dead fish floated to the surface. The smell grew each day. Tom and Johnny estimated that they'd dumped about three hundred fish into the pool by summer's end. That's when the Highlands moved out of the neighborhood. I still wonder how they got rid of all those fish. Did they call a cat food outfit or just dump their deflated pool of stinking fish into the alley?

Tom fishing in Sugar Creek at Turkey Run

The natural

Naturally well coordinated, Tom picked up on things like yo-yo tricks and juggling with no trouble. In summer, when our family relaxed on the balcony, Tom occasionally arrived by scaling the front of our brick two-flat in his "tennis shoes." That's what we called the high-top black canvas sneakers we wore. Their official brand name was PF Flyers.

Truth is, Tom was a quick study at most everything. So when Eddie O'Donnell encouraged him to play the flute Tom gave it a shot. He went along with Eddie to a few lessons given by the Flatley Irish Flute Band. Begorrah! In a few weeks Tom was entertaining us with lively hornpipes and reels. He even surprised Eddie's older brothers, who also played in the band. Bill played flute and Dave banged the big bass drum. And when the St. Patrick's Day parade marched across 79th Street, there was Tom strutting in step with the O'Donnell boys. The band's bright green pants and emerald caps couldn't have looked more Irish.

Tom's instinct to hang with his older brothers meant he even followed us when we went out to toss a football around. It was obvious that he was the best athlete of all the Murphy boys. He was throwing and catching a full-sized pigskin at age ten. In pickup games Tom amazed bigger kids when he got by them and snagged one long pass after another. In two-man games our Joe-and-Tom team beat high school kids on several occasions.

What's more, Tom could punt. Of course, he couldn't boot a football in the alley or the street for fear that it would crash through a neighbor's window. To play it safe we walked a few blocks to Calumet's practice field, where Tom could punt worry- free. He made it look easy, lofting one high spiraling kick after another. He went out for the grammar school team and became the punter. But despite his pass-catching talent, he wound up playing center on offense and linebacker on defense.

Ask and ye shall receive

On a crisp clear Saturday in November of 1960, Tom rode the "El" train with Dan up to Northwestern University in Evanston. Notre Dame was in town to play the Wildcats at Dyche Stadium. It was a hard-fought football game with the Irish losing 7-6. Afterward the Murphy boys hung around the stadium. Inspired by a scene from a movie about Knute Rockne, the legendary Notre Dame coach, Dan put Tom up to asking coach Joe Kuharich for a football.

My brothers waited at the entrance to the tunnel leading to the locker room. Kuharich stepped out of the tunnel just as the team manager approached, carrying a bag of footballs. Mimicking the kid in the Rockne movie, Tom asked, "Hey coach, you got a football?" Kuharich paused a moment, then took a ball from the bag and handed it to him. Wow — Tom came home with a new college football! We Murphy boys didn't waste any time breaking it in on the concrete alley.

Ah wilderness!

Nature excited Tom. He flipped for all manner of plants and animals — the wilder the better. That's why he loved to visit Martha and Lee's place in Mount Greenwood, a few miles west of our house. Here he could look out the kitchen window and see rabbits in the yard. Tom longed to explore places where he might encounter some new critter. He looked for muskrats or beavers in the marshy areas of nearby forest preserves. And hiking through a thick forest at a state park was ecstasy for Tom. It seemed to me that he was bound to be a naturalist or a park ranger.

Like Dan, who knew his big cats, Tom knew his flora and fauna. He could point out a silver fox, a scarlet tanager, a thistle or sedge. It was a major thrill for Tom when Martha and Lee took him on that weeklong vacation to the Ozarks. He was dazzled by Crystal Cave with its waterfalls and natural formations. Tom still talks about their rented cabin on the White River and standing on the porch before breakfast enjoying the cool morning mist.

Tom looked forward to family vacations at the Indiana State Parks. "A deer! A deer!" he'd shout as we pulled up to the lodge after dark. While Mom and Dad checked in Tom went outside and peered into the darkness, trying to spot a deer or two. Their eyes reflected the lights of cars turning into the parking lot.

Tom always took trails that were marked "RUGGED." The more creeks to cross and hills to climb the better. When he got back to the lodge he gave an excited report about the woodchucks, skunks, frogs and birds he'd seen. Then, when fall arrived, he pushed for weekend trips to places in Wisconsin, like Kettle Moraine and Horicon Marsh.

Stronger than dirt!

On a Tuesday night after supper Jim and I were headed for a Civil Air Patrol meeting at Foster Park. I had spray-starched my khaki uniform before giving it razor-sharp creases with the iron.

Exiting via the front door I stepped onto the sidewalk. Tom was barreling toward me on a bike. Shirtless and with a white swimming cap on his head, he held a bamboo fishing pole as if he were jousting. Getting closer, he sang out: "Stronger than dirt!" He dropped the pole and slammed on his brakes but ran right into my leg. Looking down at my pants I shouted a few choice cuss words at my brother. His front tire had ground an ugly black smudge into my clean pressed pants.

Seven-year-old Tom had been riding up and down the block spoofing the White Knight in a TV commercial for Ajax detergent. The knight on horseback charged as a chorus sang: "Stronger than dirt!" At the time my little brother's humor escaped me. He looked deflated as I ranted about how I couldn't go to the meeting with a big black mark on my uniform. While Jim took off for the park I ran back upstairs and rubbed the spot with a wet washrag. I showed up late for the CAP meeting, sporting a gray smudge that nobody seemed to notice.

Resurrecting my route

By the time I was a high school sophomore I was sick of delivering newspapers. I felt embarrassed when kids my age saw me pulling a coaster wagon along the sidewalk. I even ducked into the gangways between houses to get out of sight. So when Tom was willing to take over my Southtown route I was happy to pass it on to him.

My lax management had allowed the route of ninety customers to slip to about seventy. I felt bad about leaving Tom with so few customers sprinkled over such a big territory. But he showed me that I had nothing to worry about. Tom went right to work delivering extra papers to build the route back up. And within a few months he was collecting from more than a hundred paying customers.

Mother Nature's child

Tom worked smart and hard through Leo High School, winning a scholarship to college. Meanwhile, he kept in shape by running — usually through the neighborhood or at a nearby park. He especially liked getting out to the forest preserves and jogging along the trails. Tom graduated with a degree in biology and has spent most of his career working to improve the natural environment. He married a lovely girl and together they raised five children in a house right next to a forest preserve.

Chapter 20

Local originals

"Stay off my grass or I'll call the monsignor!"
—Mrs. Molloy (The monsignor's sister)

Living on Peoria Street gave us a colorful mix of neighbors. Some were wonderful; most were pretty nice; a few were real stinkers. But loveable or loathsome, certain people left indelible impressions on my memory.

The Gamowski boys

Spanky and Dicky Gamowski lived across the street about halfway up the block. They were teenagers, years older then me, so I didn't know them. But Joan remarked that they were pretty wild guys.

One summer day on my way to the A&P I saw Spanky standing on the opposite side of the street playing with a big leather whip. "Hey, stop right there!" he shouted, "I bet I can hit you in the ass with my whip from clear across the street." Before I could answer he cracked the whip. I heard a loud snap and felt a terrific sting on one cheek of my butt. It really hurt. "What'd I tell ya?" Spanky said, laughing.

Too surprised to protest, I broke into a run toward the A&P and walked home via Green Street, a block east of Peoria. Joan giggled when I told her what had happened. About a week later she found out from Spanky how his whip trick worked. As he shouted at me and I stopped to listen, his brother Dicky, hiding under the front porch, aimed his BB rifle at my rear end. And when Spanky cracked the whip, Dicky pulled the trigger. Ha ha!

Chester Schmid

After supper I occasionally bumped into Chester Schmid, who owned the two-flat just north of us. We'd stand in the gangway at the end of a cyclone fence separating our back yards and chat. For the most part, we talked about cameras and photography. Chester developed black-and-white film and printed his own photos. I liked to hear him talk about photo chemicals, developing tanks, timers, safe lights and other darkroom paraphernalia.

After developing his film Chester washed it under running water and hung it up to dry. One night he showed me the big photo enlarger in his basement. Its dome-shaped top sat over a bellows and a special enlarging lens. This whole assembly was rigged so it slid up and down a pole. A light inside the dome shone through the enlarging lens.

When Chester slid a black-and-white negative between the light and the lens, a negative image appeared at the base of the enlarger. He raised the enlarging head, making the image larger. Then he turned a small knob that brought the picture into sharp focus. I saw a bride and groom exiting the church. They were ducking their heads, as if dodging a barrage of rice.

Chester doted on his Minolta single lens reflex camera. He advised me to buy a camera with focusing to get sharper pictures. Following his suggestion I bought a used Bolsey 35mm camera at Sulian Camera on 79th Street. It only cost twelve bucks and the photos it produced were remarkably crisp and clear.

The Schmid family went on long vacations every year to Lake Delavan in Wisconsin. I was jealous of Chester's kids, Ellie and Ann — it seemed like they were gone all summer. When I asked Chester how he could take so much time off, he said that he got eight weeks' vacation from US Steel after working at the mills for so long.

The purple-haired lady

A middle-aged woman who lived a few doors north of us was always good for a laugh. She was forever sweeping the sidewalk in front of her house. Extremely territorial and vocal, she would shout and shake her broom at us if we ran onto her parkway to retrieve an errant football. This woman made a lot of noise, but her foreign accent was so thick, we couldn't understand what she was screaming at us.

We joked about who did her hair because it was always purple, year after year. And the shade was not subtle. Even if the sky was gray her hair looked intense, as if she had dyed it with neon. One fall day Jim Bradley and I had a brief encounter with her. I was riding my bike on the sidewalk with Jim sitting astride my rear fender. With one hand he was holding a harmless Daisy rifle that fired puffs of air. I didn't know that he'd stuffed a wet mashed-up cigar stub into the barrel. As I pedaled past the purple-haired lady she shouted something at us. Bradley answered by shooting her in the chest with the soggy cigar.

Richie Flanagan

The day after the Good Humor barn on 79th Street burned down I rode my bike into the alley behind the place to take a close look. The windows were already boarded up, blocking my view of the inside. But according to the morning news, the whole roof had caved in. I thought that if I climbed on top of a garbage can I could look down into the place, and that's what I did.

I'd just spotted a row of burned-up trucks when something gripped one of my ankles. Looking down I saw a husky, mean- faced kid about my age holding onto me. "Get offa there!" he shouted. I told him to let go so I could move. He released my ankle. Then, as I climbed down, he pulled me so I belly-flopped onto the alley. Smarting from the impact I got up slowly. The kid slugged me right in the solar plexus. I crumpled like a napkin and kissed the concrete for a second time.

"You're the wise ass who cut off my streamers!" he shouted. *What is he talking about?* I asked myself. Lying there struggling to catch my breath I couldn't say a word back to him. When I finally got up my assailant was gone, but a younger kid approached me. "Whatdya do ta piss off Flanagan?" he asked. "Nothing!" I gasped, still trying to catch my breath. Then I asked him about the guy who'd punched me. "That's Richie Flanagan," he said. I told him that Flanagan blamed me for cutting the streamers off his bike.

The kid informed me that somebody had clipped off the red, white and blue streamers that Richie had plugged into his handlebar grips. It struck me that Flanagan was out to blame the first kid who crossed his path. "Richie's crazy," the kid assured me. "I'd get outa here if I was you." My interest in the Good Humor barn evaporated in the afternoon sun. I mounted my bike and pumped toward home, craving a cold glass of water. Unfortunately, Flanagan and I would cross paths again.

Mrs. Glider

For years I visited Glider's Hobby Shop almost every week, buying model kits, paint, glue and other supplies. Mrs. Glider always greeted me with a smile. She was a small fragile-looking woman with black frizzy hair, wire-rimmed glasses and a kindly manner. Mrs. G. gave me feedback from other builders about the kits for different flying models, like how hard they were to assemble and how well they flew. She had the patience of Job, opening kit after kit, showing me the parts, unfolding and refolding the instructions and answering my questions.

One day I told her that I'd finally got the hang of applying lacquer paint (better known then as airplane dope). "It must be quite a thrill," she said, smiling. Pleasant comments like this made me feel welcome in her little shop. Mrs. Glider went out of her way to be helpful. She told me the right kind of glue, primer and sandpaper to use, keeping me on the right path. I felt that she cared about my little projects and wanted them to come out right. It was a good warm feeling that I don't often get today.

Chuck, ace of nice guys

In high school I built model planes designed for powered flight, but trying to start the little gas-fueled engines of the day was torture. I finally bought a new "easy-starting" model, hoping for success in the air.

Right about then, Joe Carollo, a kid I'd known through grade school, told me about a guy on his block named Chuck, who built beautiful model planes. Carollo took me over to Chuck's house and introduced me to him. Well into his thirties, Chuck looked pretty frail, except for his healthy head of wavy brown hair. He was always happy to talk to me and answer my endless questions about airplanes. His little house was decorated with some of the gorgeous flying models he'd built. My favorite was a huge Navy Corsair fighter with a wingspan of nearly three feet. Beautiful! Chuck had a pretty wife and two young boys.

I thought the world of this man — he was completely friendly and generous with his time. Chuck seemed to know everything about building, painting and flying model airplanes. Even better, he enjoyed sharing his know-how. He was good enough to build two flying models for me. I just brought him the kits, paint and glue. He did the rest.

When I came over to his house one day with a plane I'd designed myself, he was delighted. We walked to a nearby vacant lot where he started it up and flew it for me. What a great feeling to see a plane that I'd built doing dives and loops. "Flies good, Joe!" he shouted, turning to follow the craft as it circled him.

As the months passed I noticed that Chuck was always home — he never went to work. In a vague childish way I imagined that he had some kind of health problem but I never asked him about it. One afternoon at Chuck's house I was kidding around with his younger boy, who was only five or six. He said I only came over to get his daddy's airplanes. Wow! This shocked me — it hurt my feelings so much that I stopped visiting Chuck. When I bumped into Joe Carollo a few months later he told me that Chuck had been struggling with cancer and had passed away. He left his fishing boat to some kids who lived on his block.

Monsignor Patrick J. Molloy

"Certain undesirables are trying to move into this parish!" The cleric at the pulpit complained bitterly, wearing a scowl on his red jowly face. Father Molloy, pastor of St. Leo parish, voiced his opinions freely. He didn't want black families taking up residence on his turf. Always a rough reckless character, Molloy had a checkered past that spanned decades. The Minstrel Show, staged each year at the high school auditorium, flaunted Molloy's attitude toward his African American brethren. Hosting this parish talent show were three or four white men in blackface with big painted lips. They affected an accent from Catfish Row, cracking lame jokes and introducing the acts.

In her preface to *An Alley in Chicago*, a book about Monsignor Jack Egan, Margerie Frisbie describes Molloy's activities during the prohibition era in Chicago: "The then-Father Molloy fur in the 1920s as the trusted go-between between the Sou North-side gangs warring for Chicago's profitable bootlegging trade: "Al Capone, the most powerful gang boss of his day [and] Bugsy Moran...the leader of the North Side gang..."

"What Father Molloy was trusted to carry back and forth between the gangs is no longer known, but when $600,000 was "misplaced" between one gang and the other, a friendly phone caller let George Cardinal Mundelein know that if Molloy wasn't out of town by midnight, he'd be at the bottom of the Chicago River by daylight. Father Molloy was transferred fast and far away — to Argentina." Frisbee quotes Monsignor Egan's recollection that "Pat Molloy never bothered about any rules — either of God or man or Church. He was a law unto himself... a "rough and tumble boxer, friend of mobsters, foe of integration, hard-working, two-fisted pastor, friend of Archbishop O'Brien and Mayor Daley."*

Molloy stayed in South America for quite a spell. He didn't return to Chicago until after the Bugsy Moran gang had been cut down in the Valentine's Day Massacre and Al Capone had been sent to prison for income tax evasion. Then it was safe for Molloy to return to Chicago — first to Annunciation Church, then to St. Leo. On the fortieth anniversary of his ordination Father Molloy was made a monsignor.

From then on Patrick J. Molloy did whatever he wanted. He generated revenue through numerous avenues, including an annual turkey raffle and sales of Christmas cards, gift-wrappings, religious statues and rosaries. We grammar school kids were always hawking something for Molloy. We also provided the hustle for newspaper and coupon drives.

As a kid attending mass at the high school chapel I wondered about those moneymen near the entrance. They stood behind a counter tending neat little stacks of coins. One Sunday I took time to observe. All the men entering the chapel were plunking down coins. They were paying to attend mass. This was known as "seat money." Hoping to look like an adult I started paying a quarter for mass when I was seventeen. I've never seen an admission price

---

* Margerie Frisbie, *An Alley in Chicago: The Ministry of a City Priest,* Shed and Ward, 1991, p. vii.

charged in any other church. This little mass tax was just one more of our pastor's revenue builders.

While celebrating mass Molloy shouted at latecomers standing at the rear of the church. He warned them to stay away from the new doors that he'd just paid for. He mistreated altar boys in front of the congregation and even struck them. When a nervous little boy was about to receive communion and his tongue was trembling, Molloy shouted at him: "Stick it out, stick it out!"

Molloy's sister

My family had the honor of residing very near the Monsignor's sister. She lived in a two-flat on the corner of 80th & Peoria — less than half a block south of us. We called her "Mrs. Molloy," although she may have been a widow with different last name. Like her brother, who ruled St. Leo parish, she was territorial, irascible and blustery. When we were chucking a football around in the street we'd better not set foot on her property. If we intruded onto her parkway, the old bag would open a second-storey window, lean out and scream at us. "Stay off my grass or I'll call the monsignor! Do you hear me? I'll call the monsignor!"

I thought this unhappy lady was lonely and hard up for entertainment. And I doubt that she ever called her prestigious brother. What could the monsignor do to us anyway — lower the grades on our report cards? Lay some obscure church curse on us? Who knows — maybe we Murphy boys will be "personae non gratae" at the Pearly Gates. Or perhaps we'll get past St. Peter only to learn that we've been banned from playing touch football for all eternity.

The professor

There were sunny summer days when Dan, Tom and I tossed a football back and forth along a treeless strip of parkway at the end of our block. It felt good to throw the ball over grass once in a while. Better yet, the folks who lived in the corner house never complained. However, these sessions were sometimes interrupted by a tall middle-aged gent who stopped to observe us.

With his suit hanging loosely from his boney frame, this man presented a gawky image. The rim of his fedora was bent over his thick, horn-rim glasses and he carried a big bulky briefcase. His absent-minded aspect and rambling speech suggested a head stuffed with useless theoretical knowledge. He'd watch us awhile, then share his thoughts and suggestions on the mechanics of throwing a football. After a few encounters with this guy I started referring to him as "the professor."

One day, after I tossed the ball to Dan at the end of the parkway, the professor approached me, offering some serious comments about my execution: "I believe your trajectory is a bit high," he said. "Your long throws would be more efficient if they had a lower arc. You can bring it down if you grip the laces farther back and throw your arm higher. Snap your wrist smartly when you release the ball. It will travel lower and get there faster."

I thanked him for his advice, hoping he'd go away. He didn't. As soon as I caught the ball he coached me on how to throw it back to Dan: "Remember, grip it farther back. Get your arm higher!" I humored him and took his advice. Son of a gun — my toss had a lower arc! "Excellent!" he cheered. Giving me a friendly nod he continued on his way. The next time the professor came along he told me that his hobby was model railroading. We had a nice long chat.

Mr. Caroli

Mr. Caroli, who bought the "new" house across the street, was a pleasant little man with a strange gait. His footsteps were very erratic as he walked down the street — he'd take a couple of small steps and then a big one; a short skip, then two long strides. It was obvious that he was trying to avoid the cracks in the sidewalk.

When the Carolis gave their son Bill a bike speedometer for his birthday Mr. C. phoned and asked me to help him install it. The instructions weren't too helpful so we relied on our instincts, slowly coaxing the parts into place. We tightened things up and crossed our fingers. Would this thing work? The next day Bill took a test ride around the block, reporting back that he could see how fast and how far he was going. Pops was delighted.

After that, Mario (Mr. Caroli's first name) called me whenever there was a problem with the bike. Once, when it had a rear flat, he was ready to remove the back wheel, which would have involved disconnecting the coaster break and chain. I told him that it wasn't necessary and asked him to watch as I demonstrated the Jim-and-Joe Murphy wrenchless method of prying open the tire, pulling out the inner tube, inflating it, patching the hole and stuffing everything back under the wheel rim. Mr. C. beamed with gratitude and gave me half a buck. His just-as-nice wife sent Bill over to our house every Christmas with a plate of homemade cannolis.

Other unforgettables

Besides the folks we knew so well, there were memorable people who happened along every once in a while. In the summer an old black junkman came clip-clopping through the alley, driving his one-horse-powered wagon. It carried a ragtag assortment of tables, chairs, bed frames, baby buggies — you name it. One steamy July afternoon this junk collector stopped outside our yard and asked me if I'd get him a glass of water. I went back into the house, filled a glass and brought it out to him. He emptied it with a few gulps and handed me the empty glass. Then, thanking me sincerely, he set his horse into slow motion and plodded up the alley.

Twice a year an old frail-looking knife sharpener pushed his cart through the alley, ringing a little a bell to signal his approach. Mom always gave him some business, sending one of us older kids out with some knives or scissors for him to hone against his wheel. Then there was that guy who sold fruit from the back of his truck, yelling, "Straw-berries, fresh sta-rraw-berr-rries!" as he rolled slowly along. What a voice — I could hear it from a block away. And he wasn't kidding — his strawberries were fresh. They tasted great in Mom's strawberry short cake, made with baking powder biscuits.

Chapter 21

Touch football

"Interference on the telephone wires!"
— John O'Leary

When fall, 1958 arrived the scent of pigskin was in the air. Calumet High School's varsity squad was running through plays on their practice field near my house. Kids on the block were playing touch football in the street. The guys in my class at Leo were pumped for the upcoming game on Sunday: "We're playin' Carmel — this'll be a good one." "Yeah — their quarterback can throw the bomb — and he's got some good receivers."

In neighborhood taverns Notre Dame's next opponent was a hot topic. Irish Catholic males who had reached the use of reason were devoted ND fans. Still, there were a few Northwestern followers lurking in the shadows. On Sunday the Bears played their home games at Soldier Field on Chicago's lakefront. The football vibes around town were so intense, a visitor from Kazakhstan could feel them.

Despite this, I was too focused on making model airplanes to even join in a pickup game of touch football. At age fourteen I was building planes designed to fly, but mine couldn't get off the ground. The numerous coats of paint I applied for good looks made them too heavy to stay airborne. I built one Dodo bird after another.

Then one day after school, as I was heading out for the hobby shop, Dan asked me if I'd play in a game of touch football. I wasn't interested but he persisted, pleading that the group needed just more guy to even up the sides. "OK" I said reluctantly, joining the alley contest behind our house.

In these games of alley football, one player was the "rusher." He stayed at the line of scrimmage, shouting "One one thousand, two one thousand...up to five, before running in to tag the passer. He was honor bound to count at a "normal" cadence. But every kid seemed to rush at his own speed, prompting some heated arguments. "You counted way too fast — we get the down over!" "Whataya talkin' about? That was slower than you guys 'been countin'!"

In this particular contest I played on defense for one set of downs, then got a chance to throw the ball. On second down the rusher ran toward me with his arms flailing. I threw my arm high and nearly left the ground as I snapped my wrist. The ball flew straight and fast — right into the hands of my receiver, who couldn't hang onto it. "Wow," I said. "Did I throw that?" Everyone was impressed with my arm — especially me!

That toss marked the start of my obsession with touch football. I put my airplanes aside, seeing how much easier it was to make a football fly. I couldn't get enough of football in the alley. If Dan and I couldn't rustle up a game we'd toss the ball back and forth — behind our house or on 80th Street. The better I got the more I enjoyed playing. Luckily, I didn't have an after-school job that would eat up my free time and I was doing OK in school. So touch football became a priority. Homework could wait till after supper.

Dan and I threw the ball around every chance we got. And with each week I was throwing farther and more accurately. I went out for passes — did hook patterns, stopped short and ran long. I learned to haul in a long pass over my shoulder. This was more than fun — it was exhilarating! And there were plenty of kids around who wanted to play, so it was easy to get a game together. I felt a passion for touch football that I'd never felt for any other sport.

The two Johns

I don't recall exactly when John Sullivan and John O'Leary entered the picture. They were high school sophomores like me, and touch football addicts to boot. John S. and John O. were always up for an alley contest. Our Dan-and-Joe team began playing O'Leary and Sullivan on a regular basis. Dan usually played quarterback on our team. I ran out to catch his passes. On defense Dan rushed while I covered Sullivan, the taller and faster of the two Johns.

O'Leary was a good passer but his real strengths were strategy and play-calling. I didn't surprise me when, in later years, he coached high school sports. We played after school in the alley three or four days a week. There was no room to go wide, so any play that didn't go straight ahead was a quick toss to one side. Maybe I'd fake left, then cut right. Meanwhile, O'Leary rushed my brother. Waving his extended arms, he tried to block Dan's vision and, hopefully, the pass. But he had to resist the urge to jump. If his feet left the ground Dan could run right by him.

The concrete alley defined the game. It was hard and lumpy, like a long stretch of petrified cauliflower. And its narrow confines were bordered with hazards. I could go up for a high pass and come down with a wooden fence picket under my shirt. Permanent concrete garbage cans were another hazard. Bordering the alley like little brick buildings, they didn't budge. Getting shoved against their sharp corners left scrape marks and bruises.

Sometimes we started a game and found glass shards from a broken bottle on our field of play. Time out for a quick brooming. What's more, folks who were cleaning or remodeling dumped an array of junk outside their fences. This could make for some strange play-calling: "Stop short and go long — and don't trip on the mattress this time." Or "Go short. Fake to the telephone pole — I'll hit you by the water heater." Strategic use of debris could influence the outcome of a game.

Not for sissies

If a long pass was just out of reach, making a heroic dive for it meant belly flopping at full speed onto the concrete. I did this once, not really trying to — and lost the ball plus the skin off both of my elbows. A painful learning experience. Still, nothing pissed me more than having Sullivan beat on a long pass play when the ball hit some telephone wires overhead and dropped way short. "Interference on the wires!" We'd get the down over, but I knew we'd just lost six points.

By mid-October we were all taking these alley contests seriously. It was a real game if just the four of us were playing. Other guys who wanted in had better share our enthusiasm. I'd heard somewhere that "Winning isn't everything but losing isn't anything," and that was pretty much my philosophy. Dan had a

different attitude — more like, "Winning is everything every time — especially this time!"

Once in a while I came back to the huddle hurting and Dan had to take my place on defense. His thick heavy glasses gave him problems. They often flew off his face and even broke on occasion. Nevertheless, Dan was very physical when covering Sullivan. After a broken-up pass Sully would cry "Interference!" or "Foul," along with other colorful expletives, while Dan searched for his specs. But with no official ref on hand, he had to put up with Dan's tactics until I went back on defense.

One guy who could beef up a game was also named John. John Keating liked sports. I'd known him since third grade and he'd grown to be a very big boy. Keating made Leo's varsity football squad as a sophomore and played tackle on the team for three years. He showed up in the alley one afternoon, asking if he could play, so we let him step in for Dan on third down.

John called a running play — he'd block O'Leary to the right, I'd run to the left. Simple. I took the snap. John bulled into O'Leary clearing him out of the way and leveling a wooden fence in the process. I ran for a touchdown. But with our neighbor's entire fence lying in his yard and O'Leary smarting, we thought the best game plan would be to resume play on the street.

Flanagan! Again!

During one of our after-school games we all stepped out of the way while an old pickup truck crawled through the alley. As it passed, the kid on the passenger side stared at me through the open window. "What? What'd you say!" He shouted. Before I could answer, the truck had stopped and the kid had kicked the door open and plunked one foot onto the concrete.

Holy shit! It was that crazy Richie Flanagan — the kid who'd knocked me flat years earlier when he thought I'd cut the streamers off his bike. "I didn't say anything!" I blurted "Yeah? You better not say nutin!" he growled, lifting his leg back inside the cab and slamming the door. How strange — Flanagan and I had crossed paths in an alley for the second time. I hadn't seen him in eons, but he recognized me and still had it in for me! "Who was that nut?"

Dan asked. I said it was a long story, so we got back to our touch football. Luckily, I never laid eyes on Richie Flanagan again.

Hitting the street

Out on the street touch football was a different game. Even on narrow one-way Peoria Street, with cars parked on both sides, the playing surface was wider than the alley. There was more room to run and throw out to the sides. Too bad our block intersected with busy 79th Street. That major traffic artery fed a steady stream of cars through our playing field.

And even though the surface was smoother in the street, there were hazards. Coming down with a high pass, I could be stabbed in the back by the sharp tail fin of a '57 Chevy or the chrome rocket jutting from the hood of a '56 Olds. A worst-case scenario would be getting hit by a moving vehicle. On the other hand, we could *cause* some damage. A long bomb thrown out of reach could land on top of a car with a loud "THWOMP," leaving a dent. And a misfired bullet pass that hit a car antenna at its base would snap it like a pretzel.

One afternoon some telephone wires were down behind a store at the north end of our alley. They hung down in front of a brick wall, cutting through the strike zone painted there by the O'Donnell boys for their games of "fast pitching." A city crew came and sealed off the alley with a pair of wooden horses. "Hey, there's two of 'em," Sullivan shouted. "So what?" I answered. "That means we can borrow one!" "Huh?" I responded. "To block off Peoria — we'll have the whole street to ourselves!" It seemed like a good idea at the time so we moved one of the horses to the end of the street, preventing traffic from turning off 79th and interrupting our game.

We enjoyed smooth uninterrupted play for fifteen minutes or so. Then a cop car slowly rolled out of the alley next to Leo High School and stopped a few feet from me. Two officers stepped out and looked toward the misplaced barricade. The older policeman asked who moved the wooden horse that was blocking 79th. We didn't know — we said we just saw the street blocked and started playing football. Again, the officer spoke: "You wanna play football? Walk three blocks over to Calumet field! Now put that horse back where you got it! " We replaced the barricade and moved our game a block south to 80th Street.

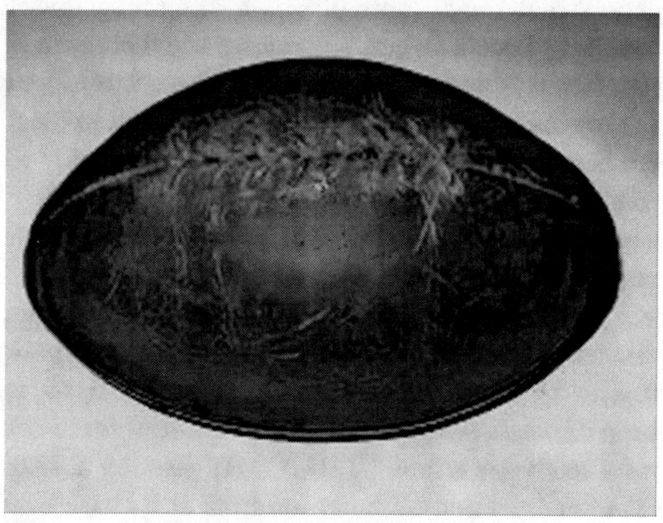

IN MEMORIAM

We got used to playing with a good leather football. Its tight regulation size and crisp square laces made it easy to grip. I could throw it farther than an old beat-up ball. Unfortunately, the concrete and asphalt we played on were not leather friendly. So after about two weeks of use in our touch games the ball's laces had lost their well-defined feel. And a couple weeks later the ends of the ball were scuffed and losing their sharpness. Soon after that the leather had worn off the ends, exposing the canvas lining underneath.

Even worse, landing in mud puddles and slush piles made the ball waterlogged. And constant wetness caused it to swell up and take on a rounder shape, so it resembled a rugby ball. A water-soaked pigskin was heavier too; it wouldn't travel as far when you tried to throw it long. Hoping to add waterproofing, we applied saddle soap, but it made the ball shiny and waxy. By this time, the cowhide's color had changed from orange-brown to dark brown with motley black splotches. Next the laces broke and up popped a herniated lump. Now the ball was too fat to grip and impossible to throw. To extend its life I did my best to restitch the ball with leather bootlaces. The results were messy, but sporting my homemade laces, the puffed-up melon ball was easier to grip. It was back in the game but its days were numbered.

Chapter 22

The balcony

"Best room in the house!"

— Joe

The architectural highlight of our house was a second-storey balcony spanning the front. It was bordered on three sides by a brick colonnade that ushered cooling breezes through on warm summer nights. That's why it was such a great place to sleep from June through September. From our den, a single step led down to the porch's concrete surface. Arching overhead, the branches of a stately elm swayed in the breeze. Their whispering leaves lulled us to sleep.

We didn't have air conditioning and electric fans didn't help much when the temperature in the house was 84° at eight p.m. Sometimes we kids would lie on the living room floor in our summer pajamas with a breeze box fan blowing over us. But the balcony was better. It always seemed cooler out there. In fact, nothing felt more refreshing to me than stretching out on a blanket under the stars.

Cousins who stayed overnight in the summer loved sleeping on our breezy balcony. Neighborhood kids liked to hang out there on warm nights. They could get a bird's eye view of our block while sipping a Coke or a glass of Mom's iced tea.

The comforting concrete

My brothers and I slept on the balcony for fourteen summers. In our prepubescent years we wore only our jockey shorts. With a thin blanket and sheet under us, plus pillows to rest our heads on, we were comfortable enough all night. If the weather turned chilly we could run inside and put on our pjs or get a blanket to cover us. Sleepers getting up to use the bathroom had to be careful where they stepped. Other family members who were sprawled haphazardly about could form an obstacle course.

Out there on the balcony my family watched sputnik traversing the night sky. It looked like a tiny silver ball moving slowly but surely through the blackness above. The space race was on and we knew from P. J. Hoff, our local TV weatherman, which nights were best for satellite gazing. As Jim and I lay on our backs staring into the heavens, we spotted the Big Dipper and the North Star — sometimes even Mars or Saturn. The night sky removed us from our earthly cares and sparked our sense of wonder. We talked about girls, trips to far away places and what to do after high school.

The highlight of our house was its breezy second-storey balcony

BALCONY CLOSED TO WIMPS

Pleasant as it was, the balcony didn't guarantee anyone a good night's sleep. Kids going inside to use the bathroom let the screen door slam behind them, waking everyone up. If it started to rain I'd hear the thud of raindrops on my pillow or someone's voice shouting, "Hey, it's raining — let's get inside!" We'd all get up, gather our bedclothes and rush into the house on the double, like a practiced drill team. What's more, mild evenings could grow chilly. On nights like that I might go inside to use the bathroom and change my mind on the way back, opting for a warm empty bed.

Certain balcony perils were impossible to escape. We kids woke up some mornings with mosquito bites in odd places, like the bottoms of our feet. These bites didn't itch — they hurt. Bites on the lips or eyelids were painful as well, and they puffed up like lumps from a fistfight.

Sitting around on the balcony was fun, although seating was limited. There was one small wooden bench out there, so kids (especially older kids) liked to sit on the limestone ledge that capped the porch's colonnade. During my teen years ledge-sitting kids made me nervous, especially if they were joking around and started rocking back and forth with laughter. I dreaded the thought of someone falling backwards off the balcony.

Untimely impacts

The balcony was a refreshing oasis on hot summer afternoons. Reclining beneath the shade of our elm I could read, think or just zonk out for a leisurely nap. Birds chirping, kids playing and cars rolling by were pleasant neutral sounds that reinforced my state of well-being. So were neighbors talking and bells from the approaching Good Humor Man.

However, our house on Peoria was near 80th Street, and that intersection was the scene of many a fender bender. Sometimes I heard squealing tires before the impact — sometimes just a loud thud. It was usually someone speeding across 80th. On more than one occasion I ran to investigate and found that one of the drivers was someone I knew.

Balcony TV

On a few sticky summer nights Dad turned the TV in our living room around so the screen faced the balcony. Centered within our parlor's big middle window, the television was easier to view than an outdoor movie. We filled a big bowl with popcorn, borrowed some chairs from the kitchen and watched contentedly. Most of the programming was from Chicago — shows like Tom Duggan and Shock Theater. On warm Friday nights we could watch movies sponsored by Courtesy Ford. Jim Moran, the Courtesy Man, interrupted frequently to hawk new and used cars with glib sincerity. On one August evening Dad and I sat outside watching the Bears slaughter the Cardinals in a practice game (at that time Chicago boasted two NFL teams).

Trouble in the night

Living near the end of the block gave us a good view of the big corner house across the street. That yellow brick structure was a mansion, out of scale with everything around it. For several years the owners rented out rooms to boarders. One summer night Jim and I were sleeping outside when loud shouting coming from the corner gave us a rude awakening. I stood up to see a lady exit a convertible, slamming the door. She and the driver shouted back and forth at each other for a good ten minutes, using colorful words I was too young to appreciate. Finally, the lady went into house and the car drove off.

The next day I slipped one of the new words I'd heard into my chat with Carol McCarthy, who lived next door. She was shocked and walked away from me. In the afternoon Mom got a phone call from Carol's mother about the word. I figured that I was in trouble, but nothing happened until after supper, when both Mom and Dad interrogated me at length about the word. After that experience I checked with older kids about colorful new additions to my vocabulary before using them.

Fire at the mansion

I was only nine years old on that spring night when my family ran out to the balcony to watch flames shooting up from the big yellow house. It was about three in the morning. Firemen blasted water at the raging fire but it didn't seem to help. I couldn't believe it. How could a place that was all brick and stone be burning up?

The Farnom family, that lived there, had to evacuate. The two Farnom sisters scampered across the street in their pajamas and

. the night with the McCarthy girls next door. Eventually the .ire Department got the flames under control. And luckily, only a small part of the house was burned, but there was water damage throughout the place. As it turned out, the blaze was started by one of the boarders who had fallen asleep while smoking in bed.

Our launching pad

Over the years my brothers and I found the balcony a great place to throw things from. We used it as a platform for hurling cap bombs, water balloons, glider planes, mini parachutes and snowballs — and those were the safer items.

Things landed on the balcony too. A calm evening could be interrupted when Jim or Tom suddenly climbed over the limestone ledge. They found it easy to scale the front of the house, their bare hands and sneakers giving them enough grip to make it all the way up. Come fall, removing elm leaves from the balcony was part of our sweeping chores. And when we shoveled snow off the balcony Mom reminded us to dump it into the front yard, not into our neighbor's gangway.

Top-notch workmanship

Detailed brickwork continued up the face of our house, rising above the balcony past the roofline. The notched edges of this brick crown were trimmed handsomely with limestone. Centered within an inner border of bricks was an ornate limestone crest. Other stone accents adorning our house had an Egyptian look, reflecting the influence that the discovery of King Tut's tomb had on architecture in the Twenties.

Balcony boogeyman

For a year or so I slept in the den on the hide-a-bed with Dan. One winter night I got up to use the bathroom and saw the huge black silhouette of someone standing outside on the balcony. Scared stiff, I shook Dan, trying to wake him up. The figure turned and walked straight toward me. My heart was pounding, "Dan, Dan!" I whisper-shouted, trying not to sound too loud. The intruder yanked the door open! Yikes!

"What's the matter?" It was Mom's voice — my heartbeat slowed. "Mom, why were you on the balcony — it's freezing out there!" I gasped. "Oh, I'm waiting for Joan," she said. "She should be home by now." The winter coat my mother was wearing had increased her bulk, adding to my initial fright. Now Dan was awake and wanted to know what was happening. "Mom was on the balcony," I told him. "You woke me up to tell me that?" he grumbled. And here I thought I'd been pretty brave trying to warn him about the dark intruder.

Chapter 23

Holidays

May your days be merry and bright
And may all your Christmases be white...
White Christmas, Irving Berlin, 1940

As I mentioned earlier, it was fun to cut through the neighborhood dime stores on the way home from school. But as Christmas approached it became more and more exciting. All that stimulation — snowy displays of white Styrofoam and candy canes; plastic holly and cardboard Santas; counters full of shiny tree ornaments and glittering little houses for Christmas villages. The toy section was beefed up with Lincoln Logs, games, dolls and air-pumped rifles that fired ping-pong balls.

By Thanksgiving the business district was decked out for the season. Giant candy canes leaned from the tops of streetlights and neighborhood storefronts became a winter wonderland. Giant snowflakes adorned the windows; ornaments hung from invisible threads. Christmas trees, flocked fluffy-white, sheltered piles of brightly wrapped gifts. Shoes, toys and toasters sat on sparkling white snowscapes. The magic day would soon arrive, but first Thanksgiving would put everyone in a cheery holiday mood (or so I imagined from my kid's perspective).

Hooray for Turkey Day!

Thanksgiving was a ball. It brought tons of good food, along with aunts and uncles. Mom and Dad got up early and went right to work. Dad chopped celery and onions for the stuffing, mixing them with pieces of stale bread and water. Next he stuffed the naked turkey, sewed it shut and lifted it into the roaster. Our Nesco electric roaster stood tall, like a jukebox without all the chrome. A small glass window on top gave a vague hint of how the bird inside was browning. As it cooked a mouth-watering aroma permeated the house.

Mom boiled regular and sweet potatoes and cooked deep red cranberries that went into the Frigidaire. She'd done her baking the day before — eight or nine pumpkin pies, two mincemeat pies and her famous French Orange Cake. Around noon on Thanksgiving Dad fried the turkey giblets and liver in a pan with butter and salt. Whoever happened to be home at the moment got to gobble them up.

Later in the afternoon my mother made whipped cream for the pies. This was the real deal, crafted in the Mixmaster with whipping cream from he milkman. Dad mashed potatoes as Mom slipped tins of dinner rolls into the oven for browning. Then the magic moment arrived when Dad removed the bird from the roaster. Placing it on a platter, he turned his attention to gravy making. He laid the roasting pan over two stovetop burners and stirred up a batch of dark tangy gravy — enough for our holiday feast and a few more meals in the days that would follow.

Our big formal dining room earned its keep on Thanksgiving. In the morning one or two of us older boys helped Dad expand the mahogany table. Standing at opposite ends and facing each other we waited for Dad to say, "One...two...three...pull!" With luck the two halves separated and slid apart. Then we added a couple of wooden leaves that stretched the table to banquet length. That chore done, Dad went back to his kitchen duties.

Our guests arrive

Aunts and uncles from Mom's side of the family started showing up about three. Uncle Mike, the bachelor ex-marine, was usually the first to appear, suited up and looking very Clark Gablesque. Aunt Theresa and Uncle Gene arrived, bearing candied yams. Martha and Lee came every year (everyone flipped for her cranberries). There were years when more of Mom's brothers and their spouses joined us. I remember that Connie and Vivian helped us celebrate a few times; so did Joe and Agatha. Looking around the table it was clear that my immediate family was much closer to the Doyles than to the Murphys.

We give thanks and chow down

With everyone seated and the feast on the table, Dad said grace slowly and solemnly. Voicing the big "Thank You" of the year, he sounded truly grateful. Then he carved the turkey, placing the white meat on one side of a big platter and the dark meat on the other. Bowls of steaming mashed potatoes, stuffing and yams were passed around, along with cranberries, green beans and rolls. Some bowls were emptied before they made one full circuit and had to be restocked so everyone had enough to be thankful for.

While we ate Mom reminisced with her siblings about growing up in Sioux City, Iowa and later years — after the Doyle family had moved to Gary, Indiana. Dad talked to Mom's brothers about pipefitting jobs they'd worked on, like the Pittsfield and Inland Steel buildings downtown. Dad and Uncle Connie hooked up pipes to the first nuclear reactor at the University of Chicago — part of the Manhattan Project that created the atomic bomb.

We all ate heartily but everyone left room for dessert. Pumpkin or mincemeat pie was coming; so was French Orange Cake — packed with nuts and dates. This heavy dessert was topped with sugary frosting, tangy with the taste of fresh-drizzled orange juice. My compulsion to eat some of everything included all the dessert items. As I pushed back from the table my stomach felt like it had been inflated by a gas station air hose. I made my way to the living room where folks were watching TV. Picking a spot among my siblings on the carpet, I reclined to view The Wizard of Oz or some other holiday broadcast.

Story hour

When we kids were growing up we enjoyed Uncle Lee's spooky after-dinner stories. We herded into a bedroom, closed the door and sat on the floor. Lee turned off the lights. Then, in a low creepy voice, he narrated a tale that was frightening but funny. The way Lee liked to kid around made him my favorite uncle. And as Jim, Dan and I outgrew his eerie tales, the younger kids — Marg, Tom and Pat — continued to savor them on Thanksgiving.

When Dan and I were in high school touch football took us outside on Thanksgiving. We rustled up enough kids to have a

"Turkey Bowl" game of touch football. And feeling that this special holiday game merited a grass surface, we hiked over to Calumet's practice field. Here we found enough other kids to make a game. If the contest wasn't over by 1:45 p.m. we bowed out so we could be home by two. It was time to get cleaned up for dinner and do some helping out. In retrospect, we boys could have done a lot more helping out.

Christmas scenes

Every holiday season a magnificent Christmas tree graced the window of Rusnak Furniture on 79th Street. It was always tall, abundantly full and dripping with tinsel. The lights were dazzling — a perfect mix of every color. And there were so many ornaments — some round, some oval and others shaped like long teardrops, not to mention little elves, snowmen and reindeer. Glistening garlands embraced the tree with perfect parabolas, and below lie hefty piles of presents, all lavishly wrapped. I stopped in front of that window many times on the way home from school. Looking at Rusnak's tree sent chills down my young spine.

The windows at Frank's Department Store were decked out for the holidays as well. Standing against a snowy background, the mannequins were bundled up for the season. It felt good to walk inside and warm up by the cosmetics counter just inside the door. The sales ladies were good about letting me loiter there, but if things got too busy I could always move. I loved going downstairs to the basement where I could check out the toys that had taken over space normally devoted to housewares. What an array — cap pistols, Gilbert chemistry sets, rocking horses, dolls and doll houses, roller skates, tinplate wind-up cars and tons of other non-electronic stuff that kids in the Fifties coveted.

The holidays on our block were magical. The windows of neighboring houses were decked with wreaths and outlined in colored lights. Manger scenes and illuminated Santas glowed in front yards. Next door, Mr. Schmid set up painted plywood reindeer on his front parkway, illuminated by spotlights. And a speaker mounted in his second-floor window played Christmas carols. As I walked home toting bags of Christmas presents his multi-media show gave me a warm holiday glow.

Anticipation and temptation

Right after Thanksgiving I started saving my paper route money for Christmas gifts. I needed enough to buy presents for everyone in my family. And though my funds were limited, I made a big deal out of holiday shopping, agonizing over what to get Mom, Dad and all my siblings. For Mom and Dad I chose practical gifts, imagining that they'd be thrilled with them. After all my searching and sweating I'd wind up giving Mom a breadbox or a set of glass tumblers. I'd get Dad something like a wallet or tie. What's more, I tried hard to imagine what each of my brothers and sisters really wanted. This took weeks. And I wasn't finished shopping until I'd bought gifts for Martha, Lee and Mike, who were so close to us Murphys.

Renting a storage locker at the North Pole would have been easier than hiding Christmas gifts in our house. There were only so many nooks and crannies where our parents could stash presents, and we kids knew where all of them were. However, as I grew up my perspective shifted, so it was more fun *not* to find presents before Christmas. Peeking just spoiled the surprise. But the younger kids snooped everywhere — in closets, under beds — even in Mom and Dad's dresser drawers. That's why they began hiding their holiday purchases in a locked basement storeroom.

One Christmas I bought three small nativity figures at Woolworth's — the Christ child, Mary and Joseph. Then, to keep them warm, I built a little a stable out of balsa wood with a hole right up front at the top for a small light. I took a single socket from an old string of tree lights, screwed in a new bulb and wired it to a plug. Things were going well. With my fingers crossed I plugged the wire into the nearest wall socket. "POP!" It blew out instantly, emitting an acrid electrical smell.

Dad was on the scene in seconds "Are you trying to electrocute yourself?" he shouted "Gimme that wire! Now get outa here and do your homework!" My enthusiasm toward an illuminated manger fizzled. Mom placed the Holy Family safely on top of the bookcase in the den.

The big wow!

When most of us kids were still small and innocent Mom believed in giving us the Big Christmas Surprise. The tree didn't go up until Christmas Eve after we were asleep. Then, in the morning, the whole Christmas scene appeared as if by magic — the tree, the presents, the stockings filled with candy... What a thrill! And Christmas couldn't start until Martha and Lee arrived. We kids gathered in the hall outside the den. We could smell the tree and see its multicolored lights, softened by the sheet tacked over the entrance. As soon as our aunt and uncle showed up the sheet came down and we ran in. On some Christmases Lee filmed the madness.

As we rushed toward the tree Mom tried to direct each of us kids to the correct pile of presents. I might get started on Jim or Dan's stuff, only to be rerouted to the mound of gifts intended for me. There was usually a tricycle, wagon or some other wheeled toy under the tree. Digging for presents, I enjoyed the combined aromas of evergreen and new rubber. Our stockings were heaped on top of the bookcase. These were our everyday stockings, filled with hard candy, nuts and an orange. Dad reminded us that all he ever got for Christmas as a kid was an orange. And he was thrilled to get it.

Christmas, 1956 (l to r) Seated: Jim, Dan, Joan holding Pat, Marg. Up front: Tom with gun, Joe with chopper

There were holiday seasons when Uncle Paul, Dad's younger brother, visited, bringing his kids, Jim and Mary Ellen, with him. They came all the way from Oklahoma City, making the rounds of Murphy relatives in the Chicagoland area. It was great to get a visit from the Murphy side of the family.

Uncle Paul was a good-natured man who really enjoyed seeing Dad, and the feeling was mutual. Paul's wife, Adeline, had died years earlier, so Paul was raising his adopted kids alone. Jim, a year older than me, had a dry sense of humor, which made me think he was very smart. Mary Ellen, who was my age, was outgoing and attractive. I kept trying to talk to her but Margaret Mary held her captive.

After supper Paul would organize a game of cards called "Hearts for Noses." I forget the rules but I remember other players slapping me on the nose with their cards. Paul also introduced us boys to *Pigskin,* a fun board game about football. One Christmas, while he was coaching us on the game, a loud scream startled us. We all ran into the living room to find Mary Ellen crying and holding her eye. She and Tom had been shooting rubber suction darts at each other with spring-loaded pistols. We thought these darts were harmless but one of them hit Mary Ellen squarely in the eye.

Mom applied a cold compress and everyone waited nervously as Mary Ellen held it in place. After a few minutes she uncovered her eye. It looked red and swollen but she said she could see. Whew! What a relief! Well, that was enough visiting for one day. We'd see Paul and his kids again before they left for Oklahoma, but it was "bye-bye" for now.

Joyous rituals

Eventually Mom and Dad relaxed the rules regarding our Christmas tree. We older kids were allowed to decorate it a week or so before Christmas. Now we could see what Mom and Dad had been doing late at night every Christmas Eve for so many years.

Dad helped us get started by dragging the tree into the house through the back door. Then, seated on the kitchen floor, he tried to fit the trunk into the stand that a welder at work had made for him. It was a piece of three-inch pipe with curved legs welded to it. The trunk was too fat, so Dad shaved it down using a hammer and chisel. This took a while and looked like work. When it finally fit into the pipe we kids helped tote the tree into the den. Dad stood it up and got one of us to hold the trunk and tip it this way or that until he thought it was straight. "Stop right there," he hollered in a non-threatening voice. Working quickly, Dad crawled beneath the bottom branches and tightened a few bolts. Tada! Our Christmas tree was ready to be trimmed.

Next we tested the lights, unraveling the knotted strings and plugging them into a wall socket. There were plenty of burned out lights that were working fine when we packed them away a year earlier. I wondered what made them die in storage. Did they have some kind of death wish? When all the lights passed muster Jim and I strung them onto the tree. Starting at the top we clipped each light to a branch, connecting one string to another as we spiraled our way downward. Oops — we ran out of lights with a foot or more of tree left to cover. No problem. We unfastened the lights and jostled them around until they covered the whole tree.

The more, the merrier

At this point I gave the tree my "blur" test by covering my good eye and using my weak one to give me a fuzzy view of the lights. This accentuated any gaping holes or color imbalances, which I pointed out to the other tree trimmers. My artistic direction was ignored — it was time to hang the ornaments.

Attaching the bulbs was easier. Joan advised us to hang the smaller ones near the top of the tree, the mid-sized ones in the middle and the largest ones at the bottom. This worked out well for the younger kids — they got to hang the big fancy ornaments on the lower branches.

When we tried to drape a garland around the tree we ran way short. But by limiting our loops to the part that folks could see, we did a first-class job. The tree looked great, and its location in the corner of the den concealed our little trick.

Finally it was tinsel time. In the Fifties tinsel was made of lead. It was heavy, hung straight and looked terrific. The younger kids dropped big wads of it over the branches. We older sibs carefully hung a few strands at a time, making long icicles. Mom liked to toss handfuls of tinsel up to the top branches. When we were finished everyone agreed that this was our best tree ever.

We couldn't let the holidays pass without getting Mom to sit at the piano and play Christmas carols. When I was in high school it started to mean something to me when the family gathered around her to sing. Year after year she played tunes from a little music book illustrated with angels, elves and snow scenes. Mom always seemed happy to squeeze a bit of music into her hectic yuletide schedule.

Back to reality

When most of us kids were still in grammar school our mother brought the holidays to a close a day or two after New Year's. She and Dad took down the tree and we helped box up the decorations. Mom vacuumed the living room floor, picking up pine needles and strands of lead tinsel that gummed up the roller brush. Then Dad put all the holiday trappings away for another year. Mom was happy to have her tidy house back.

With just a day or two left before classes resumed, it was time for us kids to tackle the homework we'd put off for a week. The weight of this grim task crushed the last spark of joy from my holidays. Sitting around the kitchen table, my brothers and I plodded through endless arithmetic, geography and history lessons. If I complained to Mom that I couldn't understand something, she'd explain it to me and move on to the next kid needing help.

Looking up answers hour after hour with no hope of escape was gut-wrenching. But glasses of eggnog and mom's holiday stockpile of pumpkin pies helped us get through this annual crisis. When school started again Mom got back to her regular routine of keeping our home clean and clutter free. If nobody was snacking or doing homework the kitchen table was completely cleared — not even a saltshaker remained. And even if we were just noshing, dirty dishes went right into the sink. If Mom happened by she'd instinctively clear them from the table.

My Christmas job

I was fifteen in 1959 when I got an after-school job at Frank's Department Store. And what luck — I went to work in the bustling basement section just in time for the Christmas crunch. There was a big Lionel train layout with two trains, bridges, towers, log loaders and other nifty accessories.

Each day more toys poured in through the shipping dock. My co-stock boy was a kid named Glen Dixon. He had a reputation as being a tough character — not someone you'd want to mix it up with — but we got along fine. Together we unloaded the flood of incoming merchandise. Slicing open big cardboard cartons, we stacked their contents onto shelves or into displays. Some toys came in boxes completely covered with colorful printing that made them downright slippery. Glen and I piled them into pyramid-like displays that flew apart when customers bumped into them. One display came undone so often that we decided to stick the boxes together with Scotch Tape loops.

We did a lot of gift wrapping in the back room, covering boxes with festive paper. Glen and I worked in synchronized motion on opposite ends of a box. And we had knot-tying down to a science. There were tons of UPS orders to go out ASAP, so we grabbed whatever we could find for cushioning — excelsior, coils of rolled-up cardboard, wrinkled-up brown wrapping paper and newspaper. But despite our efforts, certain items came back to the store broken.

My greatest shipping challenge was a large oval platter decorated with a hand-painted turkey. I found a flat box that had a few inches of room to spare and placed the platter inside, surrounding it with wrinkled newspaper. It went out via UPS and came back in a dozen pieces. Unflustered, I sent it out again, using a bigger box and more newspaper. It too came back broken, but in fewer pieces this time. Finally, my exasperated boss, Jerry Frank, packed the platter using so much padding that the box looked like it might have a TV inside. We sent it out...and Eureka! It reached the customer in one piece. After that Glen and I started packing items with layers – sometimes newspaper covered by excelsior covered by cardboard — before boxing them up. It was like dressing them for subzero weather. And to my great relief, fewer items were coming back broken.

And what do *you* want for Christmas?

As the big day approached Frank's basement became temporary headquarters for Mr. Christmas himself. Shopping parents brought their tots to see Santa Claus, who sat in front of a glistening, snowy background. He was clad in an ill-fitting, bright red suit with ragged white trim. His silver-white beard grew out of a dingy gray cord that hung an inch below his chin.

Kids lined up to sit on Santa's lap and they didn't have to wait long — the setup was much merrier than the mob scene in a downtown department store, like Marshall Field's. Inside of ten minutes a kid could sit on Santa's lap, get a free candy cane and be back shopping with mom and pop.

One day Louise, a pleasant young saleslady, asked me, "Joe, is there something wrong with our Santa?" Not quite sure of what she meant, I said I didn't think so, but a few days later I learned that our Santa had some kind of disability. This kindly middle-aged gent was unable to handle a regular job. I wanted to ask him about his condition but decided not to pry. I thought he was the perfect department store Santa — a nice guy who was a natural with kids. His hobby was carving wooden toys.

Merry glitzmas

A few steps away from Santa's realm several sparkling aluminum Christmas trees rotated on motorized stands that chimed with tinkling holiday tunes. Their branches changed hues from red to blue to green, thanks to spotlit revolving color wheels (purchased separately). The effect was very showy, like something straight from Vegas. But in the late Fifties folks went nuts over these sparkling, rotating trees with their ever-changing colors.

I carried many of these shimmering beauties, boxed and unassembled, out to customers' cars. But whenever we shipped them via UPS, they boomeranged back to the store with all their branches mashed together into a wad at one end of the box. Glen and I were given the task of pulling the mangled branches apart and fluffing them up. Our boss thought that if we could reconstitute enough branches from several returned trees we might wind up with a few saleable ones. But our best efforts to spruce up the crushed aluminum needles had ugly hairy results and left our hands red and raw.

Chapter 24

Pat

"Hey, let me help you with that!"
— Pat

Pat arrived in this world fifteen years after my mother gave birth to her first child. I was in fifth grade when my new baby brother came home from the hospital. The previous day I'd stopped at Woolworth's and bought a present for Mom — an ashtray that looked like a stubby little train engine. She pretended to love it.

Everyone at home was anxious to greet the newest member of our family, but where could we put him? All three bedrooms were filled and two kids were sleeping on a hide-a-bed in the den. Dad's solution was to set up the baby crib against a wall in the dining room. And as it turned out this location worked well. Pat thrived beneath the chandelier in his roomy makeshift bedroom.

Ahead of the curve

We kids bought rattles, balls and other baubles to keep Pat entertained. He was a happy, good-natured little blonde guy. And with all the encouragement we gave him, it wasn't long before he pulled himself up and was standing in his crib. Gripping the rail he jumped up and down, pausing to extend his arms. He wanted out of that crib and we older siblings were happy to oblige. The constant coaching we gave our baby brother may have helped him to walk and talk earlier than most kids. What's more, I think that all the attention our family heaped on Pat contributed to his poise and confidence.

Very self-propelled, Pat was never bored; he was always doing something or at least paying attention. Curious about the way things worked, Pat watched Dad fix faucets, oil hinges and patch walls. He skipped toy play tools, going straight for Dad's real ones.

Resourceful Pat was handy with screwdrivers, hammers and pliers before he could read.

Pat's bracing March excursion

One day about six weeks after Pat's birth I walked out onto the front balcony for some fresh air. It was late March but unseasonably cold. As I looked north toward the A&P I spotted Margaret Mary at the far end of the block. I was about eleven, which would make Marg about seven at the time. She was kneeling on the sidewalk wrapping something up in a blanket. Holy cripes, it was our baby brother Pat!

This scared me. Jeez, it's cold, I thought. Pat could freeze his little feet off in this weather. He had to be pretty uncomfortable lying there with nothing but a baby blanket separating his soft bald head from the frigid concrete. What the heck was Marg up to? Was she on her way home after showing Pat off to one of her girlfriends? When she lifted him from the sidewalk and turned toward our house I felt much better. Mom would be furious if she found out about this stunt.

A quick study

Pat walked so soon that I don't remember him crawling. All of us older kids took turns walking him through the house, holding his hands to help him take baby steps. Then one night while we were all in the living room watching TV, Pat surprised the lot of us. Holding himself up against a stuffed chair, he suddenly pushed off and darted across the room to the couch — with no help from anyone. At nine months old little Pat was a toddler.

Sitting in his high chair at suppertime, Pat could hardy wait for his pop to get home. He lit up when the kitchen door opened and Dad walked in. Smiling with delight, Pat reached out with both arms. John Murphy picked up his youngest son and gave him a big hug. All was well.

Just ask Pat

When Pat started scooting from one room to another we older kids helped acquaint him with his surroundings. I'd hand him a block or a rattle and tell him, "Put this in the bath tub" or "Put this on the stool." Sure enough, he would toddle to the correct room, delivering the item right on target. Pat did this so well that we gave him harder errands: "Go get the blue comb" or "Go get the puppet." He proved equally adept at these tasks. In fact, it wasn't long before we were asking him to locate things we'd misplaced and couldn't find ourselves. Pat didn't have to look for them; he knew right where they were. This kid was amazingly alert.

Pat was always energetic and curious. Barely a year old, he climbed on top of the kitchen table and jumped off. Later that day Mom noticed a slight bulge below his tummy, so she and Dad took him to the doctor. It turned out that their youngest son had an abdominal hernia. The following afternoon Pat entered the hospital to get sewn up.

When Mom and Dad went up to visit him the morning after his surgery Pat was standing in his crib smiling. The nurses commented on how much young Patrick was enjoying his stay. "No more jumping off the table," he was warned. Pat was no dummy — he heeded the advice and stayed healthy.

Pat's perils

A few months later — just two weeks before Christmas — our dining room was the scene of a very close scrape for Pat. Mom had covered the table with Christmas cards she'd received the previous year. Her ragged old address book was close at hand. Thus began her annual ritual of sending hand-signed cards to friends and relations.

Our mother's activity was contagious. We kids asked her for a few cards to send out, and before long there were three or four of us at the table writing out cards. The room grew quiet as we concentrated on addressing envelopes and adding first-class stamps (they were purple three-cent stamps illustrated with the statue of liberty).

Out of the corner of my eye I spotted Pat scampering around in his sleepers. He seemed to be sucking on something, and whatever it was, it was completely in his mouth. I thought I'd better check to make sure he didn't swallow some object he'd picked up off the floor. "Open your mouth, Pat," I said — and he obeyed. To my astonishment, lying on his tongue was a double-edged Gillette Blue

Blade — the kind Dad shaved with! In a soft voice I told Pat to be still and I gingerly lifted the blade off his tongue and out between his tender little lips. Incredibly, he didn't have any trace of a cut anywhere — on his hands, face or inside his mouth. How lucky can you get? I still wonder where he found that razor blade. Had he climbed up onto the bathroom sink and opened the medicine chest? We'll never know.

One afternoon Pat managed to pry open the top of Mom's piano and pour a can of plastic poker chips into the works. Dad was so surprised at this feat that he found it hard to get angry. He fished out most of the chips from between the strings, finding an Easter egg that had been hidden beneath the lid a month earlier. Pat, always fascinated by things mechanical, observed Dad carefully. Joan's piano pieces had an eerie underwater sound for about a week – until Mom called a piano tuner.

Where'd he go?

Pat found ways around our efforts to contain him. One Sunday morning when I returned from my paper route at about seven a.m., I noticed that his crib was empty. I checked the bedrooms to see if he'd crawled in with someone. No luck. Next I checked all the other rooms in the house. Not there either. I looked out on the balcony, then in the back yard. Still no Pat. It was time to alert Mom and Dad. I woke up them up and gave them my missing Pat report. They, in turn, awakened everyone in the house and assigned search areas to each of us kids.

I looked up Peoria and Sangamon Streets to 79th. Other brothers and sisters checked nearby streets like Green and Carpenter. When I returned from my search our little fugitive was safely home. Driving around the neighborhood, Dad found Pat a block north and a block east of our house. He was standing in front of a tavern door on 79th Street dressed only in diapers and holding an empty quart beer bottle in his hands.

For the most part Pat was safe and secure, enjoying the love and protection of us older siblings. Even so, he was easy prey for Jim and his eccentric antics. There were summer days when Jim picked up four-year-old Pat, carried him out to the back porch and dangled him over the second-storey banister or above the stairwell leading to the porch below. "Who's your friend?" Jim would ask with devilish glee. "Who do you like the most?" Of course, Pat's helpless answer was "You, you, you!" And after Jim heard that word enough times he would lift shell-shocked Pat over railing and set him back on the porch.

Pat on a homework phone conference

Man of action

As a preschooler Pat watched Dad intently when he fixed faucets, hinges or doorknobs around the house. He picked up quickly on what tools to use for various tasks. But even though he was beyond his years in some ways, Pat was still sleeping in the baby crib at age six. This was about to change. Without a word to anyone he got a screwdriver and pliers from the basement and dismantled his crib. His boldness and wherewithal amazed us. Everyone got the message, especially Mom and Dad. They decided to let Pat to sleep in a bedroom between two of us older brothers. These cramped sleeping arrangements lasted five years — until our family moved to a new house in Chicago's Mount Greenwood area farther south.

The warrior

As a young kid Pat liked to watch *Combat*, a weekly TV series starring Vic Morrow, who portrayed a tough battle-savvy sergeant in World War II. Pumped by this show, Pat and David Olsen, who lived across the alley, played "Soldiers." Together they patrolled the

79th blocks of Peoria and Green streets, armed with toy rifles and grenades from Kresge's and Woolworth's.

Getting things done

Pat was always a helpful, hands-on guy. In 1975 he married Kathy Mahoney, his high school sweetheart. They raised three terrific kids — two boys and a girl. A Murphy who looked like a leader at a tender age, Pat is now a captain on the Chicago Fire Department. Always very handy, Pat (with a little help from his friends) added a second floor to his house, finished the basement, built a big new garage and constructed a permanent deck for the swimming pool in his back yard.

Chapter 25

Vacations

"Did I ever show you the hole in my head?"
— Joan

Joan's question took me by surprise. She was sitting on the bed in our rented cabin drying her hair. "What?" I asked. "Come over and take a look," she urged me, tilting her head forward. I could see a donut of red hair funneling down into a tiny dark spot in the center. "Put your finger in there," she urged. When I gingerly touched the funnel in her hair she got more insistent. "No, push — push your finger in!" I pushed. My finger sunk an inch into her skull. I pulled it out quickly, feeling sick to my stomach. She and Marg laughed hysterically. I didn't know that Joan had put her hair into a ponytail. Ha ha — I'd just poked my finger through a rubber band.

Vacations were loaded with laughs and surprises. We usually headed for one of the Indiana State Parks, like Turkey Run, Brown County or McCormick's Creek. Many of our Turkey Run trips were weekenders. Everyone would be packed and ready on a Friday when Dad got home from work. We'd eat a quick supper, then Jim or I would help Dad strap the luggage carrier to the top the car. Using some old clothesline, we'd secure a few mismatched bags, plus a couple of cardboard boxes stuffed with clothes.

Off to Indiana

We drove east toward Indiana, passing through Whiting and Gary before hooking up with Route 41. It was a two-lane road that cut though fields of green corn and acres of wheat that glowed gold with the setting sun. Stops along the way were limited — we had to make good time to meet the deadline for late check-in. If we boys had to "go" we did so into a half-gallon milk bottle while Joan and Marg averted their eyes. It was different if Mom, Joan or Marg had to answer Nature's call — Dad stopped at a gas station. We boys didn't mind — we got to stretch our legs and buy something to munch on.

Flying diapers

The luggage on top of the car was well secured but, unfortunately, clothes packed in cardboard boxes were easy prey for wind and rain. On one trip when Pat was a toddler, a car pulled up beside us and the driver shouted at Dad, "Hey bud, you're loosing your diapers!" Looking back, I saw a trail of diapers, some flying through the air. Dad pulled over. Without saying a word he got out of the car and walked back, collecting the lost cargo as best he could. He returned a few minutes later toting a floppy pile of road-soiled diapers. He passed them to the back seat for safekeeping and tightened the ropes on top of the car. Then we continued on our way.

Joan's wet wardrobe

On another vacation trip things didn't go well for my older sister. She was in her teens and would rather have been hanging out with her girlfriends. She packed a pile of neatly pressed clothes into one of the boxes riding atop the car. For two days prior to our departure she'd been ironing shorts and blouses.

As soon as we crossed into Indiana rain hit us with gale force. Joan was beside herself. She complained to Dad that her clothes were getting soaked. As usual, he was trying to reach the state park by nightfall. I couldn't believe it when Dad told Joan that he wouldn't stop. She wasn't going to get her way — wow! Then someone, probably Jim, started chanting "Poor Joanie's clothes are wet" to the tune of *There's No Place Like Home.* We all chimed in for a few verses, before Mom and Dad shut us up. But I was amazed to see Joan in a situation that she couldn't control.

Breezy punishment

Back-seat skirmishes erupted on vacation trips. Jim wouldn't move over to make room for Marg or I wouldn't give up the window seat with its cool breezes. Dad shouted, telling us to behave. If I made trouble I'd have to ride up front, isolated from my siblings. Mom would let me sit next to the door, where I could play with the hinged no-draft window, adjusting it to direct the wind toward my face and arms. What ever happened to those terrific triangular windows? They were the best feature that any car ever had. Kids born too late will never know what a delight they were. Air conditioning will never feel that good.

Fun at Turkey Run

Though all the Indiana State Parks we visited were terrific, everyone in our family ranked Turkey Run number one. Near Marshall, Indiana, it offered the greatest variety of things to see and do. Better yet, it was the closest of the Hoosier State Parks to our house. Arriving late at night, we checked in at the lodge or got the keys to a couple of nearby cottages in the park.

The next morning we got up early and ate breakfast in the dining room at the lodge. An attractive hostess seated us as perky young waitresses scurried about, balancing huge oval trays on their shoulders. It was fun to watch — almost like a big dance number. We all got menus and ordered just what we wanted. And everything tasted better because we were on vacation. Being waited on made me feel like a big shot.

Following breakfast the whole family took a trail together. This was always a flat easy trail because Dad's bad leg (the one he'd broken) was no good for climbing. "Let's all stay together — no running ahead," Mom urged us. But Jim and Dan, the adventurers, were deaf to her plea. They were always around the next bend and out of sight.

Weekend trips to Turkey Run were short, but they worked out well for Dad because he could stay for the duration. And at least he and Mom could relax for one full day and talk together without interruption from us kids. In my late teens I came to realize that our parents needed a vacation more than we kids did. It was good to see them sitting together under a shady tree. They looked old and a bit tired but it was good to see them savoring a rare break from their hectic everyday routines.

Turkey Run snapshot, 1955: Marg in front of Jim, Tom in front of Dan

Pretty Ponytail

We had to get back to the lodge in time for lunch, served by a cute teenage waitress. One summer we had the same blonde ponytailed server several times. We kids started calling her "Ponytail." I couldn't wait for her to take my order. In fact, one afternoon when our family entered the dining room, I walked right by the hostess, heading straight for Ponytail's section. We got to sit there but Dad told me not barge in like that again. We were supposed to wait for the hostess to seat us.

Whenever we lucked out and got Ponytail I tried to make an adult-sounding menu choice and place my order in a mature decisive manner. Ponytail was sharp. She checked often to see if we needed more of this or that. I loved asking her for more of something. She'd always smile and say "Sure, right away!" We kids kept her busy, asking for more orange juice, more butter, more toast, more syrup…

A short happy nap

After lunch I went back to our cabin for a siesta. I flopped while my adventurous brothers hiked forests, climbed rocks and forded streams. Thoughts of that pretty waitress delayed my sleep. What did she do between meals? Was she bored? Did she hang around the park or go home? How much time did she spend combing her ponytail? Would she like me if I were a little older? Finally I nodded off, but my sleep was soon interrupted as Jim, Dan and Tom returned from their hike.

I enjoyed walking across the bouncy suspension bridge spanning Sugar Creek. But the most fun for me at Turkey Run was trekking through the wet rocky hollows that permeate the park. They were cool and highlighted with pools of rainwater. Tall trees bordering the cliffs above spread their branches over the canyons. Their leaves glowed a delicate green with the afternoon sun shining through them.

That killer hill

The park rented horses for trail riding but we never gave them a second thought. Renting bikes was cheaper and we could go where we wanted on them. Coasting down the park's curving hilly roads was exhilarating! One afternoon, however, I lost control on a steep, dangerously sharp curve and charged off into the woods. Thuddd! My handlebars hit two saplings, stopping my bike cold. My head flew between the young trees and my shoulders rammed into them. The pain was spectacular; I was sure that I'd broken something. But as I walked my bike up to the road the smarting subsided, and by the time I got back to the bike rental I was feeling alright. The next morning was a different story; when I woke up I could hardly lift my arms. It was weeks before the soreness went away.

The cabin on the lake

One summer we stayed for a week at Lake Van Aucken, a small lake in Michigan. Arriving after dark, we moved our bags and bamboo fishing poles into the cabin. But yuk — the place was lousy with moths. They were on the walls, the doors, the curtains — everywhere. After swatting a few of them Dad decided to turn off all the inside lights and switch on the porch light. Then he propped the door open and the moths migrated to that irresistible light bulb outside. Hooray!

In the morning Jim and I spotted the little lake about half a block from our cabin. We ran to the shore, where two or three small boats were resting on the sand. There was a clean stretch of beach, and about thirty yards offshore a small raft floated high in the water. Made of two big oil drums covered by a wooden deck, it made a great diving platform for us kids.

We scrambled to the cabin for a breakfast of pancakes and sausages. Then Dad drove us boys to an old-fashioned hardware store in town, where we stocked up on hooks, bobbers, lead sinkers and other basic fishing gear. Then, after dropping us off at the cabin, Dad left to get back to his job in Chicago.

A nice kid named Pete

Pete was a teenage boy who lived on the lake all year round. What a great guy — he went out of his way to keep us Murphy kids entertained. We first noticed him driving an old car around between the cabins, pulling three lawn mowers hooked together. He looked way too young to have a license but he had a grown-up grip on the wheel. We saw him water skiing, towing other skiers and unloading fish from his boat. Pete answered all our questions about the lake and the area around it.

One day a few of us kids hiked with Pete to a neighboring farm. He said that if we hurried we might get to milk a cow. As we passed a wheat field he picked a stalk and handed it to me. I enjoyed dislodging the kernels and rolling them around in my hand. When we arrived at the farm the milking was still in progress inside the barn. An elderly lady showed all of us how to squeeze a cow's udder, but only Joan was able to produce a healthy squirt into her bucket.

Joan's friend, Mary Frances Reen, came with us on our vacation that summer. Good thing. One sunny afternoon little Margaret Mary, who couldn't swim, drifted away from the raft into deep water. She was going under for the third time when Mary Fran spotted her and came to her rescue. Marg surely would have drowned if not for Joan's alert girlfriend.

When the Fourth of July arrived an older kid sold me a handful of small firecrackers. With Dan behind me trying to watch, I used a glowing punk to light one of them. Pulling my hand back quickly, I heard a scream. Dan was holding his eye. Oh no! I'd stabbed him in the eye with the red-hot punk! "Dan! Dan! Are you OK?" I cried. He was silent for a minute or so, before removing his hand. I was much relieved to see that the punk had missed his eye, landing a little above it.

After a week Dad came back to pick us up. I hated to leave the little lake — it seemed as though we'd just arrived. On our way home we stopped at The House of David, a religious community in Benton Harbor. It was a pretty big place but we limited our visit to their tourist shop, stocked with post cards, T-shirts, little wooden boxes and other memorabilia. The men behind the counters looked creepy to me with their long beards, black pants and suspenders. I thought they must be dying dressed like that on such a blistering afternoon. When we hit the road again I rolled down the back window to catch some cool breezes after that hot sticky stop.

Cooney's Cottage

Another summer we went up to Cooney's Cottage at Palisades Park in Michigan — right on Lake Michigan. Cooney was Frank Cooney, one of Dad's old steamfitter friends. They had worked together on construction jobs during the Thirties and Forties. Filled with nine Murphys, the little cottage was cramped but cozy. We picked the strawberries growing right outside the door and ate them on the spot.

Walking through the forest for just a short way, Joan and I could see the beach below us. The sand dropped at a steep angle toward the shore. Figuring it was time to go barefoot, I removed my shoes and socks. But the black path leading down to the beach was made of tarpaper. I took a few steps before I had to sit. That black surface felt like a frying pan. I was almost crying. Shod in sandals, Joan made it down to the beach with no problem. I put my shoes back on and followed. At the shore we enjoyed splashing around in the water, but the real fun started after sundown. Bonfire-building grownups welcomed us kids to roast weenies and marshmallows on the beach.

I learn to watch my mouth

A kid my age from a neighboring cottage came to the door, introduced himself and asked me if I wanted to play catch. We started hanging around together, hiking through the forest and exploring the beach. Walking along the shore one day, we spotted a girl who was about twenty yards out and treading water. She started talking to my new friend and for some reason I commented that she was a showoff. My remark really offended the kid because the girl happened to be his older sister. I was shocked and confused. Weren't all boys supposed to hate their big sisters?

Now my good buddy wanted to fight me. In fact, he set the time for the bout — seven p.m. And sure enough, right after supper he came over to spar with me. We squared off with our families watching from their respective porches, like the Hatfields and the McCoys. We circled and dodged; punched and tussled. We hit the ground together and wrestled. This kid was strong. I felt I wasn't going to last much longer. Luckily, a man who was walking by pulled us apart and stopped the fight. He even made us shake hands.

As we each turned toward our cottages cheers and applause came from both porches. I thought that I'd lost the contest and felt very embarrassed. Of course, Mom said I'd given a good accounting of myself. She had some antediluvian ideas about boys putting up their dukes, partly because of her brother Joe's neighborhood boxing exploits. I don't think Dad would have let the match continue if he'd been on the scene.

Mom's summer off

One summer Dad decided that our mother needed a break from her three older boys. He sent Jim, Dan and me to day camp at Foster Park. It was about a mile and a half from our house — a good walk for us kids — so we had to rise early and hustle to get there by eight.

There were about two hundred kids at camp — girls and boys aged eight to twelve. In the morning we gathered around the flagpole outside the field house. Mr. Patius, the chief counselor, led us in the Pledge of Allegiance as the flag was raised. Then we campers all threw our canvas lunch sacks into a big pile and headed off to begin the day's activities.

Each of us Murphy boys fell into a different age group, so we were separated. Jim, two years older than me, went to the Comanche Chiefs. Dan, a year my junior, was placed in the Apache Drums. I found myself among the Sioux Warriors.

Bright glaring fun

The park's recreational staff kept us busy. One hot afternoon we had to sprint forty yards in eight seconds, which I did. Another challenge was running the bases to a stopwatch. I hit home plate with a respectable time, but I'd missed one of the bases, so I didn't earn a certificate like Jim. On other afternoons my group played softball under the broiling-hot sun — not my idea of a good time. A softball coming at me was hard to keep in focus. What was worse, the game seemed very complex, with countless ways to goof up and look stupid.

So while the other kids were choosing up sides I disappeared behind some bushes and edged my way around the park, staying close to the fence. The foliage hid me until I was a safe distance from the baseball diamond. Then I darted into the field house and slipped downstairs to the basement where our lunch sacks were stored. In the very dim light I searched through them until I found the one stamped with number 168. Bag in hand, I headed for home. How I was able see in that poor light amazes me today.

"Wheel Day" at camp was a special day when kids could decorate their bikes or other vehicles and parade them around Foster Park's cinder track. Jim and I (with a little help from Dan and Joan) built a push car using scrap wood and wheels from a baby buggy. It was basically a long wide board to sit on, attached to a short one that supported the rider's back. We sawed the long board so it came to a sharp rakish point in front.

Together we painted the car bright red. It looked great. We agreed to call it "Fireball 4" after the four of us who'd worked on it. Joan painted the name on in fancy flowing letters using silver paint. When our cousin Mike dropped by that night we showed him the car and explained the "Fireball 4" name. Mike was quick to remind us that he'd done some work on the car as well — a fact that had slipped our minds. But geez, the name was already painted on. We talked it over and decided to include Mike by painting a number 1 after the 4. So the final moniker was "Fireball 41."

Riding the Fireball took practice. The driver's feet rested on the front axle, so straightening one leg or the other turned the wheels. Meanwhile, someone had to be pushing. Jim, Dan and I took turns shoving our vehicle to Foster Park but we were going nowhere slow. We wound up pulling it with a rope so we'd get there on time.

At the park we laced colored crêpe paper between the spokes of the wheels in time for the "Parade of Wheels." Then, as I pushed Jim around the track, I heard voices saying things like "Neat car" and "Way to go, Murph!" Hunched over I could only see the ground, but hearing all the kudos made me happy.

Made in the shade

Craft sessions in the field house made day camp worthwhile for me. They got me out of the scorching sun and into the fun-packed woodshop. Here we little Indians were surrounded by band saws, grinders, drill presses and other dangerous power tools. But thanks to careful supervision we used them without losing any fingers.

By the end of summer I'd made a Thunderbird-shaped thermometer, a wooden tomahawk, an Indian rattle, a shield, a tie rack and a ring-toss game. Through the shop sessions we were introduced to neat stuff like sandpaper, plywood, lacquer paint and shellac. It was great fun — not as healthy as baseball, but it gave us kids something tangible to show for our efforts.

Chapter 26

Obsessions

"Never worry worry
until worry worries you."
— Dad

"You're just supposed to put on a funny costume. You don't have to wear your dad's old coat!" Mom kept trying to get this through my head, but I knew what I had to do. The nuns at St. Columbanus School had sent us kids home with a flier promoting a big Halloween party in the auditorium. Jim, Joan and I all had a copy of the same little sheet. Joan read it out loud: "Make your own costume, wear your dad's old coat!" There it was in black and white. I was convinced that I had to follow those instructions to the letter or be the laughing stock of my kindergarten class.

My four-year-old mind was not able to fathom the note's intended message. Hell, I was too young to even *be* in kindergarten. My fragile grip on reality was no match for grownup sophisms. I had fixated on wearing Dad's old coat to the party and nothing else would do.

While I sulked by the kitchen radiator Mom helped Jim and Joan throw their costumes together. They were eager to get back to school for the afternoon party. Mom turned to me and said that I'd look great dressed as a hobo. I just cried and begged her to let me wear Dad's old coat. Finally, she gave up and said I'd have to stay home. So standing on a chair, I watched through the kitchen window as Jim and Joan exited the back yard through the alley gate. Laughing.

A happier Halloween

A few years later — after we'd moved to Auburn-Gresham — I enjoyed wandering through our neighborhood dime stores in the fall. Kresge's and Woolworth's had tons of Halloween paraphernalia on display — little jack-o-lanterns with handles for trick-or-treaters, masks, costumes, wax lips and face paint.

A huge glass case in Woolworth's was cram-packed with peanut butter kisses wrapped in orange and black waxed paper. Another held piles of colorful candy corn. Counter tops were lined with popcorn balls, candy apples and suckers shaped like pumpkins and ghosts.

I thought the ready-made costumes for kids were pretty neat. And it was fun to scan row after row of masks — simple ovals with eye holes, goofy clown masks made of stiffened cloth and rubber masks painted with black-and-blue bruises, bloody scars and dislodged eyeballs. I loved the rubber masks that would cover my whole head but their high prices scared me off.

Besides costumes and masks, the dime stores sold tons of decorations — bright cardboard pumpkins and spiders that folded open to 3-D shapes. There were life-sized, glow-in-the-dark skeletons, black cats, werewolf faces, witches on brooms and assorted goblins. In Woolworth's a string of big letters over the candy aisle spelled out HAPPY HALLOWEEN!

Our spooky little party

When I was in sixth grade Dan and I decided to throw a Halloween party. After Mom said we could use the dining room I fixated on finding decorations to cover every wall. My obsession took me to dime stores, drug stores, card shops and variety stores. I blew two week's worth of my paper route money on jack-o-lanterns, monsters, skeletons, witches and more. Then I plastered the dining room walls with all that kitch. I even hung orange-and-black streamers from the corners of the ceiling to the chandelier.

Six or eight kids from school showed up for the party. Two battery-powered plastic pumpkins cast an orange glow across the table. Munching on donuts and sipping apple cider, we talked about movie monsters — Frankenstein, Dracula, The Creature From The Black Lagoon, etc. Nobody seemed to be afraid of The Mummy, the monster I feared most. In the movie he could be summoned by burning nine tana leaves on the night of a full moon. Heck, anybody could do that. What if somebody who didn't like me lit nine tana leaves in front of my house while I was sleeping on the balcony? The Mummy might find me and...I dunno... scare me to death!

When the subject of witches came up our chatter drifted to the nuns at St. Leo. Their black outfits gave all of them a sinister look at first glance, but most of them weren't really too bad. Some were mean and some were ugly, but only a few of them were mean *and* ugly. I argued that my fourth-grade nun was both, qualifying her as a real witch.

We talked about what to wear for trick-or-treating on Halloween (just a few days off) and what turf to cover. I pushed for hitting the shops along busy 79th Street, especially the taverns. The past Halloween several guys sitting at the bar in a joint near my house had dropped quarters into my bag. So what if they broke my cookies.

Suddenly the room light snapped on and Mom appeared, reminding us that it was homework time. Holy cats — the party was over. After all my preparations, the whole shebang went by in flash.

The complete footballer

My parents gave me a football helmet and a jersey one Christmas. I tried them on and immediately wanted to tackle somebody. But with football season over I'd have to hold off until fall. A few weeks later, when our cousin Mike was visiting, he said I could have his old shoulder pads and football pants. Great! Here was more gear that I could add to my football outfit. When September finally arrived I used my paper route money to buy some hip pads. At last I felt fully equipped, although wearing all that gear made it hard for me to walk.

Then one Saturday at the Army Surplus store I spotted a cage-like contraption edged with soft leather padding. I asked the man at the counter what it was. "It's an eye protector for sports," he answered. *Darn*, I said to myself, *Here's something my football outfit is missing*! Over the next week I scrounged up a few bucks and purchased this extra protection. At home I put the eye mask on, then tried to get my helmet over it. No chance — the helmet had to go on first. So, head-in-helmet, I struggled with the awkward guard, stretching its elastic straps over the top. It stuck out like a Barcalounger from a car trunk.

The next time I went to the park, hoping to get into a pickup game of football, I looked way overdressed next to the other kids. One of them asked me about all my equipment — especially the wire cage strapped to my helmet. He said it looked weird.

With about a dozen kids, we got a game started, but my eye guard kept springing off. And putting it back on took so long that I was holding up the game. Finally, a dad who came to pick up his son asked me, "Where'd you get that thing? It's for a basketball player who wears glasses." I heard snickering behind me and felt like a dope. Back home I tossed the ugly contraption into a basement storeroom.

Cookie cutter Christmas

Early in December, right after my tenth birthday, I decided to buy Mom every Christmas cookie cutter in existence. On a mission, I hit both dime stores and all the hardware stores in the neighborhood. Within a short time I'd amassed an impressive array of brightly colored plastic cutters — Santas, snowmen, Christmas trees, gingerbread men, snowflakes and angels. I especially liked the deep star-shaped aluminum cutters I'd found.

On Christmas Mom seemed delighted as she opened each individually wrapped cutter. Unfortunately, she didn't get around to making cookies that Christmas, but there was always next year. Over the next few holiday seasons I reminded her to bake cookies so she could use all those cool cutters. But Mom's packed schedule never left time for that chore. She did put the deep aluminum cutters to use because they were actually little JELL-O molds.

More years passed. Then, when I was in high school and working at Auburn Food & Liquor, I got home late one December night to find a plate of Christmas cookies on the kitchen table. What was this? Picking one up I recognized the shape immediately. My mother had finally baked cookies using those cutters I'd given her way back when. Everybody was in bed, so those cookies were surely the only ones left. I could imagine Mom warning my brothers and sisters earlier that night, "Don't touch those cookies — they're for Joe!"

All that glitters

I was dazzled when Jim Dunbar showed me his rhinestone collection. What an array of sparkling stones he'd acquired — in so many shapes, sizes and colors. His flashy display really caught my attention. Jim said he got his gems from old buttons, earrings, broaches and such. Fascinated by Dunbar's cache of gems, I asked Mom if she had any old jewelry that she didn't want. Her answer was "No," but hooked on rhinestones, I quickly checked out other sources.

I browsed the jewelry at Frank's Department Store and visited a resale shop on Halsted. Their prices were staggering. Then I checked the neighborhood dime stores. Some of the baubles they sold were almost within my price range. One nice saleslady at Woolworth's gave me a pair of earrings that was missing a stone. And a big fake diamond came my way in a plastic ring — a prize from a gumball machine.

I even bought a kitschy plastic sword at Kresge's just to remove the large ersatz ruby from its hilt. I was acquiring stones of every hue — red, green, amber, blue. In myriad shapes — round, oval, square, rectangular. What a collection I was building. I kept my precious stones on a bed of cotton inside a tuna fish can. Protecting them was a little dome shaped lid — something I'd scavenged from a broken toy. My collection grew for several months, until one day at lunchtime.

Lunch was over. It was time to head back to school, but I was still attending to my gems. Mom told me several times to get going. "You'll be late!" she warned me. "In a minute, Mom!" I replied over and over as I rearranged my rhinestones. Suddenly she tore the tuna can from my hands and threw it at the kitchen wall. My treasured stones scattered in every direction.

I was astonished, and then I grew furious. "What'd you do that for?" I screamed, and scrambled to pick up the stones. Holding me back, she answered, "Get out of here and get back to school before I throw your rhinestones down the toilet!" I scooped up and pocketed a few of them before Mom handed me my coat, opened the kitchen door and pushed me out onto the porch.

I left for school in a terrible state of mind, not caring if I was late. That night and over the next week I found more of my lost stones, but Mom's tuna can toss had broken the gem spell. Glittering rhinestones soon lost their luster for me.

Don't sweat the small stuff

As the years passed my fixations were fewer and less intense, but certain compulsions proved useful. Some of Mom's obsession to keep things neat and clean rubbed off on me. I learned to not let things pile up or get out of control. At work I cleaned off my desk at the end of each day. From Dad I learned to finish the task at hand. I tried to follow his rule that "A job isn't finished until everything is cleaned up and all the tools are put away." Dad also taught me that no job has to be completely dreadful. There's always the reward of knowing that you did it right.

Chapter 27

Faith and morals

"I can resist everything except temptation."
— Oscar Wilde

Mom and Dad were both very religious in their own ways. When I was still in my baby crib Dad said nightly prayers with me in phrases that I repeated, one after another, "God bless Grandma and Grandpa Murphy...and Grandma and Grandpa Doyle...and all the souls in purgatory..." As the years passed I gave up the habit of saying bedtime prayers but Dad continued to kneel beside his bed each night and pray before retiring.

Mom often recited religious ejaculations when tough situations tested her strength. When her sister Theresa had brain surgery my mother went to mass and communion every morning for months. What's more, she and Aunt Martha traveled to a church miles from our neighborhood to attend nine-day novena services where they prayed for their ailing sister.

Bring flowers of the fairest

Each May Mom converted the top of her Singer sewing machine into a May Altar honoring the Blessed Virgin Mary. She laid out a white linen tablecloth and placed a lace doily in the center of it. Here she set our statue of the Blessed Virgin Mary, dressed in blue and with one of her feet crushing a serpent, Mary stood in this place of honor all through the month of May.

Everyone contributed flowers for the altar. We kids brought dandelions and peonies from the back yard, lilies of the valley from the gangway and maybe a few pink blossoms snatched from an apple tree on our route home from school. On some May evenings after supper Dad led the family in prayer as we knelt in the living room saying the rosary together.

Religion from the nuns

The Sisters of Providence drilled Catholic doctrine into us kids via the Baltimore Catechism. We memorized the Ten Commandments and learned about the Seven Sacraments. Heavy line illustrations in our catechisms helped to imprint messages into our tender minds. A sacrament was defined as "An outward sign instituted by Christ to give grace." This was reinforced by an illustration that showed Christ in the middle of a fountain with channels flowing from it in seven directions. They were labeled Baptism, Confirmation, Penance and so forth.

We learned the virtues of Faith, Hope and Charity, along with the corporal and spiritual works of mercy and the Eight Beatitudes. The seventh beatitude resonated with me. "Blessed are the peacemakers," it says, "for they shall be called the children of God." In our large family, arguments between siblings flared up frequently. Someone borrowed an item without asking or didn't want to share something. The result could be hitting, screaming, crying or name-calling. Noise and tension could replace domestic harmony at any moment. As I got older I learned how to break up skirmishes that disrupted the calm I needed to function (not that I didn't instigate my share of turmoil over the years).

At St. Leo the school day started with a little prayer called the Morning Offering: "Angel of God my guardian dear..." We also said the Our Father and Hail Mary during the day. And before we went home our nun led us in the Confiteor or the Apostles' Creed. I had to fake my way through more obscure prayers, like the Hail Holy Queen and the Memorare — I didn't have them memorized. Mom had learned all of these enigmatic prayers from the nuns who taught her in Sioux City, Iowa. And, to my astonishment, she could still recite them flawlessly.

The nuns taught us the Seven Deadly Sins — Pride, Envy, Lust, etc. We learned that venial sins were the little ones, like teasing your sister or swiping cookies from the pantry. Mortal sins were the big black ones that could send you to hell, where you would roast for all eternity.

We were cautioned to avoid "occasions of sin" that might make us falter. Cavorting with bad companions was an occasion of sin

— careful who you hang out with. I did OK on that score but with each year there were more occasions of sin, most of them involving the opposite sex.

Will the real sinner please stand up?

According to Sister Edward, my sixth grade nun, no number of venial sins could ever equal a mortal sin. I thought about this and it bothered me. To my way of thinking it meant that I could be a rude jerk, borrow money and not pay it back, loaf on the job, never do anything nice for anybody, not show up on time, refuse to pick up after myself, throw tantrums if I didn't get my way, hold grudges, not take a stand on anything, never give a penny to charity, cheat in school and tell lies to get ahead and still get a pass from God. It seemed to me that not one of the above was a mortal sin. So, in theory, I could be a total asshole for the rest of my life and then enter the Kingdom of Heaven. There was something wrong with this system.

"Bless me father for I have sinned..."

Confession is important to Catholics. They believe that by confessing their sins to a priest and receiving absolution their sins are forgiven. In fact, this telling and forgiving of sins constitutes the sacrament of Penance. And for many Catholics, unburdening themselves in the confessional also delivers the kind of peace of mind that other people seek from psychiatrists. But the confessional is free; the couch costs.

One day our nun explained "perfect contrition." This was being sorry for your sins because they offended God, not because they could send you to hell. If you were going to die with a mortal sin on your soul and couldn't confess your sins to a priest, only an act of perfect contrition could save you from everlasting flames. I didn't think I'd ever be able to make this perfect act. Fear of hell would be the overpowering motive for my repentance.

To remain in a state of grace and be worthy to receive communion we St. Leo kids were expected to confess our sins regularly. And according to guidelines set by the nuns, "regularly" meant once a week. With mass and communion scheduled for

Sunday, Saturday was confession day. The trouble was, confession scared the hell out of me.

Garden-variety sins, like calling my siblings names and fighting with them, were easy to tell. The way I saw it, there were only a few mortal sins that I was in danger of committing — sins that could send me to the fiery pit. They were: impure thoughts, taking the name of the Lord in vain and missing mass on Sunday.

❁ Dirty thoughts drove me nuts. I was never sure where a romantic fantasy ended and an impure thought began. If it felt too good I panicked. My brain froze solid. Then, before it could thaw, a gut-wrenching pang of guilt told me that I must have committed a mortal sin. Of course, the way my parents and the nuns avoided talking about sex, anything erotic had to be in the same league with murder. And so with that first mortal sin out of the way I could relax a bit, enjoying things like racy magazine covers, suggestive movie posters and dirty jokes. What the hell.

❁ Cursing didn't seem that bad. I heard neighborhood kids taking the name of God in vain all the time. It was something they picked up from their parents. I knew this because I'd heard their parents. I just couldn't see these kids burning in hell for the way they spoke every day. On the other hand, I never heard Mom or Dad say "Goddammit!" "Jesus Christ!" or even "For Chrissake!" But outside the house these expressions bombarded me like gamma rays.

❁ Missing Sunday mass was unthinkable. I always got there, although starting in fifth grade I was excused from the official nine o'clock mass for kids. My morning paper routes released me from this obligation. I went to early or late services — usually late ones at the high school chapel. Mom and Dad made sure that everyone went to church. Even on vacations our family always attended Sunday mass at the nearest Catholic church.

The ugly side of Saturday

I usually woke up on Saturday mornings feeling great. And I maintained a happy state of mind until about three p.m. when the dark, joy-killing cloud of confession rolled in. Mom would alert us, "Go to confession — you'll want to go to communion tomorrow." Walking through the house an hour or so later she'd remind us again, “Make sure you get to confession — they’re hearing till five.” The chapel was right up the block and the priests were waiting. Granted such easy access there was no reason for us to miss confession or communion the next day.

Proper preparation for confession involves a thorough examination of conscience. Accordingly, we were taught to recall the kinds of sins we’d committed, the circumstances surrounding them and the number of times we’d transgressed. Holding back sins from the priest was a serious matter. An illustration in my catechism pictured a kid kneeling in the confessional. A little devil crouched on his shoulder was talking into his ear, urging him not to tell all his sins. This made it very clear that we were not to fudge when ’fessing up.

The unforgiven

Telling my sins to a priest was never easy. But after I received Confirmation (a sacrament) in fifth grade, confession became much more of a burden. Opportunities to sin seemed to be everywhere, especially when it came to sex. Magazines at the newsstand on 79th Street and movie posters at the Capitol Theater pictured sultry females with deep dark cleavage. They gave me a delicious thrill I couldn’t control. Even a momentary glance at something erotic would come back to me when I was doing my paper route or trying to study.

Temptation ambushed me at every turn. Walking by George’s Record Shop on Halsted I might glance at the window and see Julie London on an album cover. WOW! What a skimpy dress! And that sexy look in her eyes! “Don’t look!” my conscience would scream. Turning away, I’d wonder if I did it fast enough. Oh boy, I’d probably committed mortal sin. Once again my soul was besmirched and not worthy to receive communion.

But what was I to do? Girls in tight-fitting tops were everywhere — on the street, in stores — even at church. Kneeling in my pew during mass I was aroused by the jiggling breasts of girls returning to their pews after receiving communion. I had to be the most degenerate kid alive! How was I going to explain this disgusting sin in confession?

Stewing in my sins

Kneeling in the chapel at age eleven, I tried hard to examine my conscience. The usual sins — disobeying, lying, fighting — came to mind automatically. But my clasped hands grew wet and clammy as I recalled the dirty thoughts I'd had. It was zero hour — time to describe them in detail to my confessor.

After I told my sins the "penance" required of me was usually a few Our Fathers or Hail Marys. Returning to my pew, I said these simple prayers before leaving the chapel. A year earlier this was an easy chore that took a few minutes. But now I felt compelled to say every Hail Mary perfectly, concentrating on the meaning of each word. Saying my penance took twenty minutes or half an hour. My wrenching gut told me that something in my head was out of wack.

Most of our parish priests listened patiently while we penitents rattled off our sins, occasionally questioning some detail. But there was one priest who found listening to confessions a crashing bore. I knelt quietly in the confessional box until the slide opened. In the dim light I could see the magazine on my confessor's lap. I began: "Bless me father for I have sinned..." But I'd only blurted one or two sins when I heard: "Three Hail Marys" and the slide closed, leaving me in the dark with a desperate unforgiven feeling. I had hardly begun to confess. Getting the short shrift was quite a shock. I was so upset that I got in line again and told my sins to a different priest — who listened to them.

Exiting confession one Saturday afternoon I was so distraught that I walked right by my bike, which I'd parked just outside the chapel. The next morning when Dad got home from early mass he told me that my bike was standing in front of the chapel. "Wake up!" he shouted. "Go get your bike before some kid steals it!"

Confession procession

In the Catholic Church Easter Sunday is the holiest day of the year — more sacred even than Christmas. As Easter approached the priests and nuns of St. Leo made sure that we grammar schoolers were prepared. A few days beforehand we filed out of our classrooms and walked next door to the church. Priests aplenty were waiting, not only in the dark confessional boxes but also at the front of the church, seated behind the altar railing.

Yikes! I might have to tell my sins right to the priest without the cover of darkness or even a screen hiding my face. True, the priest was facing sideways, not looking right at me. But what if he thought one of my sins was really awful? He might turn to me and shout, "You did what, Joseph Murphy? THAT IS A TERRIBLE SIN!" Oh God! Everyone in the church would hear! They'd know what a bad kid I was and blab to the multitude. Everyone would be talking behind my back. Nobody would go near me. I'd never have any friends. My family would be so disgraced and ashamed that they might have to move to another parish. What a relief it was to get that face-to-face confession over with and walk out of the dark church into God's refreshing sunshine.

A final mass was served at St. Leo Church before its demolition in 2005

Holy mackerel

In the Fifties church rules prohibited Catholics from eating meat on Friday. I grew up believing that to break this rule was a mortal sin. Even so, it was easy to forget what day of the week it was. One Friday Jim and I caught a double feature at the Capitol, then stopped at Wimpy's Grill and ordered burgers. After we'd taken a few bites one of us remembered what day it was. Oops! What to do? We talked it over and concluded that God wouldn't want us to waste food, so we finished our meals.

At home Mom fried fish for supper every Friday. She usually plunked a big slab of halibut or white fish into a cast iron skillet and turned on the burner. When it was dry and leather tough everyone at the table got a chunk of it to enjoy. This stuff was hard to chew and utterly tasteless. An extra glass of milk helped to move that stringy mass through my gullet. Dessert was a welcome part of Friday dinner. Dad tried to buy something really good to make up for the fish. It might be ice cream or cake or an apple pie. Occasionally he'd buy a cake roll — vanilla ice cream and chocolate cake rolled up together so a slice of it looked like a spiral.

Fish sticks and canned pizza

Dad must have burned out on of Mom's dry fish because he started buying fish sticks — fingers of cod with a breaded coating that kept them moist. We kids were happy with the change. And Dad decided that Open Pit barbecue sauce was the right stuff to put on them, so that's how we ate our fish sticks Friday after Friday. My father stuck with fish sticks and Open Pit for quite a while. He always brought frozen French fries home with them. Mom put everything on cookie sheets and slid them into the oven. With barbecue sauce on the fish and ketchup on the fries, the red sauces flowed freely. I ate with gusto, blocking from my mind the fierce heartburn that would soon attack.

A year or so later Dad discovered Chef Boyardee pizza mix. It came in a box that held all the ingredients. Mom made the dough, flattening it onto a cookie sheet. Then she poured on the canned sauce and added the grated cheese (also canned). This quick concoction went into the oven, and before long we had a pretty unspectacular, thin-crust pizza. Not having tasted real pizza, we kids loved this anemic imitation. In fact, we ate it every Friday night for months. Mom always served it with her lemony homemade iced tea.

When I was in eighth grade my friend John Keating joined us for Friday pizza a few times. I could see that John had a big appetite, but I didn't fully appreciate its size until one night at his house. We were high school freshmen working on our Latin homework after supper. Mrs. Keating served us a snack — a whole package of warm Parker House rolls. I had one or two. John made short work of the rest, slathering them generously with butter. No wonder he grew big enough to play tackle on Leo's varsity squad as a sophomore.

Chapter 28

The untouchables

"There are lots of cute little dolls out there with lots of cute little shapes."
— Dad

"Why would you steal something like that?" The surprised woman directed her question at me through the steel bars of her ticket booth. I'd just been caught swiping a "Girlie" magazine from a newsstand at the Jackson & State subway stop. Two black teenage boys — both older and bigger than me — had nabbed me and escorted me to the turnstile beside the lady's booth. I was in shock. My curiosity and carnal cravings had done me in.

The police will be here any minute to haul me away, I assured myself. Then suddenly a rush of subway riders herded up to the ticket booth, separating me from my captors. I turned and tore up the stairs to the sidewalk. Rounding the corner, I ran two full blocks before looking back. Nobody was chasing me. Whew! I went into a restaurant, plopped in front of the counter and ordered a Coke. After catching my breath I sat numb and drained, reflecting on my sinful ways. I decided to go home. The Latin and algebra homework waiting for me would help purge my mind of dirty thoughts.

Riding the "El" train back to 63rd & Halsted I wondered what had happened to my brain. Just a year earlier I was a good kid, bravely fighting off impure thoughts. Now I was traveling miles on a train to steal pictures of naked women. The demon hormones surging through my head were making me behave like a sex fiend. Things that had been mild erotic suggestions a year before were now powerful temptations.

The call of the blondes

To my adolescent mind a shapely peroxide blonde was the ultimate sex symbol. Movies and magazine covers bulged with buxom blondes. Not to mention posters, billboards and record album covers. Blondes were beautiful. Gentlemen preferred blondes. Marilyn Monroe, Anita Ekberg, Kim Novak and Jayne Mansfield all knocked me out. So did Connie Stephens, Diana Dors, Tuesday Weld and Sandra Dee. TV ads for Clairol blonde hair dye asked seductively, "Does she or doesn't she...?" And "Is it true blondes have more fun?"

It seemed that images of lusty busty blondes popped up wherever I traveled. In my adventures downtown I gasped at the life-sized pictures of peroxide blondes in the windows of nightclubs. And the dirty magazine I found in the alley one day was packed with bleachy blondes. After I'd flipped through its pages I stuffed the rag into a garbage can. Then it struck me that some folks were pretty careless about how they disposed of racy materials. Didn't they have any scruples about corrupting the morals of an unsuspecting youth such as myself?

Even local Chicago TV shows favored blondes. *Super Circus*, broadcast live on Sunday afternoons, featured Mary Hartline, a shapely peroxide drum majorette. Her bleached hair was whiter than Dad's. At the same time Alfred Hitchcock was casting blondes for the lead parts in his films — Janet Leigh in *Psycho*, Tippy Hedron in *The Birds*, Kim Novak in *Vertigo*...

Softer sweeter blondes

Of course, there were some classy blonde women in the movies too — stars like Grace Kelly, June Allison, Deborah Kerr and Doris Day. Doris was a honey blonde with a sweet disposition. Refreshingly clean-cut, she sang like an angel. Ah, that golden hair, those true-blue eyes, those ruby-red lips and snow-white teeth. Often called "America's Sweetheart," Doris projected a wholesome, motherly persona. How could innocence be so sexy? I don't think my fifth-grade nun could have blamed me for having a crush on this lovely lady.

There were blonde girls in my eighth grade class but they were "natural" blondes — ash blondes, strawberry blondes and such. No girl's mother would send her daughter to St. Leo with peroxide hair. It was during high school when girls started bleaching their hair. Joan was in high school but none of her girlfriends had platinum hair. No, girls with hair like that must be wild, I concluded. They, no doubt, lacked parental supervision and went to public high schools.

Endless infatuation

I had a crush on Agnes Doherty all the way through grammar school. She was so petite and cute. Her pretty blue eyes contrasted magically with her dark eyebrows. The combination sent an electric charge through my body. Of course, I dared not advertise my feelings about her. I sometimes saw Agnes on Saturday mornings shopping with her mom at the A&P. Rarely did I say anything — maybe "Hi" a few times. But on one occasion I grew incredibly bold and shouted after Agnes as she crossed the street. "You're a beautiful doll!"

In truth, I had a practical reason for hanging around the A&P on Saturday morning. It was prime shopping time and I could make a little money hauling groceries. Sitting in my coaster wagon outside the store, I waited for ladies to exit carrying overfull bags. As they passed I asked if I could deliver their groceries for a quarter. A surprising number of women took me up on my offer, placing their goods in my wagon. I followed them home, recruiting their help when going up and down curbs, so their purchases wouldn't tumble out of the wagon.

After I'd staked out the A&P for a few weeks, things got a bit rocky. As I stood near the door with my wagon, a tough-talking kid about my age approached me. He asked what the hell I was doing trying to deliver groceries. "Where's Throop? Where's Laflin? Where's Union?" he demanded to know. After the street quiz he said I wasn't strong enough to carry groceries up a flight of stairs. "You'd be shittin' in your pants," he barked. It seemed that he had a lock on the A&P delivery business and I was horning in on him. This same guy, Dave O'Donnell, wound up in my class at Leo High

School. Before long we became good friends. In fact, we still send each other Christmas cards every year.

Getting back to Agnes, my crush on her grew into an obsession in sixth grade. There were spring days when I came home from school, got on my bike and spent the next two hours riding around the block where she lived. Occasionally I stopped, pretending to check something on my bike. Once or twice I even pulled off the sidewalk onto somebody's parkway. Turning my bike upside-down on the grass, I inspected my chain or tires as if I were having some mechanical problem — all the while hoping to catch a glimpse of Agnes walking by.

About this time it dawned on me that school wasn't all that challenging. The curriculum didn't get much harder from year to year. It seemed like a re-hash of what we'd had before — especially religion and arithmetic. I never heard the word "math" until I was in high school. However, the words in our red "Spellers" got longer and trickier each year. I noticed that Agnes always got 100% on her tests.

With three years of grammar school still ahead of me I decided to buckle down and become one of the "smart" kids in my room. It steamed me when I recalled that Kathleen O'Donnell had once called me "the dumbest kid in the class!" In fact, she shouted it at me as I walked home from school with Jim Dunbar. His teasing had whipped her into a rage. And after laying into him she gave it to me. I hadn't said a word. Just being with Dunbar made me fair game for her fury.

Walking with Dunbar was never dull. Sometimes he followed close behind a group of girls in our class, mouthing smart remarks that they could hear like, "How'd we get stuck behind so many ugly legs?" I learned to take questions like these as rhetorical ones and keep my mouth shut.

The big thermometer

My eighth-grade nun picked me to draw a huge thermometer that would show the level of our room's contributions to the missions. On a piece of white poster board I drew a tall column with a big red reservoir at its base. Hash marks up to the top indicated increasing donations. As money came in more of the thermometer would be filled in with a red crayon. At the top I added some expressive lines bursting up and out. Tadah!

As I finished the poster a few other kids were still working on after-school projects. Just as I leaned the completed chart against the window Agnes walked by, pointing at my artsy lines. In an exaggerated voice, she asked: "Oh my, what do these lines mean?" I was petrified — I couldn't come up with an answer — simple, clever, sarcastic — nothing! Is she making fun of me? I wondered. But wow! She actually talked to me! Despite my lasting crush on Agnes, I never spoke a full sentence to her until one day when we bumped into each other at a CTA bus stop. I was a sophomore in college.

Judy, Judy, Judy...

In my early teens, when I was in the Civil Air Patrol, a girl in my squadron named Judy just knocked me out. I thought she was gorgeous. The form-fitting Air Force uniform she wore accentuated her wonderful shape. What's more, her gown-up sophistication dazzled me. Judy talked to the other female CAP cadets about things I couldn't fathom. She mentioned her great report card and described some guy who was "just dreamy."

Judy was alert and intelligent. She asked incisive questions during our weekly meetings at Foster Park. Her eyebrows drove me crazy. I loved the way she cocked her hat. Our Tuesday night gatherings concluded in crisp military fashion on the concrete in front of the field house. The squadron assembled in two groups. Standing at attention, I heard, "A flight, all present accounted for sir!" Then "B Flight, all present accounted for sir!" Then, "Dismissed." When we broke up the girls — Judy, Joan and Carol — headed south. Jim and I, along with Bob Schwellenbach, a classmate of mine at Leo, turned north and hiked back home.

I kept trying to talk to Judy but a conversation never resulted. My words came out in short, incoherent blurbs. I felt like a social retard, but part of the problem was the artificial setting. Our squadron leader, a year older than me, was a lieutenant who took himself very seriously. The first time I wore my uniform, he fumed at the way I'd pinned the CAP insignias onto my collars. His pimpled face was beet red as he removed and repositioned the hardware. This kid's skills with girls were zip — worse than mine. He didn't chat with girls — for him they were a nuisance. The lieutenant was so intense, I thought he might have a heart attack before finishing high school. The more I saw of the Civil Air Patrol, the more characters like him I met from other Chicago area squadrons. They were intense humorless kids trying to skip their teens and become adults. My stint in the CAP turned me off toward anything military.

The blonde from nowhere

"At last I've found a paradise...nature tamed completely and more bountiful than ever before..." The time traveler's words introduced me to the world of the Eloi in *The Time Machine.* It was late in August the summer before my senior year at Leo. I'd strolled over to the Capitol Theater by myself to see the movie version of the H.G. Wells sci-fi classic.

Everything about that film captivated me. I loved the tranquil, garden-like world the time traveler visits. Weena, the blonde girl he meets, took my breath away. In the story she's one of the Eloi people, living in the sunshine on the earth's surface. But the fair-haired Eloi are slaves to the deformed subterranean Morlocks, who raise them like cattle and eat them.

After helping the Eloi defeat their cave-dwelling masters, the time traveler revisits the present, but only briefly. He returns to the future to live out his days with the angelic Weena. *Where is my Weena?* I wondered, feeling pangs of sadness and loneliness. My soul ached to find the perfect girl but I hadn't yet been on my first date.

Chapter 29

High school days

"You're no mental giant, Murph!"
— Brother Coogan, 1958

After a summer fraught with worries about starting high school I wound up arriving two days late. Thanks to our extended visit to Jack's house both Jim and I had to get up to speed fast. I felt like an intruder walking into class. Things were already in motion and here I was interrupting the flow. Catching up in Latin and algebra was a pain in the butt. (I never did catch up in algebra.)

On my first day at Leo I learned that I couldn't go home for lunch without getting a lunch pass from the office. This little yellow card allowed me to exit the building at noon. A faculty member stationed at the alley door made sure that only students with passes left the premises during school hours. Living less than a block from Leo was a mixed blessing. On the positive side I could eat a home-cooked lunch and I didn't have to take a bus to school. On the negative side I missed out on riding the CTA with my classmates. We could have talked about girls, swapped homework and horsed around. I might have made more friends.

High School was a series of highlights and lowlights. In freshman gym class Bob Hanlon, our instructor, told everyone to do pushups like I did. "Watch Murphy, he has perfect form!" As a sophomore I got caught helping a kid on a religion quiz. We both got zeros from Brother O'Hare. In junior year I tripped in the hall and kicked a football player who was crouched at his locker. He got up and punched me in the jaw. The next year my English teacher liked my essays so much, he read them to other classes. Other episodes from my stint at Leo still come to mind now and then.

The notebook tragedy

Tall, distinguished-looking Brother Sullivan required that we freshmen maintain a notebook for his religion class. We had to outline each chapter covered by the textbook. In order to keep us honest Sullivan periodically collected our notes and checked them. He also made all the rows of kids compete against each other in contributing to the missions each week. The winning row escaped homework for one night. If someone created a disturbance in class Sullivan corrected them in a literate manner that made them feel stupid.

I was dragging my butt through religion. Moses and John the Baptist bored me to death. Keeping my notes updated seemed impossible — I was always a chapter or two behind. Then something happened that multiplied my woes. One afternoon my English teacher, Mr. Charles Byrne, checked to see if the class had written an essay that was due. I had totally forgotten about it.

Byrne walked up and down the aisles, peering over each kid's shoulder. I tried to bluff by opening my religion notebook and folding it back to make it look like a single page. I covered the title, *The Life of St. Joseph*, with my forearm. Byrne stopped at my desk and snatched the notebook. Turning beet red, he tried with all his strength to tear it in half. After three or four attempts the pages ripped. He strode to the front of the room and pitched my ravaged religion notes into the wastebasket. Then Charlie sent me to jug.

Sitting in detention after school, I wondered what to tell Brother Sullivan about my lost notes. In retrospect, I should have returned to Byrne's classroom after school, retrieved the notebook and repaired it with Scotch Tape. Instead, I went to jug, then walked home and told Mom what had happened.

"Why don't you just do your homework like you're supposed to?" she asked angrily. "Now you've got all that work to make up." As I sat at the dining room table after supper pecking at my homework I could hear Mom relating my story to Dad in the living room. She questioned the right of a teacher to destroy work that a student had done for another class. The next day Dad phoned the Leo faculty building and made an appointment to see Brother Sullivan on Saturday. He told me that we'd both be going.

Saturday morning we walked a block to the handsome brick structure that housed the Irish Christian Brothers. A nice middle-aged lady answered the door and showed us into a waiting room. When Sullivan entered a few minutes later Dad introduced himself. He explained what had transpired in Mr. Byrne's class.

My religion teacher was sympathetic but he said I'd have to do the lost work over again. Dad looked at me resignedly, then at my teacher. They agreed that I would start in on a new religion notebook, working on it at the faculty building each Saturday morning. *Saturday morning,* I thought, *That's my favorite time of the week!* Losing two hours of prime free time each Saturday morning was a drag, but with no distractions my efficiency was miraculous. I brought my religion notes up to date within a few weeks.

The joys of jug

Jug was detention. Kids at Leo went to jug for offenses like smarting off in class or not completing homework assignments. Detention meant staying after school for an hour. As a freshman I was sent to jug several times, mostly for homework violations. Every brother and lay teacher at Leo had a pack of detention slips permanently molded into the palm of one hand. They could scribble a kid's name in a flash, along with the number of days to be spent in jug. The offender received a slip and a duplicate went to the jug room, 212. During regular school hours this large room was a lecture hall.

Jug period began right after school, with Brother Ryan presiding as detention monitor. He wrote arbitrary page numbers on the blackboard — maybe 134-138. Everyone, from freshmen to seniors, copied those pages from their literature books. Meanwhile, Ryan read the jug slips aloud, including the number of days: "Morrissey, one day, Walsh three days," etc.

Sometimes a confused kid would raise his hand and ask, "Hey bro, there's a picture on page 134 in my book. How am I s'posta copy that?" A little annoyed, Ryan would answer, "Then start on page 135!" We'd sit there quietly copying parts of stories instead of doing something productive, like homework. But to be honest, I found those stories more interesting than most of my homework assignments.

When I was a freshman a big blonde kid named Jim LaDuke was in jug every time I went. And his jug slips were long ones — for several days — and from multiple teachers. Ryan would read through the pile: "LaDuke — three days...LaDuke — two days... LaDuke — indefinite! (Indefinite jug meant you went until the teacher decided you'd had enough). One day the sullen Ryan even joked, "LaDuke, you're going to earn a major letter in Jug this year. We'll have to sew a big J on your jacket."

I knew LaDuke through my cousin Mike. As kids growing up, Mike, Jim and a few other guys hung out together and played ball in their neighborhood a few miles east of Leo turf. I always thought Jim was a nice kid. His high score on Leo's entrance exam got him placed in 1A, the brightest group of freshmen. A kid in his class told me that LaDuke had separated the test's two-ply sheets so he could see which of the multiple-choice answers were the right ones. Maybe, but I think Jim was much smarter than he pretended to be.

According to my cousin, the office at Leo told LaDuke at the end of his freshman year that he still had more that a hundred days of detention left to serve. He was expected to make good on them if he came back as a sophomore. When I started my second year LaDuke was gone. He may still hold school records for the most days of jug and the highest entrance exam score.

The exploding letter

Brother Hennessey, my freshman algebra teacher, was a hefty middle-aged man with a shiny bald head and a flair for the dramatic. Looking down his nose through his wire-rimmed glasses, he pontificated in a pompous, nasal voice. He reiterated pet phrases, like, "Now boys, we must watch our signs," referring to plus and minus signs. "Low grade moron" was another expression he favored in certain contexts like, "Only a low grade moron would do that" or "You don't want to be a low grade moron do you?"

Hennessey liked to stage little entertainments featuring kids who didn't complete their homework. The slackers were summoned to the front of the room. Then, one by one, they were punished. Each kid bent over while Hennessey whacked him in the rear end with a drumstick. Hennessey had a special rhythm — bam bam...

bam! Just when the first two smacks were really starting to smart he laid in a final one that brought the exquisite pain he loved to inflict.

One day when I didn't finish my homework assignment (being clueless as to how I should approach it) I tried to buffer the sting of the drumstick waiting for me in the afternoon. While home for lunch I took a letter from the morning mail, slipped it under my jockey shorts and walked back to school. When Hennessey collected the homework I was in trouble. He called me and one other deadbeat to the front of the room. As we bent over to take our raps, one of my classmates shouted, "Hey, Murphy stuck a letter in his pants!" Instantly others chimed in: "Murphy has a letter in his pants — yeah, he stuck a letter under his pants!"

Hennessey pretended not to hear these complaints as he disciplined the kid in front of me. When he hit me, however, the letter under my pants sounded like a loud cap pistol. The class went nuts, some kids laughing and others complaining about my added protection. But, to his credit, Hennessy silenced them and told me to get back to my seat.

Coogan's Latin Club

My fifteen-year-old mind did not place a high priority on Latin. All that crap to memorize — vocab words, declensions, verb forms — yuk! Studying and translating was tedious, using up time that could have been spent playing touch football or watching TV. But on the positive side, Brother Coogan, my sophomore Latin teacher, was a bright young guy who projected energy and had a wry sense of humor that I liked.

In response to my incorrect answer Coogan once fired a barb at me in front of the class. "You're no mental giant Murph!" he said, his Ivy League accent adding a bit of extra sting. The line and its delivery made me laugh out loud. This really irritated him. "You can laugh? You can laugh at that Murphy?" He asked. "You're great Murph — you're really something, you know that?" Now everybody was laughing.

The day Coogan described the ablative absolute I thought he was joking. He tried to make this quirky Latin construction sound classy and elegant. It puts any words that are absolutely detached from the rest of the sentence into the ablative case. OK. But then there was something about a noun or pronoun and a participle... forming an adverbial phrase...that would require a subordinate clause...zzzzzzz. I drifted off to slumberland. It was the only time I ever fell asleep in a high school class. Luckily, the ablative absolute faded into Latin limbo and never showed up on a test.

Quiz scores lower than 80% put some of us in Coogan's after-school "Latin Club." We had to stay and study our vocab words, then take another quiz. If our scores didn't improve we'd be copying definitions multiple times at home that night.

One day during spring football tryouts the Latin Club was making me and another kid late for practice. When we informed Coogan of this he commented frankly on our football prospects, "You're wasting your time — you're not big enough, you're not fast enough and you're not mean enough!" As it turned out, he was right.

Morrissey's mouth

Tom Morrissey couldn't control his quips in Latin class. His off-the-cuff cracks just kept coming. Tom was a heavy-set kid who made me think of Oliver Hardy as a youngster. Coogan was pretty good at keeping him at bay, but one day Morrissey went too far. Thoroughly pissed, our young teacher decided that major humiliation was in order.

With an orange stuffed in his mouth, Morrissey had to stand in a corner holding Webster's Unabridged Dictionary over his head. He stood there like that for most of the period, so by the time the bell rang, the dictionary had sunk to the top of his head and orange juice was dripping down his chin onto his shirt and tie. Next period Tom was back up to speed with his spontaneous comments.

Rousing pep rallies

Before football or basketball games against arch rivals, like Mount Carmel or St. Rita, the entire student body streamed into Leo's tiny gym, filling the courtside bleachers and the gallery above. Standing at center court, the principal, athletic director and coach took turns talking into a microphone, trying to pump us up. Then the team captains said a few words. Next our cheerleaders (all boys) took over, shouting into their big cone-like horns.

Cheer Ldrs: *Can the big team fight?*
Students: *Yeah man!*
Cheer Ldrs: *Can they fight all night?*
Students: *Yeah man!*
Cheer Ldrs: *Well who says so?*
Students: *We say so!*
Cheer Ldrs: *And who are we?*
Students: *Leo!* (Wild cheers and applause)

Another cheer that really shook the building had us all stomping our feet in time with the band's bass drum:

Lions! Lions! Boom, boom....boom-boom-boom!
Lions! Lions! Boom, boom....boom-boom-boom!

The noise level was deafening. Our tiny gym vibrated. As a timid freshman I feared that the building might topple. Finally, the band played the Leo fight song. Everyone sang:

Oh when those Leo men fall into line
And their colors black and orange are unfurled
You see those brawny stalwarts wait the sign
And their might against the foe is hurled
For then the foe shall feel the Lion's might
And the spirit of our team's attack
For with every heart and hand
We will fight as one strong band
For the honor of the orange and the black. Rah! Rah! (More cheers and applause)

When the rally was over we returned to our classrooms, where *The Oriole*, our school paper, was distributed. We were allowed ten minutes or so to look at it before early dismissal.

Going out for football

Encouraged by my alley football friends, I tried out for the varsity squad in my sophomore year. My goal was to play quarterback. And to equip myself I bought a pair of racy, low-cut spikes at Bill Johnson's Sporting Goods on 79th Street. Walking home I pictured myself rolling right in my new low-cuts and chucking a long pass down the sideline to my wide-open receiver. He took the ball in over his shoulder, striding into the end zone for a touchdown. The crowd went wild!

Back on earth Leo High School's varsity tryouts began with sprints in the hall bordering the locker room. The fast guys covered this stretch in three seconds flat. I was maybe two tenths slower — fairly fast but not really fast. Trials continued at Shewbridge Field. Here, along with the other QB hopefuls, I conducted a pass line, tossing the football to receivers who ran out on short patterns. My passes were on target and I was glad nobody was going long. The arm sprouting from my 133-pound frame could only throw about thirty-five yards.

And since I'd never played on a helmeted football team I looked lame in blocking and tackling drills. Two weeks into the tryouts a chart was posted listing me as the fifth-string quarterback. Oh Christ! I ran my fifth-rated backfield through a few simple plays for a week but quit the tryouts without ever throwing a pass in a scrimmage.

A couple guys at school razzed me, calling me a "quitter" and it hurt. But I still enjoyed playing touch football on concrete or asphalt. Over the next year I picked up speed and became more sure-handed. Occasionally, I'd make a grab that drew applause from someone passing by on the sidewalk. Then, halfway through junior year, something possessed me to try out for football again. This time I went out for end, hoping to catch my way onto the squad. I stuck with it until the very last day of tryouts.

On that fateful final day we varsity wannabes approached coach Arneberg on the practice field. Each kid got the Yea or Nay verdict, then took off from a football stance and sprinted to the locker room. When my turn came, the coach looked at me a little embarrassed and said, "Sorry Murph, I guess you're cut." I put on my helmet and took my stance. "Hit it!" the coach barked. I dashed toward the locker room wondering why I should hurry.

Visiting the chapel

A few times a year, on Holy Days of Obligation, the entire student body herded downstairs into the chapel via a mysterious route that I could never find on my own. Somehow my class was always seated near the altar, which was raised one step above the floor and surrounded by marble railings. After sliding into the pews we knelt and said a quick prayer before sitting.

Everyone rose when the priest and altar boys emerged from the sacristy and proceeded to the altar. The service was usually a low mass (with only two candles burning and no singing) so it was over in forty minutes or so. The entire class went to communion before returning to class. It amazed me that every one of us was in a state of grace and worthy to receive the sacrament of Holy Communion.

My senior job

At the start of my senior year I got an after-school job at Auburn Food & Liquor on 81st & Halsted. Part of the Certified chain, it was a good-sized neighborhood grocery store. The place looked a little shopworn, but that gave it a comfortable character. On the day I started my very first task was hauling a load of groceries on the store's ugly beat-up delivery bike. It had a small wheel up front that made room for the giant basket above it.

It took leg strength and good balance to propel the bike when it was heavy with grocery orders. Going down a curb or hitting a pothole could make the bike cartwheel, tossing the rider and his deliveries onto the street. I learned this the hard way. On the positive side, powering a loaded delivery bike really built up my thigh muscles.

Addresses for deliveries were written on the same piece of paper that listed a customer's grocery order. Long and narrow, it came off a roll. Claude, a likeable long-time employee, took delivery orders with the phone tucked under his chin. Gripping a heavy pencil he hand-listed each item and its price, putting the total at the bottom. Claude was sharp and neat but his hearing was bad.

On more than one occasion he wrote down the wrong address and sent me on a wild goose chase. I remember a freezing-cold night when I cycled east — all the way to Vincennes Avenue — and then north for several blocks, looking for the address that Claude had given me. Had it been the address of a real customer, his house would have been located inside the CTA bus barn.

Once I had the feel of the delivery bike I had no trouble loading four cases of beer into its cavernous basket and delivering them to faithful guzzlers. On more than one occasion I was intercepted before I could get the beer to its destination. As I approached the address, two or thee teenage boys popped out of a parked car and flagged me down. One of them asked me if I had a delivery for Mr. Brown (or whoever). When I answered yes, he said that he was Mr. Brown, and paid me. Then he and his buddies moved the beer from my bike to the trunk of their car.

Snapshots of the store

I met some characters at Auburn, including Wally, the stock boy who'd worked there the longest. A muscle freak, Wally worked out to make his biceps bulge like bricks. If he didn't like someone they were a "pringding." He had a crush on a pretty girl named Chris who frequented the store. I knew her a little because our older sisters were friends. Whenever Wally tried to strike up a conversation with Chris she ignored him. Her stuck-up attitude must have enhanced her allure.

One night Chris entered the cooler to get a large bottle of pop. She went in through the big door that we used for loading. Observing this, Wally decided to have a little fun, so he locked her in. Finding the door locked, Chris acted decisively — knocking over rows of bottles so they dominoed into the glass doors used by customers. The first person that opened one of those doors would release an avalanche of glass bottles filled with beer and pop onto to the hard floor. Realizing this, Wally quickly unlocked the cooler door. Chris exited smiling. As she walked toward the checkout counter Wally scrambled into the cooler to straighten the toppled bottles before some customer opened one of the glass doors in the store.

The butcher shop at the rear of the store did a thriving business. Bob, the cheerful young butcher, cut steaks, chops and roasts with a confident flair. He also sold great pastries supplied by a local bakery. A narrow corridor led to another rear section of the store. It wasn't much more than a short passageway with a sink. Here Bernie, the diminutive produce man, washed and trimmed fruits and veggies. He was a pleasant little guy unless you left something, like a hand truck, sitting on his limited turf.

Out back there was much more to see. To the right stood a freezer with a thick door, secured at night with a padlock. (I had irrational fears that I might get locked inside and be found frozen stiff the next morning.) To the left was an oft-frequented cooler for milk. Gallon glass bottles and cardboard cartons needed constant replenishing inside the store. And down in the asphalt yard (about five feet below the cooler) was a heated garage for canned goods, beer and pop. We wheeled stock to and from the garage on hand trucks — up and down a narrow wooden ramp. There were only a few inches of width to spare for the rubber tires on our trucks.

The rat

Another experienced stock boy (I'll call him Phil for political reasons) was a stinky nasty character. He'd worked at another neighborhood grocery store where he learned to stamp prices on cans, stock shelves, keep the coolers filled and so forth. He knew about pricing as well. By checking a three-ring binder from the distributor he could figure out the correct price to be stamped on any item in the store.

This process involved finding the wholesale price and then adding the proper markup to arrive at the retail price. I wondered how he had earned his pricing privilege. Phil tried to make the process look like a problem in celestial mechanics that only his superior intellect could grasp. Even worse were the dirty tricks he pulled on me. If Phil dropped a glass jar of applesauce and it crashed to the floor, he would shout "Nice going, Joe!" I could be in some distant part of the store, but the boss would think it was me who screwed up. Phil was a rat. I had no respect for him.

That's why I was delighted with what happened when the two of us were filling the cooler one night. We had to haul big loads of beer and pop up the slippery outside ramp into the store and over to the cooler. It took heavy-duty hand trucks with fat, air-filled tires to handle the job. One guy got the cases and wheeled them into the store while his partner stayed in the cooler stacking them and putting single bottles in rows so customers could access them through the big windowed doors in the store.

When I was working the hand truck I just took one load at a time — Pepsi, 7-up, Meister Bräu beer, whatever. Phil had his own system. He went out to the garage and set up all his loads in stacks before binging any of them into the store. It was Phil's night to go get the beer. Fine with me — the temperature outside was around zero. When he left to set up his loads I knew he'd be gone for a while. This gave me time to restock rows of bottles and push them closer to the customer windows.

Where the hell is Phil?

I thought he'd be back by the time I'd tidied up the cooler. But for some reason he wasn't. *What's keeping's him?* I wondered. Well, I figured he knew what he was doing. To kill more time I sorted through some cans of imported beer in a box at the rear of the cooler. Their labels were printed in foreign languages and they were rusty with age. Finally it hit me that Phil might be in some kind of a jam, so, I decided to take a look outside.

Exiting the back door I spotted Phil immediately. He was lying with his back pressed against the slippery ramp. On top of him was a hand truck stacked with five cases of beer. He'd slipped backing up the icy incline so everything had come down on top of him. "Where the f__k you been?" he screamed. "I been stuck here for twenty minutes." "Sorry," I said. "I thought you were in the garage setting up your loads."

"Get this off me!" he commanded. I lifted the hand truck so Phil could slide out from under it. He got to his feet and took the handle, cussing about how cold he was. Phil struggled up the ramp with his load and into the store. While I loaded the beer into the cooler he warmed himself in the back room, swearing under his breath. I made extra noises as I stashed the bottles so he wouldn't hear me laughing.

Store chores

There was plenty to do to at Auburn Food & Liquor — even after closing time. Before we could leave we had to sweep the floors, and one night each week we had to swab it. Mopping up was a pain in the ass. Even worse, things got downright scary near the checkout counters. The wet floors conducted electricity from the cash registers, sending a mild electric shock through the soles of my shoes. My tingling feet told me to mop fast and get away from that part of the floor.

Saturday morning at the store was hell. Customers poured in to do their weekly grocery shopping. The checkout area, a single aisle with a register on each side, was a mob scene. It got so clogged that customers sometimes had trouble opening the door to exit.

Every few months there was a Saturday milk catastrophe. Someone leaving the store swung a gallon glass bottle into the front door, breaking the bottle, the glass pane in the door and its burglar alarm tape. Milk splattered everywhere as the alarm bell blared with ear-piercing volume. Alerted by that familiar noise, a couple of us stock boys rushed to the front with buckets and mops. We tried to avoid tripping customers as we picked up the jagged pieces of glass and sopped up the milk with our mops.

Everybody out!

The Saturday milk spills paled in comparison to The Little Bo-Peep Incident. It happened in midwinter on Thursday, which was stock day. A forty-foot truck from Certified Grocers arrived each Thursday, replenishing our supply of just about everything. We wheeled in hand trucks loaded with goods, then hurried to stamp prices on them and get them onto the shelves.

Amid this blur of activity one of the stock boys (not me) dropped a case of glass bottles filled with ammonia. The overpowering fumes spread quickly. Ken Eberly, the owner, made everybody — customers and employees — evacuate the store. Then he and Len, a long-time employee, tried running back into the place, one at a time, to mop up. They dashed in for maybe thirty seconds, then ran out, choking and gagging from the fumes. It was clear that this drill was not going to work. Amid the melee someone had the good sense to call the Fire Department.

Within a few minutes a pulmotor arrived. Two firemen stepped off the truck, put on masks and entered the store. They knew what they were doing — twenty minutes later the situation was under control. Airing out the store with fans and open doors took another hour or so. That Thursday did not rank among Auburn Food & Liquor's best days for sales. I never found out who dropped that case of Little Bo-Peep ammonia. Nobody ever owned up to it.

Congraduations!

The spring of '61 saw four Murphy graduations. Joan matriculated from Mundelein College, Jim graduated from Calumet High, I got my diploma from Leo and Margaret Mary said good-bye to St. Leo Grammar School. You couldn't swing a tassel without hitting a grad. Happy to have high school out of the way, I looked forward to a summer of earning tuition money for college. I couldn't have imagined what lie in store for me during the summer of '61.

All six Murphy brothers, August, 1961 (l to r) Front: Pat, Tom. Back: Jim, Jack, Joe, Dan

Chapter 30

Crush of a lifetime

"Do you have a rosary with you?"
— Mom

June 20th, 1961 was a beautiful sunny day. I woke up thinking about the nice 35mm camera I'd put on layaway at Polk Brothers a few days earlier. Happy to own a high school diploma, I relaxed on the balcony reading up on black-and-white developing from a Kodak darkroom manual. After lunch I decided to visit Aunt Martha, so I walked to the CTA pocket on Halsted and caught a bus bound for Mount Greenwood. Getting off at 111th, I hiked a few blocks north to her house.

As always she was happy to see me, greeting me with a kiss. I sat in her little breakfast nook while she boiled water for tea. Martha asked how everyone at home was doing and about my plans for college in the fall. We chatted for about an hour over glasses of freshly brewed iced tea. Then it was time to head for my job at Auburn Food & Liquor. "God love ya," she said as she kissed me good-bye.

I hopped off the bus in front of the store, hoping I'd be needed at the cash register. The regular grocery checkers had been training me for two or three weeks. But manning the register was not in the cards. Somebody had called in sick and a batch of bicycle deliveries had to go out pronto. I put two boxes into the deep basket of the old Schwinn delivery bike out front. One was for a lady two blocks south on Halsted, who always gave a hefty tip. The other was going someplace on Kerfoot, farther south and a bit to the east. To make that second delivery I'd have to pass under the big dark viaduct at 83rd. I got on the bike...and woke up in the hospital, looking into my mother's face.

"What happened?" I asked in a whisper. (That was all the voice I could muster.) "You were in an accident," she answered softly. She told me that I was in St. George's Catholic Hospital. The next thing I remember I was being tended to by a kindly middle-aged nurse named Bill. "How long am I going to be in here?" I gasped. "Oh, a week or ten days," he told me in a gentle reassuring voice. "That long?" I moaned. As it turned out my hospital stay would last more than six weeks.

When my head cleared I learned that I'd been hit by a Montgomery Ward truck, which had crushed me up against a parked car. I had seven broken ribs and both lungs were punctured. My pelvis was fractured in five places. A tube had been inserted into my trachea and other tubes were draining blood from my lungs. My butt was suspended a few inches above the bed in a pelvic sling. This, I learned, was to hold the broken pieces in place so they could fuse together properly.

For the first few days I lapsed in and out of consciousness. Only my immediate family was allowed to visit. I knew they were scared and worried. My bed was right near the door at the end of a ward that held half a dozen patients. For a week or so I couldn't eat solid food; my nourishment came through an IV tube. I couldn't really drink anything either, but my nurses let me suck on crushed ice wrapped in a handkerchief.

I received wonderful care at St. George's, which was run by The Nursing Order of St. Joseph, a dedicated group of Catholic nuns. Nurses watching me twenty-four hours a day included Alice Murphy, a cheery, middle-aged lady and Mary Frances Reen, my sister Joan's childhood friend, who was now a young RN. Years later she told Joan how painful it had been for her to see me in such bad shape.

I kept asking for an actual drink of water but that would be allowed only after I produced solid evidence that my GI track was working. Then one afternoon Mrs. O'Donnell from up the block paid me a visit. As she handed me a me a box of chocolates the nurse called her into the hall. This gave me just enough time to rip off the wrapping paper, open the box and stuff two or three luscious bonbons into my mouth.

"OH NO!" the nurse screamed. In a flash she darted to my bedside and wrested the box of chocolates from my grip. She tried to pry my mouth open, but I kept it clamped shut as I savored the first bit of food I'd tasted in more than a week. She turned to my visitor and snapped: "He can't have any food — didn't you know that!" A doctor was quickly summoned but it was too late. I'd already swallowed the poisonous candy. "Oh dear, oh dear!" I heard Mrs. O'Donnell say as she was ushered out of the room. The next morning my digestive system delivered. Miracle of miracles! Without delay the nurses started feeding me solid food. God bless you Mrs. O'Donnell.

My round-the-clock nursing care lasted about two weeks. On most days Alice Murphy was my first-shift nurse. She was very attentive and a bit persnickety. Alice made sure that I didn't touch anything I shouldn't — like the plastic tube sticking out of my nose, the drain hoses exiting my chest or the tracheotomy tube extending into my throat.

After I told Alice several times how much I craved a big juicy steak she promised to get one for me. On her last day my diet was still limited to soft food, but she came through as well as the situation would allow, bringing me a steak she'd cooked at home and pureed in her blender. It felt like mush on my tongue but it tasted a little like meat. I appreciated Alice's thoughtfulness.

Lying flat on my back I saw occasional flashes of color at the other end of the ward, where a teenage boy was laid up with a broken leg. After about two weeks, when I was allowed to have my bed cranked up a bit, I got a better look at all the flashy paraphernalia decorating his bed — reflectors, ribbons, cards, photos, balloons and such.

The kid's name was Dennis, and he'd hurt himself at the annual St. Leo Altar Boys' Picnic. Jumping on an in-ground trampoline, he came down awkwardly, one leg missing the canvas and plunging below ground level. Dennis had broken his femur, the biggest bone in his body. Thinking he had a charley horse, the adult in charge walked him around the park, aggravating his serious injury. Poor Dennis had been in the hospital two weeks before I got there and wasn't released until a week or two after I'd gone home.

After the 4th of July it was clear that I was out of danger. At that point I was moved to the end of the ward, far from the door and right across from Dennis. His glitzy reflectors and other colorful baubles were now clearly visible. My view of Dennis was obscured by the cat's cradle of cords, pulleys and weights that kept his leg suspended above the bed. In contrast to the garish display surrounding him, Dennis was a smallish, meek-looking kid with brush-cut reddish hair and glasses. He was almost thirteen, but looked younger.

Serious and sensitive, Dennis was a nice kid. He put a lot of energy into making jewelry out of glass beads. He fashioned quite a few pendants, attaching them to chains, but his specialty seemed to be crafting rosaries. I couldn't resist teasing Dennis about his total lack of interest in sports. This led to some verbal sparring matches that livened up quiet days at our end of the ward.

Dennis had good parents who visited every day. I liked to chat with his dad — he was a pleasant likeable guy who kept Dennis supplied with beads, chains and links for his jewelry making. When Dennis wasn't working with his pliers stringing beads together, he was playing with the little portable tape recorder his folks had given him.

My brothers and sisters usually visited in the afternoon or evening. And Dad often came by to see me in the morning on his way to work, bringing coffee and rolls. Happy to see me on the mend, he was upbeat and talked enthusiastically about my starting college at Loyola in the fall.

When a big flower arrangement came for me one morning, I asked Dad who'd sent it. He said it was from a lawyer who wanted to represent me in a lawsuit against Montgomery Ward, the owner of the truck that had nearly killed me. "Do you think I can get a big chunk of money out of this?" I asked. "Well, maybe enough to pay your college tuition," he answered reassuringly.

As my condition improved more folks were allowed to visit — people from the store, friends from the neighborhood and kids I knew from school. Two guys who had been in my grammar school class, Mike Millerick and John Connors, came up to see me. Their visit surprised me because I hadn't talked to either of them in years. In order to speak I had to put my finger over the tracheotomy opening in my throat.

Millerick said something, and as I answered him, Connors leaned forward. I thought he was looking intently at something on my chest. But he kept leaning — farther and farther — until his lips hit my chest, making a smacking sound. He collapsed to the floor. I pushed my call button and seconds later two nurses were at my bedside reviving John. He looked dazed and helpless as he came to. Millerick tried hard not to laugh. One of the nurses said that Connors might have caught a whiff of ether out in the hall from some patient on a gurney that was just up from surgery.

My old pal, John Keating, came to see me several times, bringing great chocolate shakes and hefty cheeseburgers from Skip's Drive-In. And one afternoon he brought four or five guys from the football team with him — guys who'd been my classmates a few weeks earlier. Their wishes for my speedy recovery really gave me a lift. Come fall, John would be heading to the University of Illinois on a football scholarship.

The week before I was released I got a visit from Rose Trahey. She was working at St. George's that summer, filling in for folks in the office who were taking their vacations. What a nice surprise! I'd never had a conversation with her all through grammar school. Rose was just as pleasant as I remembered her. And her hair looked redder than ever. My mother was visiting when Rose came to see me. Mom liked Rose so much that she invited her to lunch at our house later in August, when I'd be back home.

After six weeks my hips had grown back together. Finally my rear end could be freed from the pelvic sling. Assisted by a nurse, Dr. Meyer carefully lowered my backside to the terra firma of the mattress. The next day, with Meyer directing and my ward mates applauding, I was guided into a wheelchair and pushed out into the hall. The doc placed an old wooden chair in front of me with the back turned toward me so I could grip it. Then he asked me to try to stand up, which I managed to do, pushing off with my arms.

"OK now, hold on and push the chair. Try to take a few steps," he said. My legs moved stiffly. It didn't feel like I was walking but the chair was sliding ahead of me. I was happy. So was the doc.

I pushed the chair all the way to the end of the hall. "Whoa!" he shouted as I tried to turn around for a return trip. "That's enough for today."

With a few days of practice I was able to walk for short stretches on my own. "Can I get out of here now?" I kept asking. My doctors got together and agreed that I was ready for discharge. So, on the morning of August 13th, I said good-bye to Dennis and my other ward friends. After helping me into a wheelchair a nurse rolled me to the elevator. When we reached ground level she pushed me out the front door into the warm sunshine. Hallelujah! I was free!

As I looked back at the entrance a powerful rush of emotions made me shudder. I was sad to be leaving the folks who'd taken such good care of me and I'd miss the guys who'd kept me company. But I wanted to be home with my family, and it felt like a miracle to be mobile and independent again. What's more, the big adventure of college lie ahead — I was due to start classes at Loyola in less than two weeks.

It was great to be back home, safe in the world I'd almost left behind forever. When I entered the house Mom ushered me out to the balcony and showed me the nice cushioned lounge chair she'd purchased for my recuperation. I thought I'd better get in some R&R with school starting so soon. As I stretched out, shaded by our big elm, it was comforting to know that things were, more or less, back to normal. Folks came to visit — friends, neighbors, cousins, uncles and aunts. I felt like a celebrity playing host to everyone. Then the day came when Rose Trahey joined Mom and me for lunch. We all had fun getting better acquainted.

After a week or so I started taking walks around the block to exercise my legs. I'd soon be hiking to the CTA pocket on Halsted and catching a bus up to 63rd. There I'd transfer to a Howard "A" Train bound for the Loyola Lakeshore Campus on the far North Side.

Mom came out often to check on me as I relaxed on the balcony. Sometimes, when she saw a neighbor passing below, a conversation ensued. If someone asked about me Mom proudly proclaimed, "He's right here!" My cue to get up and say "hello." A favorite question was, "What exactly happened to you?" I answered that I honestly didn't know. I couldn't recall a thing about my accident (and still can't).

Occasionally, I stood up to stretch or go inside for a while. Rising from an afternoon session on my back, I spotted a nice-looking girl walking her Collie past our house. She looked like a high school freshman or sophomore. I'd never noticed her before and wondered who she was. A few days later I saw her again. There was something calm and classy about her that I liked. I meant to ask Marg about her.

As the day to start college approached I browsed through all the "get well" cards people had sent me, then put them away. It was time to focus on the future. I looked through some materials from Loyola about freshman orientation. We newcomers had to start a week early to familiarize ourselves with the campus — which building was the science hall, which was for humanities, etc.

I'd be starting in the Pre-med program. And, after receiving such good care from the nuns, nurses and doctors at St. George's Hospital, I was doubly fired up to become a first-rate MD. As it turned out my cousin Mike had been accepted at Loyola as a science major. Comparing schedules, we found that we were in the same history class. Small world. And all freshmen had the same orientation schedule, so Mike and I decided to travel together for that first "get acquainted" week. Luckily, Mike had a car and offered me free transportation.

On a pleasant Monday morning late in August of '61 I heard a horn beep out front. Donning a light jacket I said good-bye to Mom and headed down the front steps. Sure enough, there was my cousin's car out front. Mike pushed the door open for me and I hopped in. "Ready for college, José?" he asked in his usual lighthearted manner. "Just don't make me late on my first day," I joked. As we pulled away from the curb I was excited and a little scared, hoping I'd soon be back to full strength and ready for the big-time challenges of college.

John O'Leary
(630) 513-5412

LaVergne, TN USA
08 December 2010

207952LV00004B/21/P